For Marcy —

Twice A Princess

With very best regards !!!

Twice A Princess

The journey of a thousand leagues begins from beneath your feet.

—Lao Tzu, 604–531 BC

And what a journey it was!

George Willis Tate

To order additional copies of this book, contact:
Xlibris Corporation
1-888-795-4274
www.Xlibris.com
Orders@Xlibris.com
86239

Contents

Dedication

*T*his book would never have become a reality without the love, support, encouragement, and editorial assistance of my wife Catherine Hearn Tate, my very own Princess Kate.

Acknowledgments

*T*WICE A PRINCESS, the story of Princess Catherine Willis Murat, would not have been possible without the vast information and insights offered by the late professor A. J. Hanna in his seminal work, *A Prince in Their Midst: The Adventurous Life of Achille Murat on the American Frontier* which first brought the amazing tale of Achille and Catherine Murat to the broad public. His scholarship sheds an unparalleled beacon of light on these historic persons and stands for all time as the authoritative source regarding their lives and times. My offering is intended as a companion to *A Prince in Their Midst* but will forever remain in the shadow of Dr. Hanna's work.

George Willis Tate
Pensacola, Florida

Author's Notes

*T*WICE A PRINCESS is history which reads like a novel. Fashioning the book in this way stems from my deeply held belief that the world's greatest stories are history, but that too often we see only pale shadows of the full story. They need to be fleshed out to give them the richness that characterized the real events.

One cannot make up the fantastic twists, turns, and plots that have come down to us today from the real-life events of yesterday. Unfortunately many people have been programmed to think of history as boring, having reached that sad impression by dry texts, sometimes augmented with dull history teachers. Overcoming the bad rap of history as a dry subject was a central goal of this book.

To do this it was necessary to embellish available fact with the compelling psychological dimensions of Princess Kate's story and to weave them into *Twice a Princess.* These are almost universally lacking in the simple recounting of facts in a history text, but they are what provides the richness and human drama of historic tales. Inferring human motives and emotions allows the reader to peek behind the curtain of the actual moment and to glimpse the actors before they have put their makeup on. It was thus important to tell Kate's story by giving the character's feelings, such as when she realizes that her prince, for all of his royal status, is "just deeply hurt man, standing in the street and holding my hand." Or when she uncharacteristically fumes at him for leaving her alone and undefended in the face of

Indian attack. Adding the emotional dimension empowers the reader to become something of a historic voyeur as the tale unfolds.

It was also important to give these historic events an environmental backdrop to give the reader a feel for the context and the atmospherics against which it played out. If you are to understand an event, you must have a vision of it, and the atmospherics create that. For example, if an event happened on a late August afternoon in the piney woods of North Florida, it is necessary to describe the oppressive humidity, the billowing thunderhead clouds, and the buzzing sounds of cicadas. Describing the atmospherics makes the retelling of a historic event more full and textured and adds to, rather than diminishing, the accuracy of the story. In *Twice a Princess*, you are invited to touch, taste, smell, and hear the events described and it makes history more real and enjoyable in the process.

To make *Twice a Princess* more readable, it is written in the first person. You are there, not just accepting a recounting of facts in the third person. History is passionate, and to give a historic tale, authenticity requires one to put oneself into the protagonist's shoes. In writing this, I became Princess Kate, with all of her thoughts, feelings, and life events underlying the story as it evolved. It was a bold and perhaps risky step for this thoroughly male author to write from a female perspective, but aided by my wife's insights as to how a woman might think or feel about a subject, I tried. If I succeeded, the reader too will become "twice a princess."

I hope the reader will get into the story and read it for what it is, an amazing life adventure, and will not be offended by my pushing the boundaries of cold fact in ways that I might call history plus. Nothing I have added alters in any way the facts drawn from unimpeachable historic sources.

I am grateful to all of the scholars and chroniclers who preceded me in telling the tale of Kate and Achille Murat and for all of their research. I am especially indebted to the late A. J. Hanna whose 1946 book *A Prince in Their Midst* is a spellbinding account of the life of Kate's husband, the crown prince of Naples and son of Napoléon's sister Caroline Bonaparte. If I do as well with the story of the princess as he did with the prince, I shall be happy indeed.

GWT

Introduction

LYING ON THE dirt floor of the wilderness cabin, she pressed her head to her husband's chest, feeling and listening for signs of his labored breathing. He was prone to epileptic seizures, but this one had created special worry. Her usual live-in servants had taken the wagon to town for foodstuffs, and she was alone in the house save for the prostrate man who lay beside her. He would be no use in case of Indian attack. Terrified to light a candle or oil lamp for fear of inviting unwelcome attention from hostile Seminoles, the attractive ivory-skinned brunette welcomed the inky gloom of the sparse cabin's interior and reveled in its quietness. "Maybe," she thought, "they'll think we've gone to town too."

Only the tiniest ghostly glow penetrated through the partially open window as the waning crescent moon settled itself into the horizon after its nightly run across the North Florida sky. Dawn would soon creep slowly and silently over the piney woods, and the night's threats would vanish with the mist. The call of the whip-poor-will would give way to the rituals and routines of the plantation, slaves would soon appear from their shacks in the south forty to stoke the fires of Lipona and bring fresh eggs from the henhouse. Portly old Della would soon be tapping at the door to start her daily chores. The fair-skinned brunette beauty on the floor was clear that all of this was just minutes away, but her racing heart silenced any comforting thought as her night fears strengthened their grip over her heart. Alone and close to panic, the nervous palpitations she knew so well again seized her as she stroked her husband's clammy forehead, eyes darting nervously about the murky cabin. Incongruously, artifacts of silver and gold glowed in the twilight of the cabin's spartan interior, and a marble bust of the great Napoléon stared blankly from the gloom. Under threat of imminent attack, these treasures were cold comfort.

It was the 1800s, and this was Seminole country. Still bitter over their treatment at the hands of the white man, the rage of the ages smoldered just below the surface. Though she had received avowals of safety from the local chief Tiger Tail, she could not be sure that all of his clan had gotten the word, and besides, when liquored up, they might take a fancy to the woman who lived in the unusual complex of log cabins and who wore fancy dresses. Some rumored that her husband was some kind of chief, but that didn't seem likely given that he was usually dressed shabbily and affected manners, which struck even the uneducated and supposedly "primitive" Seminoles as pretty damned odd. He spoke strangely too, they thought, intoning languages they'd never heard when they ventured into the white man's settlement at Tallahassee.

Catherine, or Kate as her friends called her, startled as a branch cracked in the chilly morning air, and she couldn't resist the impulse to sneak a peek through a chink in the logs that made up the walls. "Must be just a deer," she thought anxiously, in a vain attempt to mute the fears of Indian attack, which frequently visited her in the still nights at Lipona, the plantation her husband had carved from the primeval pine forest of north central Florida. Florida was, at that time, still just a territory and far from the minds and protections of the politicians in Washington. It had been, after all, only a few years before when Spain ceded the Florida Territory to United States control via a treaty these Indians neither knew of nor cared for.

They were strangers in a strange land, these two Caucasians who called the piney woods in the middle of nowhere their home. The Native Americans who appeared and disappeared like gossamer and were downright inscrutable, she often opined. While outwardly friendly, she had come to regard them as unpredictable and unreadable, representing as they did a totally alien culture to the outsiders who called the cabin home. There had been nothing in their backgrounds, hers in Virginia and his in Austria, France, and Italy, which might prepare them for the harshness and dangers of the Florida frontier.

Frequent rumors that the Seminoles would soon arise en masse made their life always edgy. Their best efforts to create normalcy in the boondocks of the primitive Wacissa region near Tallahassee were mostly wishful thinking, for their daily realities were harsh indeed and included unaccustomed visitors ranging from armadillos to diamondback rattlers as well as lurking Seminoles. As dawn's first glow appeared after a long and fretful night, with a moribund husband of no help and death prowling at her door, it was impossible for Kate not to retrace in her mind the unlikely trajectory of life that had led her here. But for now, that would have to wait. Now, as her husband twitched a brief involuntary spasm, she pressed further against his sweaty supine body. A low groan escaped his lips. "Good," she thought, "at least he's coming around." She'd been through his seizures before, but this one had been unusually severe.

"My prince, my love, my strange comrade, how did we get here?" she mused as the first golden light of day probed the cabin.

How indeed. It had indeed been a bizarre journey for the aristocratic daughter of Virginia, barely thirty, yet at such an age, having lived a life of adventure that would pale the Arabian Nights—and as fantastic too! "My life's journey has been an odyssey that would have dazzled the great Homer," she mused as she raised herself from the floor.

She was Catherine Daingerfield Willis Murat, and the man who now stirred on the dirt floor of this rustic piney woods cabin was Charles Louis Napoléon Achille Murat, son of a king and the crown prince of the Napoleonic kingdom of Naples. Murat had pursued the young widow Catherine honorably and ardently on the Florida frontier and entrusted her with his heart. In the process, he had ensnared her into his fantasy world of royalty and eccentricity, spinning breathtaking tales of his childhood in the glittering Elysée Palace, once owned by Madame Pompadour and today celebrated as France's White House. He was given to frequent rants about lost riches, lost titles, and lost lives, sometimes in heavily accented English and, from time to time, forgetting himself and raving in one of the other seven languages he spoke. Through tear-streaked and squinted eyes and with clenched fists, Achille passionately described both his burning love and crushing sadness for his unlikely father, Joachim Murat, king of Naples, grand duke of Berg and Cleves, marshal of the empire, and mayor of Paris, the fabled City of Light. These patronage positions had come his way from years of service as Napoléon's greatest cavalry commander. He was superbly handsome, always dashing, brave beyond measure, and shrewdly political.

And husband of Caroline Bonaparte, Napoléon's youngest—and favorite—sister. But now the gallant Joachim Murat was dead, caught in the web of his own making and executed by firing squad at Pizzo.

As the death rattle of Napoléon's collapsing empire echoed over the ancient streets of Naples where King Joachim held sway, Joachim and Queen Caroline had hatched an insidious plot to loft themselves into the power vacuum, which would surely follow Napoléon's downfall. Duplicitously conspiring against Emperor Napoléon, who was both her brother and his patron, Caroline and Joachim schemed with Klemens Wenzel von Metternich of Austria, Napoléon's perpetual adversary, that Joachim's kingdom would expand northward from Naples, soak up any and all territories that may have fallen through the Napoleonic cracks, plunder the art treasures of Italy, and starting with a unified Italy, wrest the Bonaparte empire from her brother Napoléon. King Joachim would become Emperor Joachim. Queen Caroline Bonaparte Murat would become first empress of a unified Italy. Then the world would cower at their feet.

A little royalty, it seemed, was a dangerous thing, and power, as it is wont to do, was a seductive aphrodisiac to King Joachim and Queen Caroline. The fruits of their betrayal would have placed them, irrevocably or so they fantasized, at the very top of the global heap, first among equals in the cat and mouse game of the European political pecking order.

With brother Napoléon out of the way, there would then be merely the rest of the world to conquer.

Incongruously, the man moaning on the dirt floor of the darkened log cabin in "cracker" Florida was the eldest son and crown prince of all of this intrigue. Achille Murat was a favorite nephew of Emperor Napoléon I, who had teased Achille unmercifully by tugging at his ears, perhaps testing his manhood and tolerance for discomfort, characteristics he thought Murat would need to step into the gilded shoes of his swashbuckling father who had served the emperor so well in the major battles of Napoléon's conquests: the Battle of the Pyramids, Jena, Eylau, Friedland, Borodino, and more.

Never in history has there ridden such a resplendent—even ostentatious—cavalry commander. Eschewing personal safety, he invariably led from the front in outrageously ornate uniform, with his signature white ostrich plumes flowing in the thundering air of each cavalry charge. He was, aside from bravery that bordered on the foolhardy, decidedly flamboyant. Later the famous passages of Tchaikovsky's *1812 Overture* would recall the headlong charge of his cavalry into the Russian defenders at Borodino, one of music's most memorable passages celebrating his glory. Against credentials such as these did young Achille measure himself, and if he sometimes found himself wanting or seeming to fail to measure up, it is no small wonder.

The boy Achille was showered with luxury throughout his life, but never more so than amid the palazzos of his father who was styled, in Italian *Gioacchino*, king of Naples and the two Sicilies. He succeeded to that position in the footsteps of Napoléon's elder brother, Joseph Bonaparte, who had ruled the kingdom in the period 1806-1808. For both brother Joseph Bonaparte and stepbrother Joachim Murat, these were the spoils of victory, crumbs from the table of the emperor.

From the ancient Palazzo Caserta, Crown Prince Achille Murat, following his father's predispositions, loved military regalia even in childhood and was appointed at age eleven as first sovereign prince of Pontecorvo and at fourteen crown prince of Naples, a heady brew for the boy whose health plagued him from early childhood. He was to the manor born however, or more correctly, to the pomp and ceremony of martial life. Despite occasional bouts of epilepsy, he affected the egotistical air of confidence learned at the knee of his famous father and thrived on lavish uniforms and luxury like dear old dad. Along with pomp and pretense, however, young Achille received education par excellence, both academic and practical. Here he honed political skills as a child in the convoluted world of Bonaparte maneuverings; an apprentice to power. From these impressionable years under Bonapartist tutelage grew the fertile mind, which would later flower into political writings that influence European governments even today.

But now, the unlikely prince lay in the dirt beside Kate in the North Florida piney woods, far from glory and royalty, tended by his gentle patrician wife, who likewise had led a charmed life. She had brought her own credentials to the match, great-grandniece of George Washington and great-granddaughter of his sister Betty—as close to royalty as American law and custom would allow.

That morning, the physical closeness of Achille and Kate on that dirt floor at dawn was, if nothing else, a metaphor for an unmatched and improbable political tale: the marriage of the houses of Washington and Bonaparte—unprecedented, unrivalled, and transcendent. Together they joined families, continents, and political powerhouses.

Little did Kate realize in that moment that her amazing life to date was merely a prelude, that she would ride the rainbow of fame, and that she herself would become twice a princess.

Kate now tells her own story.

Catherine Daingerfield Willis Murat; at approximately the time of her marriage to Crown Prince Achille Murat. When she married Prince Murat in Tallahassee, in the Florida Territory, she was accorded the rank of princess consort of the Kingdom of Naples. Image courtesy of the Archives of the State of Florida.

Willis Hill Plantation, Fredericksburg, Virginia, Spring 1813

*I*N MY TEN-YEAR-OLD fantasies, I was a princess. I would whirl
and twirl around my bedroom of our plantation house, in my best
pink-and-cream-colored hoopskirt, clunking about in Mother's
uncomfortable shoes and eyeing the girl in the mirror. Soon I
would find myself in my mind's eye dancing at a lavish royal ball.
Scores of handsome men in flamboyant uniforms with jewel-laden
sashes, with their medals and epaulets gleaming, would bid for my
hand as a waltz began to play. "Lady Kate, may I have the honor
of this dance?" they would say. Such finery! Silks, brocades, and
diamonds glowed in the palace halls, decked out with hundreds of
candles, and tended by liveried servants bearing flutes of the finest
champagne. Whirling across marble floors until dizzy, catching
glimpses of myself in the palace's rococo mirrors, I was like a dervish
until dizziness and reality caught up with my adolescent reveries,
and I fell to the floor with a mighty flump, hoops, pantaloons,
crinolined petticoats, and dark braids flying. Snickering, George,
my brother some years junior to me, would creep from under the
bed, pinch me on my bum, and fly down the broad and squeaky
stairs to spill the beans to my older brother Lewis. "Our silly sister
is at it again," he'd yell back upstairs. "Playing queen or sump'n,
and silly as a goose!" Such make-believe waltzes with make-believe
princes were my childhood fantasies, as they are for most girls
then or now. They served to spirit me away from the reality of the
1800s in a small American town and the muddy yards, outhouses,

and homes that, however spacious and well appointed, were too hot in summer and too cold in winter.

Little could any of us have known then that my childhood daydreams would become my reality, that I would actually marry a prince, or that he would someday lead me across the stormy Atlantic to be welcomed into the bosom of European royalty as an equal. To this ten-year-old daughter of Virginia, such a life was a utopian vision beyond the pale of reality, a fanciful tale worthy of Scheherazade.

I confess that to the outsider looking in mine would appear an unlikely wisp of a life, riding as I did the whirlwind that was the saga of Napoléon's empire. But I was led to its very core when I married, in 1826, the brilliant but eccentric Achille Murat, deposed crown prince of the Napoleonic kingdom of Naples. Achille was my prince in every sense of the word, and his joie de vivre and wit helped me overcome the sadness that befell me when both my first husband, Atchison Gray of Traveler's Rest, a neighboring plantation in Fredericksburg, and my dearest baby boy died when I was barely sixteen.

Atchison and I—he actually wanted me to call him Mr. Gray—had scarcely been married a year when he passed away. His death was not unexpected as he had suffered ill health all of the time I knew him and was much older, so I fear I could not feel the depth of pain I was supposed to upon his passing. He was rigidly formal, whereas I was a happy-go-lucky girl who had been enjoying youth and playing with dolls just a year before he took me as a bride after some arranging with my parents. I tried to love him, but I was too soon married, too soon widowed, too young a mother, and much too young the grieving parent of a child called home to God in infancy. Too immature to emotionally deal with these tragedies, I was criticized in Fredericksburg's tattling social circles for what some saw as a devil-may-care attitude and not displaying more appropriate and grieving behavior. The truth was that I was devastated and hid my pain behind a mask of gaiety.

In my marriage of convenience to Mr. Gray, behind my polite social facade I always felt more like his daughter than a loving wife. Burying my infant son, however, in whom I invested the love I could not shower on my husband, was altogether different and left me flat and lifeless within. Not much more than a child myself when these tragedies struck, I was beside myself in grief for a large part of my youth and all too happy to move away to the Florida Territory with my family when father lost the family fortune and our magnificent plantation burned to the ground. I needed a new start as much as Father, and our trip south hid a certain air of desperation behind verbalized hopes for opportunity and a renaissance of both our finances and our spirit.

The Florida Territory to which we fled was brutally primitive after my sophisticated life of privilege in Virginia. Our trip via carriage, ship, wagon, and horseback was a hardship on Mother I know, but we all tried to put the best face on it, as Father had enough on his mind and didn't need a sniveling family nipping at his heels. That uncomfortable trip from our beloved Fredericksburg took over a month, and when we arrived in Tallahassee, where Father planned our new start, we were stunned to find it just a wilderness colony with a population of just a few hundred frontiersmen of all callings. We commented among ourselves that we felt like our Jamestown ancestors starting anew in the forest.

Tallahassee consisted of about forty or fifty log houses, and there were no amenities at all in the entire town save a couple of rough taverns and the statehouse, which was just a larger log house itself. In our new home, insects, snakes, armadillos, panthers, and curious Indians came to call rather than wealthy ladies and gentlemen calling to share a glass of sherry and talk politics. We lived in a log cabin on Monroe Street, but I hesitate to call it a street as it was not much more than a dirt track, and behind our house the wilderness stretched away into what seemed an infinity of pine trees and scrub growth. These were years that took a reservoir of strength for the family, requiring every one of us to reach deeply within for the fortitude we needed to deal with unaccustomed hardships on the Florida frontier.

Tallahassee we learned was the Seminole word for "beautiful land." While there were indeed some lovely attributes, when we were trying to sleep through swarms of mosquitoes on humid August nights, the beauty was sometimes hard to find.

Social diversions were hard to come by, and it was natural that we all relished a chance to attend a big picnic at the grounds of the old mission, San Luis. It was there that I met my prince, a tale on which I shall describe in detail later.

My prince, Charles Louis Napoléon Achille Murat, was the son of King Joachim Murat of the Napoleonic kingdom of Naples and his wife Queen Caroline Bonaparte, younger sister of Emperor Napoléon I. The emperor had invested Joachim Murat as king in a royal gesture of patronage resulting from the many victories Murat achieved as a marshal of the empire during Napoléon's sweeping conquests. As Napoléon's empire neared collapse, King Joachim and Queen Caroline turned on their patron, hoping to salvage Italy for themselves. The plot uncovered, Joachim was put to death by firing squad, shock from which his young son Achille never recovered. Even years later, after he grew to manhood, during our marriage the sounds of that firing squad reverberated through his persona as a source of anger and depression.

Charles Louis Napoleon Achille Murat, nephew of Emperor Napoleon I, first prince of Pontecorvo, prince of the Two Sicilies, grand duke heir of Berg and Cleves, crown prince of Naples, and husband of Catherine Daingerfield Willis (Gray) Murat; "Princess Kate". After immigration to The United States, Murat became first a planter then a lawyer and judge in the Florida Territory, colonel of the Florida Militia, postmaster of Lipona (Leon County, FL), banker, and alderman of Tallahassee. In the Territory he was often perceived as an eccentric, intellectual maverick. Image courtesy of the Archives of the State of Florida.

When Achille and I were married, my mother-in-law Caroline Bonaparte, the emperor's sister, was living in luxurious exile in Austria under the assumed title Countess of Lipona. The pleasantries we exchanged by mail could not extinguish the discomforting feeling that she remained a coiled serpent awaiting an opportune time to strike. I found her betrayal of her own brother Napoléon a self-serving act I could not forgive. Somewhere deep in the recesses of Achille's mind, I knew he too was conflicted, for in the act of her betrayal of Napoléon lay the seeds of his father Joachim's death at the hands of a firing squad when he attempted to raise an army of revolt against his own patron. The duplicitous Bonapartes seemed to make a sport of backstabbing, and I often had to bite my tongue when the subject arose with Achille.

Caroline Bonaparte Murat, sister of Napoleon I, queen consort of Naples, mother of Achille Murat and mother in law of Princess Kate. The ambitious Caroline raised the young Achille, her firstborn, to step into the power structure of Napoleon's empire but when it collapsed he immigrated to the United States, settled in the Florida Territory, and married Catherine Daingerfield Willis (Gray).

These however were the family connections that led my Achille to call the stupendous Emperor Napoléon uncle. Achille was a royal son of a king, nephew of the most powerful man in the world, and it was he who led me foursquare into the Bonaparte halls of power, wealth, and intrigue. In so doing, he gave this Virginia girl recompense for the early tragedies of life and a glimpse behind the curtain of the mightiest power struggles of the age.

When I said "I do" in that simple wedding ceremony in Tallahassee, little did I foresee the extent to which I would be swept into the Bonaparte circle of raw politics and power. Though carefully masked in polite decorum, I came to realize that the family into which I married played a high-stakes game of global politics. Behind their airs of courtesy, for all of the Bonapartes, there lay a self-serving core of raw ambition. There was nothing subtle about it at all. Every action, word, and gesture carried an unspoken subtext of personal aggrandizement.

Several years into our marriage, Achille determined to wrest the Murat fortunes from the king of France where they had been impounded since the exile of Queen Caroline and her children to Austria. Though as a member of the Bonaparte family, Achille was under edict of the allies to not return to Europe; with classic brashness, we made our way from the Florida Territory to England and thence to the Continent. We were feted by royalty and commoner alike from London to Brussels and beyond. For all of the bloodshed he had left in his wake, Napoléon remained a popular cult figure in many circles. Steeped in nostalgia, adoring crowds saw in Achille, who was a dead ringer for his uncle Napoléon, a resurgence of the real thing, a return to glory and empire.

From coronations in Westminster to common soldiers kissing his hand on the streets, the mystique of Uncle Napoléon and his lost empire hovered over our lives like an apparition from the past, at once seductive and threatening.

I shan't dwell on details here, but we lived in splendor during those halcyon days on the Continent. For months, Achille was celebrated in Brussels by King Leopold, only to find his dreams thwarted when the political pressures boiled over. The crowned heads of Europe turned the screws on Leopold to send us packing, fearing in my Achille a comeback of Napoleonic conquests and renewed bloodshed at the hands of his nephew, my husband. However, ever the conniver and politician, my Achille's flirtation with power was more intellectual than martial and, in truth, might have been good for Europe. He had tasted the fruits of American democracy and longed in his heart of hearts to install the principles of the United States Constitution among the moribund governments of Europe, many of which were dying slow deaths through the entropy of the ages.

Of course, while the common people, so long suppressed by autocratic regimes, might have benefited from this, the monarchs who clung to power by long tradition, family connections, and force were nothing less than terrified by the twin notions of personal freedom and elected government that crept over the horizon from America. As I looked back on this in later years, I realized the immense threat my husband represented to centuries of royalty. To them, he stood for nothing less than a revolution of the mind, the unleashing of the limitless powers of "We the people."

As a practical matter, Achille returned to the Continent hoping to recover the Murats' lost titles and fortunes at a time when, for many heads of state, their crowns sat uneasily on their heads. Though his family had been formally exiled to Austria, he had fled to America in a sort of self-imposed exile abetted by youthful enthusiasm and a yen for adventure. As a member of the Bonaparte family, he was forbidden from reentering the Continent and could return only surreptitiously. With classic Bonaparte vanity, he vowed to return anyway, flaunting the travel restrictions that had locked him away from his heritage and his family's fortune for years.

As we made our way from the Florida Territory to Europe, it was a stormy time generally and literally. Political storms crackled about the Continent while actual storms buffeted us for a month on the North Atlantic aboard the packet ship *Ontario*.

For a time, the royals watched nervously from the sidelines cutting backroom deals to suppress the will of their own peoples and stifle the many rebellions, which bubbled just beneath the surface. Countless commoners on the Continent remained sympathetic to the ideals of *liberté, égalité, fraternité*, which had produced such bloodshed in France, producing in their autocratic royal leaders a sort of political paranoia.

Europe's monarchs were never quite sure what to think of the volatile Achille. On the one hand, he represented a very real threat of recreating the juggernaut of the Bonaparte empire from its ashes. Equally threatening, at the other end of the scale, he inflamed masses with American populist themes and notions of democratic government. Either of these opposing threats might cause them to lose their crowns, their wealth, their status, and their heads.

Neither populism nor return to Bonaparte power sat well with monarchies entrenched in power for centuries, indeed throughout European history.

In truth, I never knew from day to day whether the man I loved would wake up as promoter of democratic reforms or a hard-driving autocrat of the Bonaparte stripe. Because he was both brilliant and mentally troubled on occasion, affecting the occasional epileptic seizure, I suspect that my Achille never knew either, but was nevertheless able to hold comfortably in his teeming brain these two opposing views of governance. Although it was not in his nature to be gloomy, I have many times seen him retreat to the innermost recesses of his mind where I know he wrestled with his conscience to the very edge of schizophrenia, trying to reconcile opposites without going mad. From this cognitive dissonance, in moments like these, his most eloquent writings would take place. They also drove him to instability and depression. As they took their toll, these bouts of mental turmoil became more frequently fueled by alcohol and deteriorated occasionally into incoherent babble. But I loved him still, and for the very passion he brought to the political debate and for his vain attempts to bridge the old and new worlds.

He was the most passionate man of his age about the philosophical core of the raucous American style of democracy, the freedoms it granted to citizens, and the energies such freedoms released upon the land. My Achille loudly proclaimed these egalitarian beliefs in his many writings, in courtrooms, and from rowdy political rallies to quiet intellectual debate with the likes of the Marquis de Lafayette, Ralph Waldo Emerson, and Alexis de Toqueville.

Yet despite Achille's profound intellectualizing about democratic ideals, I never doubted for one moment that he sought, with equal passion, to pick up the tattered mantle of empire from his Uncle Napoléon and to create a new and united Europe under, of course, his leadership. Memories of childhood in the Elysée Palace, the heady ascent of his father from peasant to king, and unlimited wealth, and power on a grand scale died hard for my Achille. Always in the quiet recesses of memory, these memories were baked in a cake of revenge for the execution of his beloved father as the empire gasped its last convoluted breaths. Was he at his core a liberalizing democrat or was he an autocrat, forever seduced by the absolute powers of kingship? I never knew. Achille was an honest man, not given to dissembling. If he publicly advocated democratic causes while secretly harboring the dream of a Bonapartist renaissance with himself at the helm, it was not a deliberate deception but rather an inability to see the innate conflict within himself. His mind was such a complex tangle of ideas that it probably didn't seem contradictory to him.

Such opposing beliefs concerning governance formed but one dichotomy of my prince. Another, which would fester in our nation and our personal lives, was slavery.

Though raised in the slave-based economy of the South, I myself felt quite conflicted about the subject. As a practical matter, our entire economy and lifestyle rested on the institution of slavery as generations of my family before me. At some deep and unspoken level, I knew it to be wrong yet saw no alternatives in the agrarian South to which I was born and in which Achille and I made our home. I had been raised on an aristocratic Virginia plantation where my family owned hundreds of slaves, a practice vocally condemned in many circles and for which we would later fight the American Civil War. Throughout the 1800s, I grew up with the belief, not shared by my Achille, that our greatest responsibility in the world was to care for our slaves, not abuse them. To help them, not harm them. It was almost as if they were our children, and our greatest duty was to protect them and give them shelter and livelihood however meager.

Throughout our many conversations on the subject, Achille and I never broached the untouchable subject that these were fellow human beings who had been brutally ripped from tribal cultures across Africa to be transported to an alien land in chains and there face a life of involuntary servitude. Neither did we verbalize the thought that for one human being to own another was anathema to the beliefs on which America was founded. Such an admission would have been too entirely uncomfortable and dissonant to the genteel and altogether patrician lives we led. Deep down, we knew that slavery did violence to the lofty ideals of the Declaration of Independence, but neither the Founding Fathers nor Achille and I could deal with it. We would put it off for later generations. Thousands would die.

I suppose that in deferring the slavery question, we salved our consciences by practicing a form of benevolent dictatorship over our slaves, not unlike the rulers of Europe practiced regarding their subjects. Noblesse oblige! Let them eat cake or at least cornbread. I was wrong about this, and so was Achille, but we were products of our era and our environment.

Back in Europe, American populism as seen through the eyes of an autocratic continental monarch in the 1820s was a radical concept. Once unleashed, it could easily spin out of control as had happened in France. The power elites of Europe, with whom we rubbed elbows, had after all only recently seen the bloodlust into which the French Revolution had descended and watched royal heads fall to the guillotine as ravenous mobs sought their revenge for centuries of royal excesses.

My Achille, in his most ambitious dreams to recover his father's kingly mantle, would never have allowed this to happen, but in their paranoia, the royal houses of Europe would take no chances. Thus while we were living in luxury in the elegance of the Hotel Belle Vue in Brussels, a royal cabal formed that would turn up the heat on our host, King Leopold, and drive us from the Continent. Tragically for millions of European commoners, this would deprive my Achille of his noble goals of introducing American-style governance and push democratic reforms further down the road of European history.

It was thus that Achille, with sadness and frustration, saw the handwriting on the wall. He packed our dreams of empire in my sea trunks after a few years of gaiety and intrigue on the Continent and in 1832 sent me home to our mortgaged plantation on the Florida frontier. He remained in Europe to tie up a few loose ends and write yet more critical essays promoting American-style self-government over European models, which he found stultifying. In 1832, his controversial *Esquisse Morale et Politique des Etats-Unis de l'Amerique du Nord* was published in Paris and translated into English and German shortly thereafter. Commentary on this salutary work by many literary journals on the Continent raised him to prominence as a political writer, but his hoped-for breakthroughs in actual governments were stonewalled by the monarchs whose powers he challenged. Unable to secure compensation for the Murat's confiscated riches and thwarted in his efforts to liberalize Europe's hidebound governments, he sailed with heavy heart for his adopted home in the spring of 1833.

There we found neither royalty nor immense wealth, but the matchless gifts of freedom and equality afforded by American democracy. We ceded, not without regret and second thoughts, the glittering halls of European courtly life for our little complex of log cabins outside Tallahassee. Lipona, an anagram for Napoli—Naples—the lost kingdom of Achille's father. There we set about to achieve in this blessed nation, still less than a half century old, a life that was denied us across the ocean.

Hoping to influence from afar the old hidebound systems of his native Europe, Achille would passionately write reams about American politics and government, rooted always in gratitude for his blessings as an American citizen. Some compared his discourses on American government and democratic traditions to his better-known countryman and colleague Alexis de Toqueville.

Many of my Achille's writings were to take root across the Atlantic long after his death and serve as models for the democracies of Western Europe as they emerged from centuries of royal autocracy. It was thus that his fertile mind helped to shape the destinies of millions who had heretofore known only servitude to their governments and a social strata based on family rather than on personal achievements, notions he found akin to slavery. So while his physical presence on the Continent threatened many European governments, his European mind, expansive and expressive as it was, was able to bridge the gap between rigid traditional monarchies and the more freewheeling and egalitarian style of American democracy. From his new and humble home in America, he was able to do for millions of Europeans what he was unable to do for them while living in Europe itself. This, I know, he fervently believed to be his most important legacy, and he would feel vindicated as I write this today.

I was always moved especially by a line from his *America and the Americans*, which read, "I came to America poor, friendless, and an exile, and have here found a home and country which Europe refused me." That summed up my Achille simply and elegantly.

Prince Charles Louis Napoleon Achille Murat. Evidently the prince took after his father King Joachim Murat of the Napoleonic Kingdom of Naples in his fondness for ornate uniforms. This portrait was painted in New Orleans in the late 1830's by French portrait artist Jacques Amans at a time when Murat held no military appointments at all, yet he appears in flamboyant military attire. Image from the book, "Louisiana Painters and Paintings From the Collection of W.E. Groves", Pelican Publishing Company, Gretna, LA, 1998.

My Virginia Youth, Early 1800s

LONG BEFORE THE royal travels and travails just described, I was just an ordinary American girl blissfully living out her childhood years with family and friends in Fredericksburg, Virginia, with studies and with parties, and under Mother's tutelage, forever apprenticing in the role of Virginia aristocrat to which I was born. It was a sweet life, and there was little to want for.

In my childhood, I always had a vivid imagination, the private fantasy world to which I could withdraw. I sometimes had the disquieting sense that despite the affluence of our home atop Willis Hill, my daily world of rutted dirt roads, reading Latin, and doing needlepoint with Mother left me unfulfilled. Socially, my world consisted of foxhunts, gossipy neighbors, political rallies, and mandatory Sunday churchgoing. Once I became aware of the big world beyond, after trips to Washington and Williamsburg, my daily world seemed not enough, but even in my wildest dreams, I could never have written for the ages the script by which my life played out.

I paid no heed to the dozens of guests who'd come to call and talk politics with my father, Byrd Charles Willis, who was, I was told, the best-known man in Virginia except of course for the really big Virginia names, such as my venerated great-uncle George Washington and of our recent president Thomas Jefferson. And always in Virginia lore, there were the aristocratic Byrds for whom my father was named, the Carters, the Warners, the Randolphs, and so many more it just became one big genealogical blur to me.

I was more interested in childlike pursuits and had my own horse on our plantation when I was ten, a twelve-hand dapple gray filly named Lizzie, and would sometimes ride with my father when he'd go down our big hill into town. On special occasions, he'd take me to point-to-point races at the Jockey Club, and I felt so big and grown-up among the men and a few women who'd chitchat for hours, hardly even noticing the races. I could never quite understand what they could find to talk about for so long, especially the wives, who were always fretting about their hair or their latest dress or so-and-so's new baby. It seemed so inane but was not mine to question. It was times like these when I'd just find myself drifting off into my dream world, and the horsemen about me would, in my imagination, become the gallant knights I'd read of in the new Waverley novels that Father adored. Even the author's name, Sir Walter Scott, was exciting in small town Virginia, and everyone was quite caught up in reading the new Scottish author's works, especially Father. I think that even at his age and even though he was overweight, he'd get caught up in his own fantasy world of chivalry and jousting and damsels in distress as he read by firelight on quiet evenings.

Father was a big man, some said fat, but he was just one of those always-happy affable people that everybody gravitated to. Later I would come to realize that he loved partying and socializing and foxhunting to the detriment of family business, and we'd pay a heavy price for his forgetting to tend to the family's money, which he bet freely at the Jockey Club. He loved to bet on the races and even asked me what I thought sometimes, especially when one of our thoroughbreds was running. Father was committed to only the highest quality horseflesh and had the money and wherewithal to indulge. I remember, for example, a beautiful chestnut mare named Maid of the Oaks that brought the huge sum of $15,000 when we sold her about 1820.

Even though we had lots of servants, mostly slaves who'd been with the family for years, I loved saddling my Lizzie up myself and can still smell the pungent leather as I'd cinch up her girth. Funny how aromas are so evocative; things like a big drenching summer rain, and the smell of the year's first big snowstorm when the leaden skies leach all the color from the land. Then the last brown leaves skitter away on sudden gusts, and the smell of the frigid air makes everything seem more intense. You know that smell; I know you do!

Sometimes I'd even sneak out after dark and take my Lizzie carrots and apples and just talk with her. I swear she could understand me. She'd nicker back at me and nuzzle her big head against me as if to say we were best friends. And who knows, maybe we were in that, my tenth year on Willis Hill. Like dozens of our other horses down on the flat pasture who were bought, bred, and trained for the foxhunt and race, my Lizzie was a thoroughbred too, and I swelled with pride when my father told his friends that I was his best thoroughbred of all!

Father was always big into horses, and I liked cantering across our fields with him just when the morning mists was burning off. Oh, the air was sweet, and I'd leave my hair down unless we were going somewhere and let it fly in the cool morning air fragrant with the sweet aromas of fresh dewy grass and deer's tongue. I was a good rider, everybody said, and since I tended to be sort of a tomboy, sometimes enjoyed riding more than being cooped up in the carriages, which ladies were supposed to flit about in. I found them slow, uncomfortable, and bumpy, so I'd saddle up my Lizzie and follow the rest of the family over the field and down rutted roads. To everyone's horror, I wouldn't even ride sidesaddle, and there were concerns about my ladyhood, whatever that meant.

We had about six hundred acres then, just on the edge of Fredericksburg, the town that my grandfather Henry Willis founded. Before that, it was just a little crossroads by the river. Many is the time I've heard important people say that Grandfather was personally responsible that there even was a Fredericksburg, and that even that really aristocratic folks like William Byrd, master of Westover on the James River, called him "the top man of the place."

I know I've been rattling on about my father, and that's just because he was such a warm and happy man, outgoing, bursting at the seams, and boisterous while mother was so much reserved, almost too proper for my tomboyish tastes. She was Mary Willis Lewis, an old-school Virginia lady through and through, and when she married father in 1800, she took on the tongue twister name, Mary Willis Lewis Willis. Everybody took this in stride though, as most of the upper crust Virginia families we knew had intermarried somewhere along the way. Mother spoke with the distinctive Virginia accent, which I fear I've lost. *House* was *ha-oose*, not *howse*, and it was just one of many ways that my gentle mother's patrician Virginia roots were on permanent display, the role model that I was expected to emulate.

We were all pretty proud of Mother's family. Her father, Major George Lewis, had protected George Washington during the Revolution as commander of his personal bodyguard. But for my grandfather George Lewis, Washington might not have lived to defeat the British and become our first president. His sword still hung on the wall of their plantation house nearby, Marmion, and I went with Mother to call sometimes. Of course, twenty-two miles by carriage or on my Lizzie took all day on the little paths that passed for roads and always meant staying overnight or several days. In those impressionable days, I always enjoyed hearing Grandfather's stories of the great Washington and his exploits. People were still worried about the English and thought them not honorable since they'd surrendered at Yorktown, but kept troops where they could threaten the fragile new United States. Who knew when war might erupt again. In fact, they attacked Washington and burned the White House long after we had defeated them at Yorktown. I was twelve and afraid when the British sacked Washington.

Betty Washington, only sister of George Washington, married Colonel Fielding Lewis. Their son Major George Lewis served as commander of George Washington's Lifeguard (3rd Regiment Light Dragoons) during the American Revolution, charged with protecting the life of the Commander in Chief who would go on to become the first president of the United States. George Lewis was Princess Kate's grandfather.

As a child, it was hard for me to fully appreciate the importance of our hard-won victory over the yoke of our English masters, but I listened attentively to the stories told by my family. To me, it seemed a God-given right that people should govern themselves. The notion of representative government came naturally to me since, in colonial days, many of my family had served in the House of Burgesses at Williamsburg. Why a king should be able to rule a nation with absolute authority was an alien idea, and the right to choose the pathways of my life was deeply embedded in my psyche. It was admittedly a childish understanding of a concept at once simple yet complex, an idea that my very own forefathers had fought and died for.

I knew that I was an American through and through.

The parameters of what being an American meant had not yet fully evolved since we were still a new country. In my youth, America's promise was not yet fleshed out, yet my faith in my country was so deep and abiding that it would remain with me always. My American patriotism would stir especially deeply within me in future years to the point where I would refuse a château and riches in France and even a place at the court of Emperor Napoléon III. Even with its hardships, freedom in America was preferable to wealth in the structured artifice of an emperor's court abroad.

From my own Virginia upbringing and experiences, from the heritage of my patriotic family, and from the depths of a passion for America, which burned instinctively in me, I knew where my heart lay, and I could not be bought with all the riches in the world.

Bonaparte-Murat Background, Early 1800s

THAT I ACTUALLY married into the immediate family of one of history's most famous men was, for this daughter of Virginia, an event to defy my wildest dreams. I have spent the better part of my adult life searching for a deeper understanding of the combination of people, places, and events that drew me into the maelstrom of the Bonapartes' world. As the product of the Commonwealth of Virginia, I was sadly lacking in experiences of the sort that were commonplace among my Bonaparte in-laws. I might have been aristocratic in Virginia society, but that hardly prepared me for their nuanced social world of royalty power, and intrigue. To compensate for this and to better understand my husband and his relatives of high station who would be my family, I read extensively, seeking to make up with acquired knowledge what I had missed out on as first-person observations.

Achille Murat, husband of "Princess Kate", was the nephew of Emperor Napoleon Bonaparte.

I started this quest for learning with some fundamentals about my uncle-in-law, the great Napoléon the First. The more I knew, the less I understood. Never in history has there been such a complex character. A brilliant egomaniac, driven, devious, intimidating, paranoid, a tyrant, manipulative, a natural leader, self-serving, a genius bordering on insanity are some of the descriptions I tried to rationalize as I delved into the most famous of my new marital relatives; my uncle-in-law, Emperor Napoléon I. How was I to internalize enough about the Bonapartes generally, or Uncle Napoléon particularly, in order to prevent being ostracized, laughed at, or driven from the family as a foolish naive outsider? Or worse. It was daunting to make the psychosocial leap from my simple upbringing in Fredericksburg, Virginia to the highest councils of Europe, and I was understandably intimidated. While I never actually feared for my personal safety, I well knew that one did not cross the Bonapartes, so prudence was the order of the day. Being well-informed was an important precautionary measure.

The safest course of action, therefore, was simply to stick with the facts and not wander into the minefields of opinion. And so I began my foray into the arcane world of the Bonapartes, with a natural focus on the interplay between the families of Bonapartes and Murats into whom I married. At the end of the day, I hoped these inquiries would help me better understand my husband, Crown Prince Murat, and help us achieve a happy, stable marriage. My own roots in Virginia have been explored, so please indulge this look back at my husband's roots.

Amid the rubble of the French Revolution, on 13 Vendémiaire, a royalist uprising in Paris threatened the popular assembly. Urgently, Barras and a young Corsican general named Bonaparte called for a volunteer to retrieve cannons from nearby Sablons. Captain Joachim Murat, a dashingly handsome former aide and cavalry leader stepped forward. Forty cannons were brought up in haste, Napoléon's famous "whiff of grapeshot" ensued, and Murat led the Grenadiers into the Council of Five Hundred. With Murat's help, Napoléon's coup d'état was complete. The event provided the catapult for Bonaparte and earned for Murat promotion to *chef de brigade*.

It also paved the way for the marriage on January 20, 1800, of the swashbuckling Murat to Marie Annunziata Carolina Bonaparte, the seductive, ambitious younger sister of Napoléon, better known as Caroline, who was then only seventeen.

Joachim and Caroline Bonaparte Murat at the time of their wedding.

At the time, Napoléon had not yet achieved the battlefield successes that would later crown his reputation. Neither had Murat blazed his way across Europe as Napoléon's greatest cavalry commander, earning along the way millions of francs, dukedoms, kingdoms, and the title First Horseman of Europe. In all battles, but especially in Russia, Murat drove his men hard, sometimes in the saddle from three in the morning until ten at night. His personal daring and aggressive tactics virtually created the fast-moving shock role for which cavalry is now known. *Maréchal* Joachim Murat virtually created the reputation for courage and audacity for later generations of cavalrymen.

As Joachim's battlefield prowess grew, by marrying into the immediate family of Napoléon, Murat's inside track to power was abetted and strengthened by the scheming Caroline, whose knack for intrigue knew no bounds. As one married into the powerful Bonapartes myself, I knew something about the potential of running afoul of the in-laws and could actually empathize with my father-in-law, Joachim.

Joachim Murat, father-in-law of "Princess Kate" led Napoleon's cavalry with aggressive tactics, always leading from the front with his signature white ostrich plumes. His valor and leadership gave Napoleon many of his most famous victories and led to a patronage appointment by the emperor as King of Naples.

After audacious success at the summertime battle of Marengo, Joachim Murat, who would later become my father-in-law, was appointed governor of Paris and basked in a welcome period of calm and the unfamiliar limelight of the City of Light. But now, as Napoléon's sister Caroline followed the carriage of her brother the first consul on Christmas Eve 1800 to attend the opera, the tranquil Yule season was shattered.

The Rue St. Nicaise was narrow and poorly lit, long before the grand avenues and boulevards for which Paris is famous today. Bone-chilling wintry fog hug over the hushed city like a cloud, and sloppy wet snow lay on the ground. Iron-rimmed wheels clattered over the narrow cobbled street as the festive party of Bonaparte carriages hastened to the opera—it was to be one by Haydn. The mood was one of celebration. Though Napoléon had not yet crowned himself emperor, his shadow hung apocalyptically over the Continent and the jovial holiday mood of the Bonapartes had more to do with recent battlefield successes than with the Christ child.

The festive group formed a veritable cavalcade of power. Elegant carriages with their sidelights flickering in the gloom were accompanied by lavishly attired outriders in Napoleonic livery, affirming the identities of the occupants. The ornate carriage immediately following Napoléon bore a very pregnant Caroline Bonaparte Murat, younger sister of Napoléon and wife of the young officer who had, a few short years ago, earned the attention and gratitude of her brother.

It was then that a massive bomb exploded in close proximity. Napoléon, Josephine, Caroline, and other family members in the cortege were showered with falling debris and the gory dismembered body parts of bystanders. With the force of the blast canalized by the buildings, the effect was overwhelming and many died. Hortense de Beauharnais was cut by flying metal, but it was Caroline, far advanced in her first pregnancy, whose physical and psychological symptoms were most severe. The fright, abetted by a wildly careening carriage, shattered her nerves and sent her to hospital fearing for her own health and that of the baby she carried.

Caroline was "laid in" at the Hotel de Brienne apartments in the Tuileries where a sallow premature baby boy, with characteristically Mediterranean features of his Corsican and French parents, drew his first breaths a few weeks later on January 21, 1801. His name was Charles Louis Napoléon Achille Murat, and I knew him lovingly as my Achille. The Bonaparte genes were strong, and as he grew to manhood, Achille would become, in the eyes of many, a dead ringer for his Uncle Napoléon.

Caroline's frenetic stress shortly before Achille's birth laid her low for many weeks and left her son, it is widely believed, with physical and psychological issues which would haunt him throughout his life. Whether the effects on his mother of the explosion of the "infernal machine" shortly before his birth led to his later seizures or hypertension, I cannot say. Caroline, however, was convinced beyond all doubt that the child suffered trauma in the womb, which left him moody, high-strung, and epileptic. I saw these tendencies in him frequently but was less certain than she of their origin. Sometimes I suspected that the "infernal machine" had provided a palatable excuse for negligent parenting, but it was not mine to know, and I would surely not risk Bonaparte wrath by such a suggestion.

Sister of Emperor Napoleon Bonaparte I and queen consort Caroline Bonaparte Murat of the Napoleonic kingdom of Naples, which comprised roughly the southern third of Italy. This original engraving depicts Queen Murat at approximately the time of her marriage to Joachim Murat. Etching by J. Champagne.

Achille's early childhood was spent in glamour at the governor's lavish estate of Villiers in Neuilly. Even more posh, in 1805, Achille's father, Joachim Murat, bought the fabled Elysée Palace once occupied by Madame Pompadour. Now highly placed amidst the tight inner circle of Napoléon's key advisers, the elder Murat had it refurbished by the famous architect Vignon and moved the family into the most famous residence in all of France. For the son of an innkeeper from La Bastide-Fortunière, Joachim Murat had arrived!

Achille Murat, husband of Catherine Willis Murat, was raised in France's most famous residence, the Elysee Palace. Today it is the residence of the President of France.

My Achille's youth was luxurious but pompous, artificial in the extreme, and lacking in warmth; a childhood environment that I believe contributed to his high-strung moodiness. In my later appraisal, I would come to regard his youth as a mere caricature of childhood—pretentious, vain, and cold. It was not of his making but was the bedrock of his life.

It was a very flimsy bedrock, which did not serve him well. I tried, for all of our years together, to empathize with him when he fell under the alternating gray depression and flights of fancy that overcame him from time to time. Modern psychologists would likely diagnose him as bipolar.

When he was but six, his mother Caroline fell into, perhaps even sought out, an amorous liaison with General Junot, who had replaced her husband as governor of Paris. From this and similar examples, I am led to understand from others, never from Achille himself, that motherhood was never her long suit. From stories told by other family members, Caroline appeared more in her element as a Machiavellian political operative than as a doting mother.

There are reliable reports that Caroline also flaunted her flagrant dalliance with Austrian ambassador Metternich while her husband was away on campaign with Napoléon. This liaison would be inflamed in future years when Metternich brokered her into a home-in-exile at Schloss Frohsdorf, a castle in Lanzenkirchen, Austria, where he promptly placed her under house arrest. There, as Achille grew into manhood in palatial exile, he and his mother were constantly under Metternich's microscopic suspicions. Whether Caroline still, under these drastically altered circumstances, warmed the bed of her former lover is a matter for speculation.

From my conservative upbringing in the strictures of Virginia society, my background was positively puritanical when it came to the freewheeling sexual attitudes of the French. Their lifestyles seemed an outrageous counterpoint to my upbringing as a churchgoing Southerner. To this naive daughter of the American South, it was all positively scandalous but scarcely a subject to be discussed with my husband whose own mother was the subject. That Achille and his mother loved each other is not in doubt. That she was good for him is another matter entirely.

Rumors abounded that my mother-in-law, Caroline, was promiscuous with any number of the handsome young officers who came and went during Joachim's long absences. Perhaps. Perhaps not. In any case, she was my mother-in-law and raised with an altogether different code of morality, and it was not my place to gossip about her. I render the above as observations, not as judgments.

As with telling my own family story, I know that the bloodline of one's family and the experiences of one's early years set the predicate for our later lives. I relate these stories of Achille's youth not to judge or criticize but merely to explain some of his moods and behavioral tendencies learned in a most unusual childhood. His propensity to emotional outbursts and periods of deep depression can, I believe, be laid at Caroline and Joachim's feet due to being shunted off to nannies, tutors, and strangers rather than enjoying a supportive family environment such as the one with which I was blessed.

My Achille adored his father, yet Joachim was scarcely around during his formative years and, when present, presented himself as a peacock on flamboyant display. He played lavishly the role of marshal of the empire, grand duke, and eventually king but, from the many stories to which I have been privy, was not always an appropriate role model for his son. Forever engaged in political intrigue in garish uniforms of his own design, Joachim was more of an operatic character than a wholesome father figure.

Joachim too had romances outside marriage, which titillated the gossipy crowd and were not lost on the young Achille. As Achille matured, he surely saw behind the curtain of his parents' faux marriage. Though love was ever in the air and loudly proclaimed, in the world of the Bonapartes, nothing was as it seemed.

Achille had an abnormal childhood to say the least, and it affected our lives in ways I will never fully understand. Notwithstanding our diverse upbringings, we forged a life of satisfaction and adventure on a grand scale. Tragically, in his glittering childhood were sown seeds of hypertension, moodiness, and the worrisome seizures that would afflict him forever. From many a deep and draining conversation, I know that his low point was the execution of his father by firing squad after a youth spent in adoration of the man. And what child would not brood over such a terrible event, filing its imprint deep within the soul? That Achille was a celebrated royal in no way excused him from the full range of human emotion and, in my opinion, may have even exacerbated his feelings. The higher the status, the further the fall.

It is an axiom of the human condition that we are all products of our experience. From a boyhood that bordered on the bizarre, it was a wonder that he found enough emotional stability to fashion a functioning life, much less to author great tomes of political wisdom, which earned the respect of scholars and government officials the world over.

Vainly substituting pomp and hollow titles for parental love, his parents maneuvered Achille at a young age into several of the shell titles, which rang loudly but hollow in the halcyon years of empire. Together with gaudy uniforms designed by his father, he acquired, before he was twelve, the honorary titles of Prince Royal of the Two Sicilies, First Prince of Pontecorvo, and Grand Duke Heir of Berg and Cleves. These high-sounding honorifics made him, however, no more than a political pawn on the Bonaparte chessboard, manipulated at will by the elders who wrote the rules of the game. In later life, recognizing the futility of these vanities, he would disdain the empire from which he sprang and become its most vocal critic. In a gesture of contempt for the vainglories of courtly life upon residence in the Florida Territory where we spent our years in the wilderness, he wore the shabbiest of clothes, sometimes even frontier buckskin and never changed shoes until they were worn out. One habit I especially frowned upon was his disdain for bathing, which with the hot, humid clime of our Florida home resulted in odors that can be charitably described as gamy.

Without consciously realizing the role he was playing, Achille was very much a rebel who relished thumbing his nose at the pretensions of life in the courts of Europe.

The young Achille was widely celebrated in his father's kingdom of Naples. His birthday was made a national holiday and loudly feted by Neapolitan children. Like his father before him, he learned to play the courtly role and did it well. His young ego grew in step with his stature as a young man.

Catherine (Kate) Willis Murat's husband Charles Louis Napoleon Achille Murat as a child in the uniform of a midshipman of the navy of the Napoleonic Kingdom of Naples over which his father ruled as king. His mother was Caroline Bonaparte, the sister of Napoleon and queen of Naples which constituted the southern third of Italy. (Image from a contemporaneously painted locket painted during the Napoleonic rule of Naples.)

At age eight, with much ado as a diminutive honorary colonel of lancers in pretentious uniform like his father, Achille accompanied Joachim on a military mission to assault the British garrison on Capri. Like most of his young life, it was largely a stage show for his father's Neapolitan subjects, and Achille reveled in it. Feasting on a reputation for military bravado, much like his father's diamond-studded sword and ostrich plume hats, the young Murat may be seen today in works of art at museums and palaces in Naples, ever playing the royal roles: driving chariots, scaling cliffs, and visually affirming the fictions of his childhood. Though he largely succeeded in subduing his ego, throughout life he would sometimes revert to childhood glories, however contrived they may have been, and marvel that the world did not flock to his door or march lockstep to his beliefs. At times like this, I reminded my crown prince that he was still the prince of my heart.

If, in later life, my Achille affected some unusual manners and idiosyncrasies from such a bizarre childhood, who, one must wonder, would not? The wonder was that we found enough commonality of life from which to piece together a marriage.

One of the few common denominators of our lives was a passion for learning. While I had been well schooled in Virginia and developed a lifelong craving for reading, my Achille's education in the European model was one of privilege and excellence. Whatever mental/emotional handicaps he may (or may not) have had paled under the severe academic regimens of his private tutors. In his father's court at Napoli, Achille's prodigious brain was cultivated by some of Europe's most famous scholars. One example I can recall is that he learned geography from the distinguished Alexander von Humboldt, one of the first to bring true scientific method to the study of our planet.

Achille wanted for nothing in his lessons except consistent motivation. As in all other avenues of his life, his studies were characterized by flashes of energetic brilliance, alternating with periods of boredom and malaise.

His amazing mind seemed to soak up knowledge with such ease that confinement to a study room with a tutor seemed self-limiting. He had a penchant for experimental learning where he himself was engaged. This he preferred over readings and discussions with his tutors. He would follow this inquisitive mind to the frontiers of the natural world at our home in the Florida wilderness, ever seeking to know all he could about its plants, animals, and mysteries. He probed the frontiers of the latest advances in scientific disciplines with tutors who were often the original proponents for them. Though imbued with the mind of a scientist, he nonetheless studied the classics to an uncommon level of mastery. Complementing these educational achievements, Achille was a natural linguist and spoke fluently in no less than seven languages. This skill would later serve him well as he matured and interacted with leaders on the Continent.

Let me just say as plainly as I can, and without embellishment, that my Achille was the smartest person I ever met. His intellectual world was so complex that it was almost like there were multiple minds inhabiting the same prodigious brain. I actually believe that it was this aspect of the man that caused many to regard him as mentally unstable. In my Achille, I observed the full gamut, from courtly European sophistication in the company of world leaders to such coarseness of person and manner in Florida that townspeople would scarcely have anything to do with him.

Of course, I did not know Achille in childhood. He was growing into manhood in the salons and palaces of Europe while I was being groomed into the role of demure Virginia gentle lady atop Willis Hill in Fredericksburg. The United States, in which my youth was spent, was still a relatively new nation, and in many respects, I and my country grew up together. My prince and I could have scarcely had more different experiences during childhood and adolescence.

My beliefs concerning his childhood and how it affected his later life come from years of imagining his youth more than from firsthand knowledge. I have the luxury of hindsight and of seeing the result of his upbringing by way of proof in the pudding. My empirical observations of Achille in later life validate with observed fact the beliefs I report to you, so they are probably more reliable than had I actually grown up with him. Please believe me when I tell you that he was so enigmatic in manhood that I spent much time imagining his childhood and how that shaped the man who became my prince.

The young Crown Prince Achille was especially adept at politics of all sorts. Some of his political acumen was learned by reading, and some was learned by conversation and debate with his tutors. Most of his razor-keen grasp of politics, however, was learned in the witches' brew of Napoleonic maneuverings, practical lessons in survival of the fittest, where the astute thrived and lesser combatants in the political game died, quite literally. Even in his childhood, an attempt was made on his life, and according to family lore, the poison left him affected in odd ways for the rest of his days.

He learned firsthand the value of trustworthy information from trustworthy allies and how to parlay that into political doctrines and personal advantage while reducing the power base of adversaries. He saw at close range the quicksands of relationships. At the feet of his royal parents, he learned that alliances of today often become the enemies of tomorrow. He learned cynicism and duplicity from the best of them and saw that in order to survive in the Bonaparte regime, even in the Bonaparte family, one must ruthlessly rewrite the rules to suit the moment.

Fortunately, Achille did not subscribe to the more diabolical traits affected by some of the Bonapartes, such as Caroline's perpetual scheming against Josephine. Caroline was positively paranoid that that Napoléon's wife, Josephine, while not related by blood, held the upper hand over herself and other members of the family. Had Achille been so devious, I should not have been able to be his wife, I fear.

How Achille outgrew these early life lessons of self-centered expediency is to me a testament to his strength of character. His behavior may have been strange at times, but he was honest to a fault. Even his detractors begrudgingly admired his integrity.

Achille conversed comfortably with kings and commoners about political theories and developed a questioning mind regarding the philosophical underpinnings of governance. He especially like to debate the relative merits of various forms of governing and developed early a keen appreciation for the humanist thought springing tentatively from the drawing rooms, lecture halls, and taverns of Europe. These early seeds of humanist political thought would not blossom fully until planted in the rich soils of his adopted home in America. In the bosom of the Bonaparte world, he couldn't breathe a word of these radical thoughts concerning popular government.

Many is the time I have heard my Achille ponder aloud the essential political question: "Is the wisdom of an anointed sovereign greater than that of the collective wisdom of his people?" Even asking this was akin to heresy, for it challenged the legitimacy of all of the kings, of all of the queens, and of all of the nobles of all of the countries, fiefdoms, and political divisions of Europe back into the mists of time. Something of a rabble-rouser, he enjoyed nothing more than baiting a political conversation with the radical notion that the people, from the lowest ragamuffin to the highest lord, have the innate wisdom to choose what is best. I especially remember a quote from a letter to his friend Count Thibaudeau in 1832: "This principle from which so much good has emanated, and which is destined to govern the world, is what is called in America 'self government'; government by the people themselves."

I ask you, what could be further from the power-hungry centralized government enforced at cannon-point upon the hordes of Europe by his very family? Is it any wonder that he developed a persona of near schizophrenic proportion, toeing the Bonaparte line yet espousing government by the people? I often wondered if his European education and worldview led to a warped perception of America or if it gave him instead the more dispassionate and detached insights of an outsider.

One thing was to me abundantly clear about my Achille's youth. The democratic ideals he vociferously espoused grew from the antitheistic nineteenth century humanist movement, which denied the infallibility of God and set man in His place. The humanism of the eighteenth and nineteenth centuries gave to every man the certain "inalienable rights" of which America's founders had written, rights staked out in Philadelphia by my ancestors. These rights of the common man stood in the starkest contrast to the royal status, wealth, and power into which my Achille was born. In his world, there seemed little need for a God. As royals, they got to play that role for themselves. Of course, this was forever a bone of contention in Catholic France, and the tug of war for hearts and minds went on for centuries and still existed in the 1820s when I married Achille.

Achille found the humanist gospel appealing while remaining an elitist—a royal by birth. His facile mind found some convoluted logic by which to subscribe to a profound belief in the common man while still glowing white hot in the Bonapartist furnace and railing against the fates that had done in his family and confiscated their wealth and titles. He never relented in his zeal to restore the perquisites of royalty.

After the fall of Naples, only a bitter brew remained for the Murats who had ruled it. The same Count Metternich, with whom Caroline had carried on a dalliance in bygone years, now ruled Austria, and under his mandate, he ensconced Caroline and her four children in the castle of Frohsdorf near Lanzenkirchen. In pretended splendor, there she affected the title Countess of Lipona and, with no political intrigues to occupy her time, assumed some of the motherly duties she had so long shirked.

Achille Murat was exiled, along with his family, to Schloss Frohsdorf in Austria after the fall of Napoleon and execution of his father.

After Naples and her brother Napoléon's downfall, there was, of course, nothing to be countess of, but the fabricated title salved Caroline's ego while, like everything else in the latter days of empire, it had nothing to do with reality.

Under the humanist thought, which now dominated Achille's philosophy, people could and should govern themselves. Those beliefs evolved, along with furtherance of his other educational pursuits into his complex worldview while he impatiently waited out eight interminable years under Metternich's house arrest at the cheerless Castle Frohsdorf.

Now in his early twenties, the humanist movement also fed Achille's growing disenchantment with religion generally, and by the time we married in 1826, he was at least an agonistic, if not an out-and-out atheist. I quietly and privately maintained my Episcopal beliefs, but the role of religion fell into subtle decline in our marriage as the years wore on. Achille merely humored those of a religious bent, and later singled out the South's fundamentalist religions, largely the Baptists, for cynical comment.

These polar opposites of childhood thought, democracy versus monarchy, created in Achille a tangled skein of contradictory political beliefs, which forever lurked in the background like a tiger pacing a cage. While the caged tiger wrote eloquently of democratic ideals, it also snarled that the mantle of wealth and power was torn from his family, leaving them at the mercy of others. The anti-Bonapartist cabal that dethroned the Murats had left them powerless, confiscated their fortunes, and stripped them of their titles. Achille wanted it all back.

Achille's theology of the rights of man—his democratic streak—arose in stark opposition to the greed and insatiable egos of not only his Bonaparte in-laws, but also of all old-world monarchs who remained comfortably ensconced in absolute power and insulated from their own people. The two could not be reconciled, no matter what mental tightrope he walked.

As a practical matter, Achille had a point regarding the confiscated millions taken from his family as Naples fell. To him, this smacked of theft on a grand scale, and he didn't care who knew it. For years to come, Achille pressed his suit in any forum that might offer a sympathetic ear, but there no sympathies were to be found among the allies who sought to not only rub the Bonaparte's noses in defeat, but also to keep a boot on their neck.

Adding to this financial insult, of course, was the death of his father at the hands of the same coalition of nations. He might someday forgive the loss of the family fortune, but asking him to forgive his father's death was pushing him into an impossible corner.

Knowing as I did of Achille's zeal to avenge his father's death, recover the Murat fortunes from a hostile France, and lurk in the wings awaiting a Bonaparte resurgence, I actually feared for our safety sometimes. Would some agent of a secretive foreign power track us down in Florida, or did they care at all?

It would have been humiliating to my husband, who had sprung from proud Bonaparte loins, to know that he was perceived as totally inconsequential, yet as that family's sun went into eclipse, so too did his. Achille's ego would have been wounded to know just how little the movers and shakers of Europe cared about his fate. If he was "out of sight, out of mind," his mother, the deposed queen, was not.

My Husband's European Backdrop, 1800-1821

*I*F EVENTS HAD left my Achille's childhood topsy turvy before 1815, they ratcheted up to a crescendo as Uncle Napoleon's fortunes went into eclipse. This is the saga of the end of empire and of the royal Murats as told to me by my husband and forms a backdrop for his persona and for our marriage. I did not live these moments and spin the tale second-hand here just to provide insights. All of this, from the grandeur to the ignominious betrayals was woven into the fabric of our lives and so must be taken into account. For a daughter of Virginia, of a simpler time and place, it all seemed so unreal . . . yet behind this curtain lay the truths of my Achille and thus of our marriage.

First came Uncle Napoleon's disastrous Russian Campaign. In despair and defeat as the remnants of the Grande Armee trudged painfully homeward in the vicious winter he turned once more, as history tells us, to the senior leader who had bailed him out before, Achille's beloved father Marshal Joachim Murat.

Was it an act of trust which caused Napoleon to delegate the tatters of the Grande Armee to Marshal Murat, or was it simply desperation bordering on cowardice? Did he seriously think he would regroup and fight another day?

What would his people think? If he still had any allies left, what would they think? The courtiers and administrators? Uncle Napoleon sulked his was back to Paris in atypical silence, the gloom of his mood perfectly captured in the famous painting by Adolph Northen.

What did it matter? The Grande Armee was for all intents and purposes finished and the First French Empire began to totter on it's last legs.

Violating the trust Napoleon had placed in him, and not wanting to be seen at the head of an army which had been soundly defeated, soon after Napoleon himself abandoned the Grande Armee so too did Marshal Joachim Murat, my father in law. With some grain of truth to the story that his kingdom needed him straightaway in Naples, on January 16, 1813 at Posen, in East Prussia Marshal Murat slipped away toward Naples in disguise. The remaining artillery and supply wagons of the Russian expedition were abandoned in a dump. Temperatures fell to 34 degrees below zero. There was no food, no warmth, no transport, no chain of command, and worst of all, no morale for the Grande Armee. It became a disgraceful "every man for himself" rout as the once mighty force straggled leaderless back to France.

A gloomy Napoleon delegated to Achille Murat's father, Marshal Joachim Murat, the mission of shepherding the remains of the defeated Grande Armee' back to France after the disastrous Russian campaign.

This was an inconvenient topic for Achille to come to grips with and was never spoken of. He worshiped his father, preferring, as any son would, the heroic image of the dashing cavalry commander thundering into the mouth of the cannon with ostrich plumes flying. Joachim's betrayal of his patron Napoleon, complete with desertion of his post under less than honorable conditions, was the eight hundred pound gorilla in our room.

As Napoleon's fortunes waned, there were further betrayals. It was and is my assessment that Caroline and Joachim's actions reached a level somewhere on a continuum between shameful and traitorous. For a simple Virginia girl married to the son of all of this, it was more than one could fathom yet I dare not voice any critical opinion for fear of repercussions.

After Russia and the desertion of his army by Napoleon himself, the myth of infallibility which had surrounded the once-mighty emperor faltered. Old enemies and even a few friends formed new coalitions to oppose him. Some of his own generals turned against him. Given a virtual ultimatum from Marshal Ney, and the terms imposed by the allies under the Treaty of Fontainebleau, Napoleon abdicated in the spring of 1814. Under the treaty, he renounced the thrones of France and Italy and was sent into genteel exile on Elba, just twenty miles off the Tuscan coast. There he brooded and schemed in the Villa Mulini overlooking the sea and ruminated about unfulfilled destiny.

Never one for passivity and inaction, Napoleon's delusions prompted his escape from Elba and clandestine return to the continent. He was either the supreme optimist or blissfully ignorant of the extent of the overwhelming opposition which he faced. No doubt his certitude of success was fueled by the massive Bonaparte ego which to date knew no bounds. At first it appeared that his confidence was not misplaced. In France old forces rallied to his side, and new ones were recruited. On the surface one might have presumed that a miracle of resurgence was in the offing with the return of the old cockiness. Simultaneously however, a coalition of Great Britain, Prussia, Russia, and Austria were assembling the machine for his final defeat and pledged massive forces to achieve that end. In that moment, the seeds of his downfall flowered into a massive million man army fielded by the allies under the seventh coalition. All of central Europe was in thrall as major maneuver forces clashed at Quatre Bras and Ligny, setting the stage for final defeat by the coalition, led by the British at Waterloo in a battle now synonymous with ignominy.

At Waterloo, the classic Bonaparte ego, laced with wishful thinking, had failed to visualize both the strategic environment and the tactical reality of the battlefield. Wellington's forces, with Blucher's Prussians on the flank, carried the day on July 15, 1815 and a sulking Napoleon fell back on Paris. In desperation he planned an escape to the United States where allies in French-friendly New Orleans awaited. A British naval blockade at Rochefort would thwart the scheme. Boxed in and completely out of options, it was there that the once invincible emperor surrendered to the British aboard HMS *Bellerophon*.

In that act the first notes of the funeral dirge sounded for the once-mighty empire. Tricked once, the allies would brook no chances this time, and sent the imprisoned emperor aboard the HMS *Northumberland* to the wind-swept rock of St. Helena off the coast of Africa where he would be surrounded by a small cadre of followers until his death in Longwood House on May 5, 1821.

With the emperor's death on that remote island, his empire gasped its last breath, as did the many powerful hangers-on who fed from crumbs of the emperor's table.

Once the dominos began to fall, the entire Bonaparte clan became a clan of wealthy political pariahs. Not only was the emperor himself brought low, but so too were all who were his adherents, including his puppet king of Naples, Achille's father, Joachim. Without the patronage of the emperor, it was not difficult for King Murat to foresee on the immediate horizon an inglorious end to his rule. Queen Caroline was slower to admit to their precarious position. As the self-appointed grand strategist for Murat interests, she still clung to delusions that they and their kingdom could survive without the emperor. It was classic Bonaparte ego.

It would have been supremely interesting to me if I had had opportunity to meet my uncle-in-law the emperor and once the most powerful man on earth. All the world held its breath throughout the years of my childhood as he went about conquering one country after another. Without a doubt, his legacy of brilliance and bloodshed reshaped the world, and to this day it seems implausible that I actually married into his family. I can scarcely reconcile the news reports read up on Willis Hill with the fact that I personally became caught up in the web of Napoleonic politics. But I have digressed.

Shortly before the end of Napoleon's empire, King Murat deserted the Bonapartist cause. The traitorous sister of the emperor, Caroline, prompted a duplicitous alliance with her former over Prince Klemens Wenzel von Metternich of the House of Habsburg, in Austria. Under their scheme, an alliance of Metternich and Achille's father King Murat would prevail, a weakened or dethroned Napoleon would be the odd man out, and King Murat would expand his reign over a unified Italy.

The allies, as history shows, had other ideas. When the allies in assembly at the Congress of Vienna threatened his throne, a cornered King Murat turned on his supposed new allies the Austrians and marched to do battle with them with whatever forces he could cobble together. In the only significant battle against his would-be allies, King Murat was soundly defeated at Tolentino. Both Murat and Metternich played a grand game of duplicity in this the eleventh hour of the empire. Murat lost. Metternich won.

There was something quite irrational about this. Having joined forces with Prince Metternich against his patron Napoleon, and with no Army forthcoming from his own Kingdom of Naples, King Murat's attack on his only ally Metternich, might not have been the wisest strategy. Though official histories are obsessed with the grandeur of clashing armies and venal politics, and logically see in Murat's attack on Austria his attempt to preserve his kingly crown, I always wondered if there wasn't a more personal subtext. I think my perspective as a family member empowers me to proffer a different insight, one overlooked by historians.

Never mind the politics of nations, at the human level when Murat attacked Metternich, did he see his wife in their sexual embrace? Was a proud and vindictive Murat actually avenging his wounded masculine ego? Men and armies have died for less, and I believe this a plausible motive for such an illogical act as throwing his inferior force against the well trained army of an ally. Jealous rage is not a rational creature.

The dashing Joachim Murat, father-in-law of "Princess Kate" and Napoleon's greatest cavalry commander. He was known for resplendent military uniforms and regalia of his own design and for audacious cavalry tactics on behalf of Napoleon's armies.

While all of the above skullduggery was taking place in Austria, Achilles' mother Queen Caroline, was still in Naples with her family including my husband-to-be. There she vainly tried to generate public support by a showy uniformed appearance on horseback amidst the operatic pomp which had always rallied her subjects before. Despite best efforts, she too was unable to build a fire under old loyalties or generate military support for their ill-fated venture. The Napoli which the Murats had loved and ruled with a benevolent hand spurned their last desperate overtures. The Neapolitans soundly rejected Queen Caroline's pleas to join her husband to fight for a unified Italy. The ominous sound of falling dominos echoed over the streets of Naples and throughout the empire of Napoleon I. The mighty Murats had at last failed.

After being trounced at Tolentino, in an uncharacteristically meek retreat the flamboyant King of Naples, once "First Horseman of Europe" and Napoleon's greatest cavalry commander, sneaked away on a small fishing boat to save his skin.

Was the heroic leader of so many battles now to quail in cowardice, or was he simply being practical, living to fight another day as he had done on the retreat from Moscow?

During his ignominious flight, the King of Naples, my Achille's father, was captured by the legitimate King of Naples, Ferdinand IV, recently restored to power by the Congress of Vienna. After the brief formalities of a kangaroo court martial, the death sentence against King Murat was quickly handed down. The vainglorious Joachim Murat, never much more than a puppet king anyway, refused a blindfold at his execution in Pizzo and directed his own firing squad. In a final expression of vanity, he implored his executioners to aim for the heart and spare his face. It was Greek tragedy and grand opera wrapped into one.

Achille Murat's father, the dashing Marshal Joachim Murat, was considered by some a peacock general for his taste in dazzling self-designed uniforms.

I found this verbatim account of his last hours in a journal, and herewith present this to illustrate the man.

"PIZZO, OCTOBER 15, 1815.

The following is a brief account of the unfortunate end of Joachim Murat.

On Thursday last (the 12th instant) arrived an Estafette from Naples, and another at 9 o'clock, directed to Marshal Nunziante, with orders to assemble a Military Commission to try Murat. They immediately began to call the witnesses to depose what Murat had said on his arrival in this place. In the meantime the commission was formed, consisting of Marshal Nunziante, a Lieutenant-Colonel and Captain, with the Procurator General of Monteleone. The suite of Murat was then placed in close confinement, and he was left in a room with a guard upon him. An hour before the reading of the sentence, he knew the commission was sitting, and through me, desired to speak with General Nunziante, but he was informed he was not then present. Murat impatient, wrote a note to the said General, but it was not received, it being intimated to him, that no letter could be admitted. At length, the process finished, not more than twelve hours having elapsed, as the Estafettes arrived in the evening of the 12th, and it was terminated at 9 o'clock in the morning of the 13th. By the decision of the Procurator General, he was condemned to die, which sentence was agreed to by the votes of the whole commission. It was then read to him by one of those who composed the said commission, on which he exclaimed, " How does Ferdinand IVth wish my death ? What have I done? It displeases me much to find the violence with which the Court of Naples has treated this affair." A confessor then entered the apartment, and exhorted him to confess but Murat answered him, " My sins are so heavy, that none but God himself can pardon them." At least", said the confessor, "make some confession"; he seemed much affected—The confessor again pressed it, in order to do away what might be said. He then took a pen, and wrote in the last moments of his life, " I have lived a Christian, and die a true Christian." He desired a pair of scissors, to cut off some hair to be sent to his wife, but it was not permitted. The time for putting the sentence into execution being elapsed, (orders from Naples not to exceed a quarter of an hour after it was passed) he was told to move towards the place destined for his execution, in the same prison, and coming out of the room, a Neapolitan Officer gave him a handkerchief to blind himself, but he refused it. Arrived at the destined spot, with an intrepid countenance, turning immediately his face to the soldiers, and placing his hand upon his breast, he gave the word " Fire." They fired twelve shots at his breast, which killed him instantaneously, and three in the head after he fell. His body was placed in a rough wooden box and carried to the Church, without a bier or any religious ceremony, on the shoulders of six soldiers, accompanied by fifteen or twenty others, and buried in a pit where they throw the most despicable felons. The trial of this unfortunate man has been similar to that of the most infamous brigands. This is a correct account of the miserable end of Joachim Murat.

After betrayal of Napoleon, King Joachim Murat was executed at Pizzo, Calabria, Italy October 15, 1813. Brave but vain until the end, Murat, the father-in-law of "Princess Kate", refused a blindfold but implored the firing squad to spare his face with their fusillade.

The populace, not sufficiently satiated, dug up Murat's body, and attempted to burn it; upon the interference of a respectable magistrate, they shot him, and consumed their bodies together. Ferdinand has pardoned all Murat's suite.— This act does him honour."

For the young and impressionable Achille, when his father was executed it was almost like his own death. It painfully ripped from him the role model he adored, his mentor who epitomized for the son the chivalric ideal of old. The psychological impact on Achille was almost as brutal as the physical impact of those twelve bullets at Pizzo and the moodiness which closed in upon him in recollections of his beloved father would remain a characteristic of his personality forever.

With the King and his kingdom now dead, Queen Caroline's ambitions and schemes reached a dead end and she had only to save herself and her children. Just as it was for Napoleon, it was the final straw of humiliation that the hated British came to the rescue, perhaps saving the entire Murat family from a fate similar to the dead king. The populace had turned against their rulers and if King Joachim's death had not been at the hands of the Bourbons, I believe that the deposed Murats would have been done in anyway. With their ostentatious wealth it seems probable that they might have been targeted by any number of brigand bands which roamed ancient Napoli. In the ebb and flow of public sentiment the king and queen whom the people of Naples had once celebrated were now *persona non grata.*

Such were the political fates in the final tumultuous days of Napoleon's empire when rumor prevailed over reason and passions over practicality.

At Gaeta however, Achille and his brothers and sisters joined their mother Caroline aboard the British man-of-war, *HMS Tremendous,* and were whisked away to safety albeit as prisoners of war. In this interlude Achille recalls the humorous story that his mother implored the captain, Captain Campbell, to allow her to bring aboard a favorite cow named Caroline in order that her children might have milk during the voyage. Humorous moments were scarce at that time and this one seems especially poignant.

But for this British intervention, given the turbulent environment and fear of anyone with Bonaparte connections, I believe there would have been a tragic end for all the Murat family, with mother Caroline and children following father to the grave.

If Queen Caroline and the Murat family had died as their kingdom did, the turn of fate would have been so vastly different. Achille and the rest of the family would likely have been executed or just plain murdered in Naples.

There would have been no flight to America.

He would not have made his unlikely move to the Florida wilderness.

I would never have met him or fallen in love with him.

The only intersection of the Washington and Bonaparte families in all of history would not have taken place.

Destiny would have consigned my life to a different path and I should not have become a princess. Twice.

And I would not be writing this story which you have chosen to read. Such is the unseen hand of fate which invariably writes the script by which our lives play out.

But the fates were kind and had a different life in mind for me. Achille Murat, his mother Queen Caroline, and his siblings did live on though neither King Murat nor uncle Napoleon would survive.

Together with his siblings and his uncle Emperor Napoleon Bonaparte I, the young boy in uniform in this painting is Charles Louis Napoleon Achille Murat. He would later immigrate to America where he married Catherine Daingerfield Willis (Gray) and engaged in unsuccessful business ventures in the Florida Territory and in Louisiana.

Napoleon, risen from peasant Corsican stock to become the world's most powerful leader, would die on St. Helena, not from poisoning as was rumored, but of gastrointestinal bleeding. The First French Empire died not with a bang but with a whimper.

The dashing cavalry leader Joachim Murat, son of a French innkeeper, whose legendary exploits made him a king, died at the hands of a firing squad after betraying the very regime which had created him.

Marshal of the Empire Joachim Murat, seen here in white ostrich plumes accompanying Napoleon at the Battle of Jena, was the father of Achille Murat, husband of Catherine Willis Murat. He was later rewarded by Napoleon with a patronage appointment as King of Naples, roughly the southern third of Italy.

The great Napoleon was gone and with him the puppet kings and kingdoms. The royal youth of my Achille, indeed the entire royal saga of the Murats, was over. It was a mere prelude to what would follow.

Joachim Murat, King of Naples, Grand Duke of Berg and Cleves, Marshal of the Empire, Grand Admiral of the Napoleonic Navy, and Governor of Paris. Born a commoner, his elevation to positions of power resulted from the patronage of Emperor Napoleon I. Murat's valor as a cavalry commander was legendary and he gave Napoleon many of his most famous victories but betrayed him as the First Empire began to crumble. He wrote wistfully to his son and daughter-in-law in America, Achille and "Princess Kate" Murat who made their home in territorial Florida. Image from the 1831 edition of No. VIII in the Family Library, "The Court and Camp of Napoleon".

Royal Roots, Early 1800s

CAROLINE BONAPARTE MURAT, queen consort of Naples, and her husband, King Joachim, raised their children in the classic royal mode, which is to say, all of the material advantages money could buy but scarcely a warm, "normal" childhood. There were four of them: Charles Louis Napoléon Achille Murat, Marie Letizia Josephine Annonciade Murat, Lucien Charles Joseph Napoléon Murat, and Louise Julie Caroline Murat. Each was raised to the privileges and pretensions of life in a Bonaparte court. Each was expected to assume a position of influence in the Bonaparte empire, which was intended to continue its conquests and bring new realms under its sway. Nothing less than ruling the world was enough for Uncle Napoléon and his minions, especially family members were expected to participate in the grand global conquest.

To achieve their part, royal educations for the Murat children, under the very best tutors, were designed to prepare them for future positions of nobility. Presumably, they would elevate to these levels under the aegis of Queen Caroline despite her having spurned her brother, the emperor. Frankly, Caroline's presumptions that she would forever be doled out pieces of the imperial pie seemed preposterous to me after she betrayed her famous brother Napoléon as the kingdom of Naples collapsed.

I was to learn that, with the Bonapartes, the depths of family loyalty often overcame fits of imperious pique. Family ties had always been important to me, but with the Bonapartes, it was an obsession.

Queen Caroline Bonaparte Murat and her four royal children ensconced in the lavish trappings of the Kingdom of Naples. The young boy in uniform is Prince Charles Louis Napoleon Achille Murat who would later immigrate to America, marry Catherine Daingerfield Willis (Gray), and settle in the Florida Territory near Tallahassee.

As Napoléon's empire crumbled, none of the Bonapartes could be certain how the future would play out. In Caroline's case, the crystal ball was especially cloudy. She had no way of knowing if she would remain in favor with her brother the emperor or if he might order her arrest for her eleventh-hour betrayal. It was a turbulent, even frightening time, in the Murat household.

If neither Queen Caroline would not be in position to oversee her children's preparation for power, the four Murat's were to be tutored as skilled, independent manipulators. The goal of this was to school them in avoiding the political quicksands and bring them up in the opportunistic creed of the Bonapartes. In order to survive in the cutthroat world of Napoleonic politics, it was necessary for all of the Murat children to become practitioners of realpolitik in the extreme. This took on greater urgency when the money dried up after Uncle Napoléon's exile and the demise of their kingdom of Naples.

In 1816, the post-Napoleonic government of France had banished the entire Bonaparte family and seized their possessions and incomes, leaving Caroline and the others stranded and facing an uncertain financial future. She had only what she could marshal on her own from the collapsing kingdom of Naples.

With the death knell of empire echoing across Europe, each disenfranchised Bonaparte reacted differently. Many of the family looked longingly toward the United States for salvation. In 1815, Joseph, ex-king of Spain, for example, hightailed it for America with a fortune in bank orders, traveling incognito under the assumed name Lazare Carnot. He would later send an emissary back to Switzerland to recover the crown jewels of Spain with which he had absconded.

Younger brother to both Napoléon and Joseph, Jérôme Bonaparte had also immigrated to the United States. Jérôme married Elizabeth "Betsy" Patterson of New Jersey, whose claim as an American princess precedes mine but was never recognized as valid by the ultimate authority in such matters, Napoléon himself. The marriage of would-be princess Betsy Patterson was annulled by edict of the emperor, who carefully orchestrated familial marriages for political purposes. Napoléon was incensed that brother Jérôme sought to marry for love! In a final insult, under Napoléon's unrelenting pressure, Jérôme abandoned Betsy, a sad ending for my predecessor as a Napoleonic princess. She died embittered and vitriolic at her treatment by the Bonapartes. Who could blame her! As a reward for toeing the imperial line and dumping his wife Betsy, Jérôme was rewarded with the puppet kingdom of Westphalia. Thus was love dealt with amid the Bonapartes.

My marriage into the Bonaparte family, I am proud to say, did last. I am offended when some compare me to the hapless Betsy Patterson. We could hardly have had more different experiences.

I have always held the belief that we create our own realities, and for me, the reality of life as an in-law among the Bonapartes was rewarding and exciting. I was allowed, even expected, to participate fully as a member of the royal Murat household and to bask in the reflected glory of the Bonapartes. So far as I know, I remain the only American in all of history to be so honored

Exile in Austria, 1815-1821

*I*N THE WAKE of the final collapse of the First Empire, the Bonaparte clan scattered before the four winds, but none of them tried harder to preserve the illusion of royalty than my mother-in-law Caroline. Caroline led the formerly royal Murats in flight to their new life in Trieste and Austria after the fall of Naples. She managed to secret away some of its royal treasury of Naples in the kingdom's last days, ill-gotten money with which she would secure a future for herself and her children. While regent of the kingdom in its last days, the crafty Caroline had taken opportunity to line her pockets from the coffers of the kingdom. Three million francs were diverted to her personal accounts as a hedge against the uncertainties that defined life under the dying empire.

After being forcefully deposed from power in Naples, the first few years of their life after the kingdom the lifestyle of Caroline and the Murat children scarcely skipped a beat from the lavish court of Napoli. Their so-called exile was one of wealth and privilege until the coffers began to run dry. The French had impounded more than ten million Murat francs upon the ouster of brother Napoléon, and there was no ready source of income after the Neapolitan funds ran out. Never previously having to concern herself with finances, they ran out rather quickly given Caroline's royal tastes and limited funds.

Caroline found herself a queen without a throne, a politician without a constituency, and at Trieste, a royal without a title. Poor thing! Feeling thus deprived, she assumed with a flamboyance characteristic of her dead husband, the nostalgic title Countess of Lipona, an anagram for Napoli, the lost kingdom of the Murats. After Trieste, the "countess" moved her entourage to Hainberg in the Niederosterreich region of Austria but kept a weather eye for more suitable royal accommodations.

Under the watchful surveillance and protections of her old lover Prince Metternich of the House of Habsburg, who oversaw the smothering of Bonaparte ambitions for the allies, the ambitious Caroline set her sights on Schloss Frohsdorf in the Lanzenkirchen area near Vienna. Built in the 1500s on the ruins of an even earlier castle, when the castle's present owner, Graf von Hoyos, named the exorbitant sum of four hundred thousand silver florins for the property, Caroline accepted without hesitation. She was determined to complete the hegira from defeat to new glories for herself and family.

Caroline Bonaparte Murat, Queen of Naples.

One might speculate that the deposed queen sought, by owning a castle, to cultivate an image of respectability and royalty for herself and children. Possibly. Perhaps though it was no more than an ego of pretentious proportion. One wonders, in this remarkable display of chutzpah, if there was even a trace of sadness for her recently executed husband.

If so, it was not obvious, and after 1817, Caroline continued apace to craft a new presence of faux nobility in Austria. Ever the master of the political chess game, she determined that she would carry the imperial Bonaparte mantle of her defeated brother where he had failed. Caroline, Countess of Lipona, with a characteristic overdose of Bonaparte ego, approached her new status in life with an air of entitlement. It was clear that she was unable to accept her changed circumstances, to regard her royal status in the past tense, or to live within her means.

From outward appearances, the once-royal Caroline gave every indication that this hiatus in Austria was merely a temporary inconvenience, an interregnum in her royal aspirations. However delusional the phantom throne of her dreams may have been, in her mind she fancied that the Bonaparte phoenix would rise from its own ashes.

The truth was that, in defeat, the fractious Bonaparte clan fought with each other over the crumbs of empire even more than they had in the glory days. To the allies, and probably to everyone but the Bonapartes, the very notion of a resurgence, however ludicrous, mandated close watch over the family, which was now dispersed over the Continent and beyond. The victorious allies in their powerful coalition were determined that the hegemony of the now-prostrate First Empire never be allowed to rise again.

If the mother affected that attitude of Bonaparte superiority and entitlement, she applied the same philosophy to her children's preparation the nobility she believed rightfully theirs. Before his death, her own brother, the Emperor Napoléon, said of Caroline that "her ambition was inordinate," and he was right. Some even opined that it was Caroline's ambitions and duplicitous dealings with Prince Metternich that led directly to her husband's arrest and death. In the world of the Bonapartes, relationships and people, even spouses, were expendable. As a pliant daughter-in-law, I never believed that even the ambitious Caroline could or would go that far. But who knew?

Prince Metternich of the Habsburg dynasty and Caroline had a long history dating back to a romantic liaison in Paris at the time when he served as ambassador to the court of Napoléon. They were two of a kind, venal, aggressively ambitious, supremely egotistical, but star-crossed. The difference now was that he was the ruler and she the ruled.

Insight into the Metternich persona is found in this quotation attributed to him. It sums up the aggrandized sense of self, which characterized both Caroline and Metternich. "There is a wide sweep about my mind. I am always above and beyond the preoccupations of most public men . . . I cannot help myself from saying about twenty times a day: how right I am and how wrong they are." Humility was not the long suit of either Metternich or his "guest," Caroline.

Metternich had outwitted Napoléon by brokering the Congress of Vienna and restored the Habsburg Empire to its former glory as the geographical and political center of Europe, while Caroline, his paramour, now out of power, coveted the royal trappings he represented. Might she have become so caught up in that that her husband became expendable?

Hapsburg Prince Klemens Wenzel von Metternich remained the nemesis of the
Murat's after Napoleon's defeat but maintained an amorous relationship with
Napoleon's sister Caroline, Achille Murat's mother.

For Queen Caroline and Prince Metternich, theirs was a dance of
illusions. Caroline, self-serving and power-hungry but out of power,
rekindled the relationship of years before, throwing herself and her
family on the Habsburg state's protections and largesse. The equally
arrogant Metternich, with real power and an effective police state
at his control, took advantage of this to watch her every move. On
behalf of the allies and perhaps from personal jealousies, he sought
to contain the smoldering Bonaparte embers she represented while
maintaining a diplomatic protocol and quite possibly her sexual
favors.

It was thus that the deposed queen and her offspring, under the
protections of the very empire that had done in both her brother and
her husband, achieved a sort of luxurious checkmate in exile during
their years in Austria.

As I was not there to participate with my mother-in-law in the last days
of her regency in the kingdom of Naples or her new life in Austria,
I have only Achille's biased observations to rely on. It is difficult for

me to interpret that period of his life, yet I must. These were Achille's impressionable teenage years and were the seeds from which his adult life and our marriage would grow.

If understanding Caroline's actions was difficult enough, understanding her deep underlying motives was altogether impossible. She evidently had a deep streak of the Bonaparte propensity to keep her own counsel and to share her deepest thoughts with no one. Just as well. As her daughter-in-law, it was not my role or purpose to impugn my mother-in-law; I was simply not raised that way in the genteel South, and my parents would have been horrified. As I never had opportunity to meet my mother-in-law, the ex-queen, these must be of necessity mere impressions. However imperfect, I knew it was necessary to look at the shadow world behind my husband's surface persona to his convoluted royal youth.

With my strong belief that one's family forms the basis for their lives, I knew that I had to plumb the depths of the Bonaparte psyche. My Achille was a tree that had grown from Bonaparte roots, and I was determined to understand his complex, sometimes conflicted personality.

Luxurious House Arrest at Frohsdorf, 1815-1821

*I*T WAS DURING his teenage years at Frohsdorf that Achille and the other Murat children received their first-class educations. No expense was spared, and the adolescent Murat children enjoyed superior educations at the expense of the former treasury of Naples. In these most impressionable years, all of the Murat offspring must surely have looked wistfully over their shoulders at the halcyon days of Naples where they occupied the highest pedestals of fame and adoration. Deep in their psyches, the four Murats of the younger generation, despite comfortable lives, must have known that all they could do now was to make the best of the situation.

Not all of the new world of the Murat children was pleasant. In particular, Achille suffered long illnesses. The seizures I would later learn to nurse in Florida afflicted him at Frohsdorf for months in 1818, evolving into something like paralysis. Achille did some nursing too. During his Frohsdorf years, he nursed a simmering hatred for the French who had confiscated the family fortunes and implemented smothering restrictions on their travel! He mouthed constantly, I am told, about his distaste for France and the French, always opining that he was raised an Italian and remained so. Together with the omnipresent surveillance by Metternich's secret police under Count Seidlitz, who sifted every move for traces of Bonaparte sympathy, Frohsdorf was an oppressive atmosphere, which fed the innate moodiness of my husband-to-be.

By now, the family's finances continued their slide, and Caroline was reduced to selling some of her paintings and dresses. From the sidelines, grieving for his mother's unaccustomed poverty, the teenage firstborn son Achille, with all of the bravado of his father's cavalry charges, swore he would never cease pressing the Murat claims against the French. He was true to his word.

As he reached his majority, the restless Achille, chafing under the strictures imposed by the allies looked to the New World. Motivated by correspondence with his Uncle Joseph, now ensconced in his lavish Point Breeze estate near Bordentown, New Jersey, he wheedled his mother and the Austrian authorities into a passport for America. After my marriage to Achille, I actually visited King Joseph at Point Breeze with my family, so I feel most comfortable in sharing these insights.

Achille's Uncle Joseph's manner, while distinctly European, was warmer and more cordial than I had expected a king to be. It was not much different from the high society of Virginia into which I was raised. I was thankful that my mother, Mary Willis Lewis Willis, had been such a stickler for insisting on proper manners and conduct, as her training would stand me in good stead on many an occasion.

I found it interesting that King Joseph no longer affected that title, and like his sister, the Countess of Lipona, Joseph assumed a new title invented from thin air. Joseph Bonaparte, brother of the emperor and ex-king of Spain, now styled himself the Count of Survilliers. I surmised that he chose not to overwhelm his neighbors and countrymen with the title of king but couldn't quite give up the formalities and trappings of his former life of nobility.

As I was privileged to visit with King Joseph at Point Breeze, I can vouch that it was a palatial domain of over one thousand acres, suitable for an ex-king, featuring lakes, winding carriage trails through elegant landscaping, guesthouses, and of course, the mansion itself. On the exterior, lavish statuary throughout the grounds helped create an illusion that one was in Europe rather than the United States. The fantasy was continued inside with an art gallery featuring paintings by Rubens, Canaletto, Velasquez, Rembrandt, da Vinci, and other masters, along with several portraits of Bonaparte family members by Francois Gerard including a grand one of Joseph in his coronation robes. A library, state dining room, and grand staircase left no doubt that Point Breeze was designed to impress and constructed to keep alive memories of imperial grandeur.

At Point Breeze, the Bonaparte mystique was on ostentatious display, and Joseph offered it as a retreat and rallying point for Bonaparte family members who came to America seeking a renaissance of the family or simply a respite from oppressive surveillance. I was blessed that I saw it when I did, and to get to know other members of my new family of famous in-laws. Unfortunately, that excluded Joseph's queen, Julie Clary, from whom he was separated and who remained in Europe. In the melancholy of old age, Julie and Joseph, the former king of both Naples and Spain, now Count of Survilleirs and master of Point Breeze, reconciled late in life. He returned to Europe where he poetically died in her arms in Florence in 1845.

Joseph Bonaparte, ex King of Spain, immigrated to the United States and built a
lavish 1000 acre estate in Bordentown, New Jersey named Point Breeze.
Achille and Kate as well as her Virginia-born family visited the
deposed king. Point Breeze became a rallying point for members of the
Bonaparte family who relocated to the United States.

The Fates Are in Motion, Early 1820s

*T*HE BONAPARTES AND Murats were not the only family coping with hard times and a major adjustment of lifestyle. My journey from a luxurious upbringing in Virginia to the virtually unknown Florida frontier was a difficult time for the Willis family, though not to the extent of exiles and executions experienced by Achille. It was harsh nevertheless and tested the family's mettle.

Father, the now destitute socialite Byrd Charles Willis whom we all adored, had spent months deciding to roll the dice of fortune and strike out anew. He had spoken at length with family and friends about the risks and consequences of uprooting us from centuries of Willis residence in Virginia, and though he was upbeat on the surface, I know that he was saddened by his losses and conflicted that he must ask so much of his family. Though we had personal choices and any one of us, except the youngest, could have opted to remain in familiar surroundings, we all chose to go together as a family and to support him. Father's ego was badly damaged by loss of the family fortune and his precipitous fall from status as a social lion of Virginia. His normally ebullient personality was deflated by this turn of events, and we all prayed that he would return soon to his jovial self. He needed to retreat to a new place where he could start anew and recover his damaged pride and, with any luck, some money as well. Our journey to a new life in the Florida Territory seemed just the thing.

Though Father was quick to point out his shortcomings as an entrepreneur, even to poke fun at himself for his lack of business acumen, he spoke with enthusiasm of the opportunities that awaited. Thus forearmed and hopeful, though not wildly enthusiastic about the inconveniences and harsh conditions which awaited us, we respected his decision. We knew not what we would face, but we were not leaving our country of birth or setting forth like Achille into a new nation whose very language was alien. Despite our many questions and apprehensions, we knew the United States, and it knew us.

While the Willis family had lost our money and our elegant home, Achille had lost all of that plus his royal status, his father, and even his country. His mother, Queen Caroline, had lost her husband, her throne, and the riches that a kingdom afforded. She had also lost the status that accrued to being sister to the world's most powerful man.

As Achille and I later compared notes on our respective journeys into an unknown future, I was quick to concede that as difficult as ours was, it was not nearly as traumatic as his.

On our trek to the frontier, we had each other—a mutually supportive family group determined that we would transit together whatever difficulties lay ahead of us. When we Willises left Virginia, it was not only with apprehension but also with high hopes that our new life would allow Father to recover his pride and his financial losses to an extent that we might someday return to the familiar comforts of the Old Dominion.

Achille had none of the above. His prodigious language skills included English, but it was not his first language, and he spoke it haltingly. He stared into a far more intimidating abyss than we, for he was changing countries and cultures and faced the likelihood that he would never see his family again. As you might have guessed from earlier comments, I am big on family.

Achille was crossing an ocean to seek a new start while we were simply moving south. Most daunting of all, he would undertake it alone, far from the royal status of his youth, with the pot of gold at the end of the rainbow a mere chimera. He obviously had inherited some of his father's bravery as he faced the world alone.

Seven years of house arrest at Schloss Frohsdorf at the very height of his adolescence had surely left him eager to experience the world. However elegant his lifestyle, his years of restricted movement and intense scrutiny merely heightened the natural instinct of the boy-become-man to spread his wings.

This natural penchant for establishing his independence and setting out on his own was heightened by tantalizing invitations from his Uncle Joseph, Napoléon's brother and the former king of both Naples and Spain. Joseph was now comfortably and securely established in the United States at his estate in New Jersey.

If nothing else, Joseph represented a transitional safety net for Achille until he could truly find his own way. As another motivator, Achille was well informed by a voracious reading habit that kept him abreast of the post-Bonaparte world, which was growing more reactionary by the day. The more he learned, the more he grew embittered at the direction his life would take if he remained in Europe. That inquisitive mind of his chafed at Europe's backsliding into despotic regimes rooted in a totalitarian past after brief flirtations with democracy. The freethinking Achille readily saw that in the emerging world across the Atlantic democracy was in the air, and it called to him persuasively. To the young intellectual and humanist, the rights of Europeans were endangered by the same old top-down governmental and social structures that had stifled the Continent for centuries. Achille, the liberal thinker, could not stomach the state of European politics and made no bones about it.

Having grown up under the rigid restrictions of his Austrian exile, the chance to reunite with Uncle Joseph represented a siren song. The very idea of becoming not just an observer of American democracy but to actually live under its freedoms flamed brightly in Achille's mind. Unable to resist the temptation any longer, once he attained his majority in 1822, he petitioned for a passport to leave Austria.

For his part, Prince Metternich, in whose captivity the Murat's lived, viewed Achille's departure as good riddance.

Even the powerful Metternich was not the final authority however. The Congress of Vienna had established strict controls on all of the Bonapartes' movements fearing that a flare-up of sympathy might embolden a Bonaparte renaissance. With good reason, Europe's leaders sought to avoid plunging the Continent into turmoil and bloodshed once more.

With Metternich's urgings, the allies reluctantly granted Achille a passport on the strict condition that he travel anonymously and, most importantly, swear to never return to Europe without their permission. The near-paranoid allies saw in his departure the dilution of "the Bonaparte threat," though one never really existed. The long-sought passport to freedom was in hand, and the spirit of America burned in his heart.

Bittersweet was the moment. The twenty-one-year-old Achille was now free to pursue his dream but might in the process never see his family again. It was a price he was willing to pay to transform his dreams into his truth.

So determined was he to reinvent himself as an American that on December 17, 1822, in the dark of night, Achille stole away from Frohsdorf without telling anyone. He was vague always about the reasons for his clandestine departure. I suspect he never knew his heart's dark secret here. Was it to preclude a tearful farewell scene with Mother and siblings, or did he want to avoid the risk that he might lose his nerve and remain ensconced in the stifling safety of Frohsdorf and familiar Europe?

In Vienna the next morning, the adventure began in earnest. Both excited and apprehensive, Achille called first at the famous bank of the Rothschilds where he withdrew from his mother's accounts several bags of gold and silver with which to finance his American adventure. Again he was vague with me about the extent to which Caroline had approved of this or even knew of it. He was her eldest son and the apple of her eye, so I think it unlikely that the transaction was done underhandedly. If you ask me, I think Caroline had mortgaged Schloss Frohsdorf expressly to finance her son's flight, for she saw in him a restless lion pacing its cage. Like any mother, she was reluctant to let him go but knew she could not prevent it.

As impetuous as one of his father's cavalry charges, Achille was off, accompanied by Baron Lindt, an old family friend. Ten days of winter travel by horse-drawn coach brought him at last to the port of Hamburg where he purchased passage to New York aboard the bark *Daphne*. True to the demands of the allies, he traveled under the assumed name of Mr. de Frohsdorf. Impatiently, Achille chafed at the bit to start his new life in the New World. The bitterly cold weather refused to cooperate, however, and the harbor remained frozen. For three months, he whiled away time and money with the pleasures of the city, free after so long a confinement and reveling in the freedom and anonymity of his first solo adventure as an adult.

On April 3, 1822, the thaw allowed the *Daphne* to sail, and Achille's—Mr. de Frohsdorf's—excitement reached a fever pitch. It was soon tempered by the chilly and damp reality of a late-spring passage on a small boat in the stormy seas of the North Atlantic.

There was not a storm in the world, however, that could dampen his enthusiasm for his new adventure and nothing could dissuade the eager passenger. My Achille was at last bound for the New World in a manner not very different from my own Willis ancestors in their own transatlantic voyages of old, searching too for a new start in the brave New World of America. Achille had at last thrown off the conflicts, the turbulence, and the sadness of his youth and, with pride, was an adult making his own way to a new future, unshackled from all of his complaints about Europe and Europeans.

When the bark *Daphne* arrived at the port of New York, Achille walked through the door of his new life into the sunlight of America, no longer fettered by the social and cultural strictures of the Old World. Under the constant thumb of the allies while exiled at Frohsdorf, he had become a rebel, yearning to throw off both the Austrian's intimidating surveillance and the excruciating formalities and protocols of European custom.

The achievement of his dream now well underway, Achille arrived in New York an excited bundle of opposing viewpoints stewing in the American melting pot. Was he a royal? Yes, but sovereign rulers who governed with an iron hand were his nemesis. Was he a Bonaparte? Yes, but he disliked the Bonapartes. Was he a freethinking liberal smitten with democratic ideals of America? Yes, but he would spend decades trying to restore the lost royal powers and fortunes of the Murats.

How could he balance these contradictions without becoming schizophrenic?

I am not sure. Maybe he didn't.

Early days in New York were a whirlwind of pleasure. He could hardly contain his excitement and took great joy in thumbing his nose at

Europe by applying immediately for American citizenship. The young and impressionable Achille had always balanced precariously on the knife-edge of his own identity. Was he French? Italian? Corsican? It no longer mattered, for now he was an American!

From pretentious royal wealth in Naples, through oppressive house arrest in Austria, to the welcoming springtime environment of New York, his days were filled with wonder. Sunny spring days in the unaccustomed freedoms of America were an apt metaphor for this long-awaited moment, for it was the springtime of his life, and he couldn't have been more content.

Though impressed with the multifaceted world of New York, especially its business climate, it was the psychological and social environment more than the physical that appealed to Achille. He at last felt that he had complete control of his destiny, a heady notion for any young adult but especially so for this one who had to date lived a life completely structured by others. He had made good his escape. With money in his pocket and the winds of freedom at his back, his Bonaparte confidence swelled, and his destiny loomed larger than life itself.

After a brief stint at the Astor's City Hotel, the lure of being reunited with family called strong. Achille now shed the Mr. de Frohsdorf disguise, hastened to nearby New Jersey and his Uncle Joseph to be welcomed into the bosom of the American Bonaparte family. Despite unspoken malaise between the two, they were still family. The reunion of these close Bonaparte family members, who had successfully escaped the trials and treacheries of Europe, was a welcoming one. The wealthy Joseph maintained an open door for any Bonaparte seeking escape and appealed vociferously to Achille to follow his lead and settle into a simpler life in America, devoid of political intrigues and simply enjoy the residue of Bonaparte splendor with which he surrounded himself. While such hedonism no doubt called seductively to the young adventurer, to his credit he maintained a single-minded focus on his dream of succeeding on his own in America.

Had Achille succumbed to the temptations of the easy life by accepting Joseph's invitation in 1822, how different my life would have been. As I look back in retrospect, the catalog of what-ifs is overwhelming.

* I would never have met this most wonderful man or reveled in his love and attentions.

* We could never have built a life together from the raw fabric of the Florida frontier.
* He would likely have never pursued his goal of shaping Europe's destiny through his writings.
* The historic Bonaparte-Washington linkage of our families would never have occurred.
* Our halcyon years in Europe and all of the wonders I experienced there would never have been. I should never have known royal friendships such as with Leopold of Belgium or Emperor Louis-Napoléon and Empress Eugenie of France. My life would have lacked the rich texture it took on from personal relationships with these world figures.
* I would never have become a princess, not just once but twice.

During Achille's visit with Joseph, the impetuous young Murat learned that Spanish liberals were in revolt against their Bourbon rule. Because it was the Bourbons who had ousted his family from power, Achille's simmering hatred ignited. Without a thought for his oath to never return to the Continent, he dashed back across the Atlantic hoping to lead the reform-minded liberals of Spain in revolt against the Bourbons. In Achille's mind, he pictured himself as his father: gallant, dashing, impetuous, a leader in time of crisis. Never having experienced glory in battle, he saw this as the perfect opportunity to establish a reputation and to vindicate the Murat name. In grandiose imagination, he envisioned that Europe would welcome a Murat to lead them to victory. As the younger generation Murat, he fancied himself riding on waves of adoring followers.

It may have been only an unlikely pipe dream, but to Achille it was his foreordained destiny.

This was exactly what the allies feared, a Bonaparte back in command of military forces in Europe, and Achille would have faced certain execution if caught. He nevertheless summarily announced that he was off to participate, presumably under his leadership, in a venture that, as he wrote, would bring him "immortal glory."

Not exactly.

By the time he arrived at Gibraltar, the revolt of the Spanish liberals had been quashed and Achille's dreams of following his father's footsteps to "immortal glory" were stillborn. Older and wiser, the deposed royal Bonapartes, King Joseph and Queen Caroline, were aghast. Achille's rash behavior at throwing in the face of the allies the oath to never return, which he had sworn in order to receive a passport, was sure to blow up in their faces.

But there was a more pragmatic reason as well.

Achille's blatant violation of his oath stood squarely in the path of Caroline's efforts to recover her impounded fortune from the very people her son had gone to fight. Mother and son were at painful odds, and she rebuked him sternly while continuing her ingratiating ways with Prince Metternich, who was the allies' spokesman on the matter.

Were bedroom politics involved between the former lovers? No one would confess to it, but the two had a long history of mixing personal and political passions.

Caroline was livid at her son's rash behavior as were other members of the family who were trying to rinse the stain of Napoleonic bloodshed from their reputations. My sense of my mother-in-law, Caroline, was that she would stop at nothing to achieve her ends and that one never wanted to be on her bad side. Achille now was. There were examples from Caroline's past of her vindictiveness, and for the son who had flown the nest and cost her her fortune, there would be hell to pay. In a pique, she wrote him that there would be "no peace of mind until you are back with Joseph."

Tail between his legs, a chastened Achille sulked back to the United States in late 1823, this time without the bravado of his first voyage. Alas, the Murats were never very good at eating humble pie. A gloomy Achille fumed and fretted. First nursing the failure of his quixotic expedition then chastised like a naughty child, Achille was stung to the core and, for some time, pouted as only a Bonaparte temper can.

He was still in a bad mood when he arrived back to his uncle Joseph Bonaparte's home at Point Breeze. With Caroline's consent, even urgings, Joseph offered Achille the hand of his daughter Charlotte in hopes that marriage might settle him down and dampen his tendency to race off into harebrained schemes such as the ill-fated romp to aid the Spanish liberal cause.

This notion of an intrafamily marriage was straight from the Bonaparte playbook. Marriage was about power, politics, and money. As with royal families down the ages, royal power was to be kept concentrated by keeping it in the family. When it came to Bonaparte marriages, love was merely a distraction.

Forced on them as it were, there may have been the pretense of a dalliance between Charlotte and Achille, but it was not much more than that. I believe my Achille when he says that his fling with Charlotte was no more than a flirtation. Since they were forced on each other by the political manipulations of the family rather than by love, I am inclined to accept his account of the ill-fated match, especially since Achille was more determined than ever to be his own man. His rebel streak was in full view for all to see, and he thumbed his nose at the arranged marriage to Joseph's daughter. If he was out of favor in the family after his Spanish gambit, he was a near pariah now.

The fortunes smiled upon me once more, and Achille remained a bachelor.

I at the time remained in Fredericksburg as the young and star-crossed bride of a far older Atchison Gray and mistress of his plantation, Traveler's Rest. I had succumbed to that arranged marriage while Achille had slipped that noose.

By the time I was seventeen, my husband, Mr. Gray, was dead and so was our infant son. I lacked the coping skills to handle either. In my immaturity, I proceeded to sully my reputation with outward pretense that things were normal. Because I had married so young and had never experienced the normal social life of a teenager, after Mr. Gray's demise I sought out a gay adolescent social life, which polite Fredericksburg society criticized considering how recently my husband had expired. The truth was that I was devastated by losing my precious baby boy. I was no more than an immature teenager, and my merry front was an ill-conceived facade to hide my grief.

The family mansion atop Willis Hill had long since burned, and my parents and siblings were making a valiant effort to salvage their lives. Though it was an abnormal environment, after Mr. Gray's death, I rejoined them to live in the hotel where they had moved after the fire.

These were grim years as the Willis family clung precariously to the ghost of an aristocratic past; Father now slid further into financial ruin just on the heels of the fire, which demolished the home that had been the family seat for a century. The cumulative impact of all of this was crushing. We tried our hardest, especially my mother, to keep a bright face on things as we watched the clouds roll in, decades of our family fortune slipping away like quicksilver. Inside, Mother's heart must have been broken, but she kept us all together as a financial and emotional tempest roared about us. Actually, there were more tears than tempest.

By 1825, it was clear that things were going from bad to worse. Father sold off our remaining possessions, and the intrepid little band of Willises, minus sister Anne who remained in Virginia with her husband, set off to some newly acquired territory of the United States, Florida. We were going to a place named Tallahassee, a new town of log cabins loudly touted as a land of opportunity. Maybe to a perpetual optimist, but I wondered.

My husband was dead. My infant son was dead. My father was broke and dispirited. Our home was burned to the ground. We scratched our way southward by taking coaches to Newport News where, with trepidation at leaving our beloved Virginia, we boarded a small coastal packet boat, which was bound for St. Augustine in the Florida Territory. Father had descended from aristocratic bon vivant gentleman, the "best known man in Virginia" to refugee in two short years, and we had gone with him. The rains that drenched us and the storms that beset us were an apt metaphor for the mood that infected us all. Along our way to our final destination, Tallahassee, we would fight dysentery, bugs, weather, snakes, terrible food, unsanitary conditions, broken axles, lack of accommodations at night, and hardships for which none of us were prepared.

Most of all, we fought depression.

As we entered the Florida Territory by coastal packet at the old and run-down Spanish settlement at St. Augustine, we encountered a new world, unimagined from the comforts of Fredericksburg. We had no frame of reference for this. Under a sun so glaring it hurt the eyes, in the shadow of the ancient Castillo de San Marcos there was marshland as far as the eye could see, more even than the

Virginia tidewater. Stinging flies. Muck that sucked at your shoes and stained your clothing. I even saw my first alligator, a giant about ten feet long hung from a rafter and being skinned and dressed for food. The people who swirled around us on the narrow streets with overhanging balconies were definitely not the Virginia aristocracy we were accustomed to.

There were many of Spanish descent (mostly from Minorca), a few French, some Seminole Indians, and free men of color (so they said; many were probably runaway slaves). There were some obvious half-breeds, the product of black and Seminole interbreeding, but few whites of any note. Most of those seemed to be hucksters, opportunists, and speculators who had migrated here in search of the elusive fast dollar, which everyone spoke of but no one had. It would not have surprised me to find a criminal element in some of these evident social outcasts, some of whom were wearing sidearms or carrying a rifle. Some, both Indian and white, were dressed in filthy buckskin and had large knives strapped to their hips. Funny little roughly plaited hats of palm fronds were ubiquitous on many of the white men, and I giggled privately to think of the 350-pound Virginia aristocrat Byrd Charles Willis—my father—wearing one.

I had never seen Indians before, though some remained about the woodlands near Fredericksburg. These men were large and, if I may say, quite handsome. They mostly wore a sort of long shirt gathered about the waist by a belt, several knotted kerchiefs around the neck and a funny turbanlike little hat. The women, for the most part, wore long embroidered skirts, very short little vestlike blouses, and were adorned with dozens of strands of tiny glass beads. The items they displayed most proudly on their person, however, appeared to be thin silver disks hung as necklaces with pride from their handsome frames. Though the name *Seminole* was used to describe these people, I learned while we were at St. Augustine that they disdained that name, applying it only to those of their tribes who had been pushed westward by the white man's government in Washington. *Seminole* to them was an insulting term.

I wondered how they felt about the whole experience of interaction with the white settlers who claimed to own lands they had roamed forever. Their anger had boiled over in the First Seminole War and I felt it simmering just below the surface among the Indians who came to trade at St. Augustine while we were there.

What, I wondered, might we face in the primal forests through which we were we to travel and which we were later to call home?

In contrast to the elegance of dress and manner of our associates in Virginia, I must admit that it was the polyglot people who seemed most intimidating. If these were to be our colleagues, friends, and neighbors, we feared an abrupt adjustment to life in Florida. The lure of the Florida frontier, as promoted by the Marquis de Lafayette, by Andrew Jackson, and by General Call, seemed as remote as the place itself.

Thus immersed in an alien environment, we each wondered about the Florida Territory to which we were committed. Each of us that muggy September morning was blanketed with unspoken trepidation and unanswered questions, but we had miles to go before our new home in Tallahassee and gamely put on a show of excitement.

False bravado is more like it.

Mother led us in a prayer for our safety, and our three newly purchased wagons started to roll. By noon, it was ninety-eight degrees.

I asked Father why he had chosen the new town of Tallahassee rather than better established settlements. Enigmatically, he replied that it was all about politics. With encouragement from Andrew Jackson, whose election Father had assisted, he hoped that his powerful connections in the national government in Washington might open some doors in the rough-and-tumble new capital of the Florida Territory.

Primitive Tallahassee, only now being carved from the wilderness, had been named the capital of the Florida Territory because it was located halfway between the two most prominent settlements at St. Augustine and Pensacola. Tallahassee was halfway between the two and was a geographical compromise for the legislators agreed to meet at that halfway point.

We were to learn that even though the legislature met there, it was not much more than a desolate frontier outpost. Tallahassee, in 1826, had little to recommend it and was so isolated from civilization that it might as well have been on the moon.

Our roadway to Tallahassee was called the New Bellamy Road and was recently completed though much of it followed ancient Indian paths. We were greatly encouraged that our first few hours of travel passed over well-constructed roads, paved with the oyster shells that were ubiquitous at St. Augustine. The farther we traveled, however, the worse our travel became. We encountered stumps to inhibit our wagons, brush that grew to the very edge of the road and clutched at the wagons, and boggy sloughs infested with water moccasins. We could not have anticipated a less accommodating passage, and I am sure that from the comforts of Fredericksburg, this is not what Father expected. As we set out, we were little aware that the Bellamy Road would be so arduous or that there were no amenities such as inns or coach stops.

Mother particularly, a close Washington descendant and true blue-blooded aristocrat, gulped at what lay ahead but spoke with her usual comforting tones, urging us onward along the bumpy dirt road toward Tallahassee over two hundred primitive miles to the west. I am certain she would have preferred to be sipping sherry at a social gathering in Fredericksburg, decked out in some of the fine silken clothing of her wardrobe, but here she was, the uncomplaining rock of the family.

Attempts to rally the family's spirits by singing familiar hymns and ballads seemed not up to the task as we trekked into what we were warned was the territory of the Seminole, usually friendly but unpredictable. They were rumored to harbor ill will toward the white man, and who wouldn't, after some of their settlements were destroyed in the first Seminole War. My teenage brother George was not amusing as he teased about scalpings and jumped at us from behind moss-hung trees with make-believe tomahawks. It was his boyish way of expressing the nervous energy and honest fears we all felt.

As our three wagons lumbered westward, after a few miles the oyster-shell-paved roadway came to an abrupt end, and from there on to Tallahassee, it would be slow progress for our wagons and horses along rutted dirt tracks with such holes that six times along our route we had to repair broken axles or wheels.

The heat and humidity of the coast gave way to the heat and humidity of the piney woods. With the help of the three slaves who had accompanied us, we sometimes were forced to make camp beneath our wagons at night. A few times, we were fortunate to pay for a night's lodging at the home of some accommodating family along the way. So new and primitive was this Florida and the Bellamy Road that only once on our two-week trip did we find a commercial establishment at which to pass the night. Though the owners called it an inn—it surely wouldn't have passed for that in Virginia—it was really just a fleabag boarding house. There were just a few rooms, and they had no comforts to speak of. The furniture, such as it was, was all roughly hewn and of such poor construction that we wouldn't have given it to our slaves back home. There were four beds of Spanish moss mattresses over rope-strung frames, three "real" beds, and a big rustic table where they served us grits, beans, corn, and some roasted meat of unknown origin. Those who slept on the Spanish moss belatedly learned the Florida lesson that it is infested with red bugs, and they itched and scratched their way onward the next few days.

The last bed I had slept in was a week ago, so while our so-called inn was a spartan environment, it was all we had, and we girls didn't mind doubling or tripling up in tiny hard beds. As a drenching rain that night drummed on the roof, snug in the rustic comfort of our inn, Mother and Father broke out a precious bottle of port they had been hoarding. In a moment of show, for benefit of each other I am sure, they toasted the moment and allowed that this Florida wasn't going to be so bad after all. A brave statement by brave people.

I wondered briefly where my parents got such optimism and courage, and then in a flash, I knew. Each and every one of our ancestors had also endured similar hardships in the settling of America. Each of them too had left the comforts of home and hearth. Each of them had experienced the same anxiety we felt. The blood of Jamestown settlers flowed in our veins, and we drew courage from that. And so like our ancestors, we realized that we too were real pioneers, and thus fortified, we reached deep within for the extra ounce of determination that allowed us to move forward day by day, making the best of things and cheering each other onward.

It wasn't easy. Twice in our two-week journey toward Tallahassee we encountered snakes stowed away in our belongings, but it was the insects that drove us near crazy. There was no escaping them. We came to long for morning when we could get up and start a new day, hoping that the mosquitoes had left some flesh on our bones. Father, the jolly giant of Willis Hill, the denizen of Fredericksburg's taverns, the proud descendant of George Washington, who still hobnobbed with presidents, the once-wealthy breeder of Virginia's finest thoroughbreds, rarely spoke. Once in a while, we'd find him rereading a well-worn news clipping from the Fredericksburg newspaper describing the lavish party given him by his friends before we left. At such times I suspected that behind the faraway look in his eyes was both unspoken trepidation about what he'd gotten us into and longing for the gentlemanly camaraderie to which he was accustomed. There would be no elegant plantation parties or foxhunts in Florida!

Father was quite heavy, and the oppressive heat made him perspire profusely. Without complaint, he would lose quite a bit of weight struggling toward our unknown future. When we finally arrived, his clothes hung about him like a bedraggled sack and showed rips from the briars and undergrowth that plagued our way.

Father had sold off most of our slaves to pay his accounts in Fredericksburg, but we had brought along three of them, William, Bessie, and young Bucky to work for us in Tallahassee. Their presence among us was an inspiration. The three of them were such great help on our trek along the austere trail from St. Augustine to Tallahassee that I vowed to never look condescendingly at our servants again!

Bessie had been Mother's favorite in the house and still, in this most primitive setting in the piney woods, wore the uniform she had proudly worn on Willis Hill. Though it was an anachronism in the 1820s, Father still insisted that our house servants be attired in livery bearing the family coat of arms. I think that as we slid into graceful poverty, these little reminders of our former lofty status reinforced his wounded ego and assumed disproportionate importance in the private world of his self-esteem.

Never would he need that esteem more than struggling through the North Florida wilderness headed toward God knows what.

Bless Bessie's heart, in her own unassuming way, she considered herself more of a family member than a slave. Both her mother and her grandmother had also worked the Willis Hill mansion, serving my grandfather Lewis and his father Henry before him. We did nothing to disabuse her of that sense of family loyalty and found it endearing.

William was a field hand who knew all there was to know about the outdoors, and young Bucky tended our horses. Sharing with them at close range the new world of the Florida frontier gave us all a newfound appreciation for these gentle and loyal people. In Virginia, we lived at distance from them and saw them only when needed. On the road to Tallahassee, they were *always* needed. As we struggled together in this primordial wilderness, their cheerfulness in adversity enabled us to see them for their essential humanness. They would go ahead with their wagon each day, set up a primitive campsite for us, and have supper waiting when we rejoined them for the night. But for them, our grueling trip would have been intolerable.

This experience forever changed the way that I saw blacks. Their stoic manner and good humor remained with me forever. In later life, when I was to settle in after Achille's death in a new home named Belle Vue, my servants and I depended on each other in ways that harked back to these days on the Tallahassee trail. There at Belle Vue, the synergistic relationship of master and slave came full turn as I shared all I had with them and they, in their sweet and generous way, with me. We were all Americans after all.

On the road to Tallahassee, even with William, Bessie, and Bucky's support, we were rudely taught the meaning of the word *primitive*. One could take nothing for granted, and daily survival took great resiliency and patience from everyone. For example, during our long days on the trail, there were no facilities, of course, in the wilderness. Every few hours, Mother would take my sisters Mary Byrd, Ellen (whom we called Attie), and me off into the undergrowth in search of some privacy for tending to our natural functions. These little moments were always somewhat embarrassing, but we needed to keep our little group close together. Little Attie was nine then and filled with childish curiosity. As she sought out a felled log from which to hang her backside, she commented on a buzzing sound. The next sound we heard was the most curdling scream I ever did hear. Just behind her log, there was a huge snake with dark diamond-shape patterns on its back all coiled up and, in Attie's childish description, "wagging its tail." Clothes askew, we urgently pulled Attie to safety. Father, having heard her scream, rushed to the scene and shot the terrible thing. We had not seen such a serpent in Virginia and, though repulsed, took its still-writhing body back to a wagon. Later we would learn that precious little Attie had had a close call with an eight-foot diamondback rattler.

We had had a relatively easy trip by two of our coaches from Fredericksburg to the coastal packet boat at Newport News, which started our southward trip. William, Bessie, and Bucky followed with two wagonloads of our possessions, all we could reasonably take to our new home. Most of our possessions had been sold in anticipation of the move, but we had brought, of course, the family silver—some over a hundred years old—crystal, and a beautiful set of dishes given to Father by Andrew Jackson. Our boat journey was pleasant, but now in the virgin woods of the Florida Territory, the overland trip was coarse, uncomfortable, and intimidating. As we neared Tallahassee, a stranger along the road asked if we had seen the springs nearby. Not having bathed in almost two weeks, we jumped for joy at the prospects of a proper bath, even a wilderness one.

Never have I seen such crystal clear water! It bubbled from deep underground, we were told, filtered through limestone, and it was the most gorgeous sight I ever beheld. No one had bathing clothes, of course, so we all—the Willis children ranging in age from nine to twenty-four, my portly father normally the soul of propriety, and mother, the Virginia aristocrat—plunged with abandon, fully clad, into the chilly spring waters. Wide-eyed, William, Bessie, and Bucky declined the experience with a polite, "No suh, ah can't swim, but y'all be careful now."

Nothing ever felt so good. Not even the two alligators on the bank could stay us from this joyous intermission in our journey. I freely admit that we kept a wary eye on them however.

It had been hard, far harder than we had anticipated, but we were almost there, to our new home in Tallahassee. After our swim, and refreshed in body and spirit, we finally understood its Indian meaning "beautiful land."

As we struggled southward, Achille too was exploring his new world. After the debacle over the proposed arranged marriage to Joseph's daughter, he was eager to once more fly the familial coop. In 1824, he was eager to see firsthand the American government he so admired and struck out for the capital city at Washington. Never was there a man so passionate about the world of legislatures, courts, and the administrative branches of government. Despite having a family history where we were much involved in government, I myself took it too much for granted and never gave it much thought. Achille, however, studied and debated it with anyone who would listen. Somewhere in the course of his life, he had changed his political stripes. Raised, of course, as a royal in a world where a single word from a single monarch could send a man to his death or change the fate of nations, he was wholly committed now to a form of government where it was the people who reigned supreme. It was altogether reactionary for a Bonaparte to enthusiastically embrace the downfall of the world's autocrats while raising up the common man.

Once again, Achille's rebel streak was in control. His royal parents, one dead, one alive, would hardly have recognized him

As he arrived in the capital city, he was willing enough to use the Bonaparte name and connections to provide the essential entrée. Upon introduction by Jérôme Bonaparte to well-connected friends, Achille spent several weeks in the neighborhood known as Georgetown in a polished cultured setting akin to his European upbringing. There, as well as pursuing his passion for learning more of American democracy, he was feted lavishly as a social dignitary by the Washington upper crust. The pampering reminded him that he was a product of well-heeled elegance and provided welcome salve for his bruised feelings. He was still pouting over being so upbraided by Caroline and Joseph for his hasty, ill-fated, and altogether illegal rush back to Spain. For his ego, it was a comforting reminder that he really was something of a minor celebrity.

Princes, even deposed ones, caused a stir among Washington society.

For a national capital, the District of Columbia was still rudimentary in the 1820s. Achille was appalled that the main thoroughfare, Pennsylvania Avenue, was mostly a rutted quagmire and the gutters still contained the burned-out roots of trees. It was a far cry from the elegant capitals to which he was accustomed—Paris, where he was born, and Naples, where he was raised. Even Frohsdorf, which he had come to hate, looked quite elegant and sophisticated by comparison. Though the nation's capital had moved from Philadelphia in 1790, Washington remained a relative backwater with a population of only thirteen thousand.

During Achille's visit, the presidency was held by James Monroe, and it was then that Monroe announced his famous doctrine of hemispheric defense. Needless to say, Achille was thrilled to hear formal pronouncement that further interference in American affairs by the clutching, avaricious powers of Europe would not be tolerated. He could not have agreed more.

Achille regarded the Monroe Doctrine as evidence that the United States was maturing into a true sense of national identity despite a sometimes fractious relationship among and between individual states. He relished visits to the Capitol where he met many legislators of the day and learned at the knee of the U.S. Congress the practical lessons of the democracy which he held so dear. No one impressed him so much as the dynamic Richard Keith Call, the delegate from the Florida Territory.

After serving with Andrew Jackson at the Battle of New Orleans, Call accompanied Jackson to Pensacola in 1821 to accept the Florida Territory from Spain and remained on with him during his tenure as governor. So impressed was Call that he established a law practice in Pensacola and was elected delegate to the United States Congress. It was not these credentials that lured young Achille, however, but Call's mesmerizing descriptions of the frontier territory and its opportunities. Call's mission in Washington was as much that of a salesman as a delegate. Charged with attracting settlers, he was known for spinning castles in the air from the dense Florida undergrowth. Just Achille's kind of man, a well-educated fellow dreamer with a yen for adventure!

But Call was more than that; he was a mover and shaker who had risen rapidly in the political structure of both Florida and the United States. Later, Achille would remark that Richard Keith Call was a sort of role model for him: military leader, politician, businessman, and attorney, a veritable Renaissance man, the very model of an American citizen as Achille saw it. Call was a self-made man, grown from the soil of America, the antithesis of the European leaders, whom Achille detested. In direct contrast to Richard Keith Call, Achille derided those European leaders who held their positions only by virtue of heredity. He knew many of them personally, and quite astutely, he observed that they had little to offer in the way of real credentials of accomplishment. As Achille saw it, they would have fallen flat if forced to compete in the crucible of America.

American statesman and prominent Floridian Richard Keith Call was a patron and friend of Prince Achille Murat. Murat served as his aide-de-camp in the Seminole Wars.

Achille was plainly in thrall with America and Americans, and Call was the personification of it. Their affinity and respect for each other would continue for years to come. Though now representing the Florida Territory, Call was born a Virginian, one of many Achille would come to know and respect. The Old Dominion, the cradle of American democracy, bred something into its sons that Achille admired. It would please all of the Willises in later years when Achille wistfully described Virginians as "the only real aristocrats in the Union." Without their saying a word, I know that my mother and father both felt a bit more kindly toward him for that most generous observation.

They, of course, epitomized the Virginia aristocracy but were now relocated by fate, fortune, and circumstance to a log house on Monroe Street in Tallahassee, surrounded on all sides by the Florida wilderness. We had known such luxury in Virginia that this rugged little frontier town came as a shock. I must say that we were at first quite let down, as we had such high hopes. The human mind and spirit being what it is, I think we reinforced those high hopes along the way by substituting hopes and dreams for reality.

Charleston was a good example. As we worked our way southward, our coastal packet had called there. At Charleston, we encountered a cultured city of stately homes with the most spectacular gardens we had ever seen, brick-paved streets with gas lamps, elegant churches, shops, and even museums and art galleries. Our spirits soared on these most favorable images and perceptions of Charleston. Would Tallahassee be like this? We were most impressed and greatly encouraged! We even implored our ship's captain to let us remain an extra day so that we might enjoy exploring the city, attend church, and have a meal at a most splendid inn. The wealth of the city was on lavish display, echoes of that day not so long ago when we had been at the center of an equally sophisticated Virginia plantation society with its foxhunts, lavish balls, concerts, museums, and galleries. Without a word from my parents, I knew that in Charleston they were saddened and bitterly reminded of our financial reversals.

I fear we were all guilty of imagining something like Charleston when we envisioned Tallahassee. It was wishful thinking. What we got instead was a diamond in the rough, spectacular natural beauty cradling a town of log buildings and rutted dirt streets. The year after our arrival, Ralph Waldo Emerson would describe it as "a grotesque place of land speculators and desperados."

Such was the place the Willises would call home for six years. Except for a three year stint in Europe, I would call it home for the rest of my life.

Achille the American, Mid-1820s

*W*HEN ACHILLE JOURNEYED southward to the Florida Territory in 1823, he too had stopped in Charleston, which he pronounced the most agreeable city he had ever visited. That universe of cities included some impressive names, Paris, London, Berlin, Rome, Vienna, and Naples, so it was evident that his favorable impression of Charleston exceeded even that of ours. The Murat name was still on the lips of the world due to his father's exploits and thus carried great cachet in the loftiest social circles of Charleston society. No one seemed to mind that Uncle Napoléon had wrought the greatest bloodshed in recent European history or that the cavalry of Achille's father had ripped through hapless armies before him like a knife through butter.

Achille brought excitement to a sleepy southern city. Residents seemed eager to rub elbows with one of greater lights of the Napoleonic era and the only one of Bonaparte ancestry to so far grace the aristocratic southern city. Achille, who still affected the title Prince Murat when it suited him, played these cards brilliantly. No less than General Charles Cotesworth Pinckney hosted a lavish gala for him. Achille chatted with the famous Rutledges in multiple languages and was generally accorded a reception of glitter and pomp, the very thing he professed to be trying to escape! A little social pampering and kowtowing by local leaders, however, was good for the ego, but it didn't satisfy for long.

Bored with the refined culture of Charleston and suffering itchy feet, the now-vagabond Achille set out for St. Augustine aboard the sloop *Rapid* in 1826. We had been there a few short months previous, but the fates were not yet ready for us to meet.

The St. Augustine in which Achille arrived was exactly as we had found it, run-down after years of neglect in the Spanish occupation and populated with the varied castoffs from many a northern city and some even from abroad. The Spanish, of course, had been there, as had the French, British, Seminoles, American ne'er-do-wells, and yellow fever. Each of these invaders had taken a toll and left the town underdeveloped considering its long history.

So enamored was Achille with his newfound freedoms and with America, however, that he could not bring himself to criticize, and he was soon swept up into the local society. He rented a small coquina-rock house on the main street and gave in briefly to a phenomenon alien to his nature, relaxation.

The Saint Augustine home of Prince Achille Murat still stands.
Image from the Rollins College Archives.

Never one to rest on his oars though, his energetic nature soon overwhelmed the moment, and in one of his fits of spontaneity, this child of royalty, who had never turned a spade of earth, bought a 2,800 acre plantation along the Matanzas River for the exorbitant sum of $1,960. The young adventurer, who professed disdain for all things European, promptly chose a European name for his new purchase.

What a romanticist! Wistfully, he selected the Greek name Parthenope, after the legendary siren who tried her best to seduce Ulysses. When the seduction failed, she threw herself in the sea and washed up on the shores of Naples. Parthenope thus became the ancient name for Naples, the Murat's lost kingdom, and in choosing the name Parthenope, Achille chose a daily reminder of the glories of his youth.

I thought that the name he chose for his plantation suited Achille in other ways as well. As had the Greek siren Parthenope after failing to snare Ulysses, he too had washed up on the shores of Florida after his failed love match with Charlotte Bonaparte.

Achille had brought one male slave with him from Washington but soon added to his ownership of Africans in order to work his plantation along the Matanzas River. He tried cattle. He tried tobacco. He tried cotton. He even tried oranges. When the wealth he sought failed to materialize in just a few months, however, and the reality of life in an uncultured wilderness set in, with typical Murat impatience, he cast about for new adventures.

A temporary respite from boredom came when he sailed for Savannah to serve as a part of the welcome committee for one of his great heroes, the distinguished Marquis de Lafayette. Without Lafayette's assistance, the America he so admired might have still been a British colony, and the flames of democracy he worshipped might have been extinguished at birth.

Like the highly respected Lafayette, Achille was passionately committed to liberty and the rights of man. In Lafayette, he saw the same traits of his father: bravery, skill as a strategist and leader of men, and commitment to cause. Lafayette's fame, in support of the American Revolution, was the very stuff of which Achille dreamed. This, he opined, was the sort of Frenchman he could admire!

The United States Congress settled on Lafayette a grant of $200,000 and 24,000 acres in the new Florida Territory acquired by the United States just a few years previous. At President Monroe's invitation, Lafayette was embarked on a fourteen-month grand tour of the United States, a sort of victory lap of historic proportion, and it was that which occasioned the momentous meeting of Achille Murat and Lafayette in Savannah in the spring of 1825.

The Marquis de Lafayette, hero of the American Revolution and close colleague of George Washington, was also a hero of Prince Achille Murat. Congress awarded Lafayette a large tract of land in northwest Florida. His enthusiasm for the Territory of Florida motivated Prince Achille Murat to seek his own fortune on America's southern frontier.

An official member of the welcoming committee, Achille availed himself of every opportunity to associate with his hero, who was now approaching the age of seventy. Particularly warm was his relationship with Lafayette's secretary, Auguste Levasseur. One can imagine the bonhomie that characterized the little circle of Frenchmen. When Lafayette spoke in glowing terms of Achille's father, Joachim, it was a moment that especially endeared the aging warrior to the young adventurer. Achille in turn praised the gallantry and selflessness of Lafayette's role in the Revolution, and a small but effusive mutual admiration society ensued. To Lafayette, the mercurial Murat was an interesting diversion. To Murat, in return, esteem for Lafayette reached a proportion of hero worship and one that he would attempt to cultivate again in both Florida and at Joseph's estate in New Jersey. His adulation of Lafayette to me seemed a bit unseemly and one-sided. Perhaps it was just Achille the politician, but to me it appeared as Achille the favor seeker.

When at last they parted, Lafayette headed west from Savannah to the interior of Georgia while Achille hastened north to Washington to help his brother out of a tight spot. Lucien Murat, Achille's twenty-two-year-old brother, had in classic Murat fashion blundered into a political minefield. Rejected in Austria, he was now held captive by the Spanish, who held a serious anti-Murat grudge stemming from his father's bloody put-down of a popular revolt. Brother Lucien was now imprisoned in Gibraltar.

Using his princely title to advantage, Achille sought and was granted audience with President John Quincy Adams, who interceded, and Lucien became the second Murat to flee to a new life in America. The Murat brothers, united after years of separation, fell in once more to the bosom of Bonaparte hospitality in America, Joseph's estate at Point Breeze. Old wounds and hard feelings were put aside, and the familial glories on the Continent were reprised over many a bottle of Bordeaux. Navigating both the roads and the bureaucracy, Achille accompanied his brother Lucien to apply for American citizenship in Philadelphia. A Bonaparte king and now two princes contented themselves under the protections of America, a security not afforded them across the Atlantic where they were still cast as pariahs.

To these halcyon days at Point Breeze for the reunited brothers was added yet another treat of grand proportion. After having recently served as a host for the Marquis de Lafayette in Savannah, Achille was overjoyed at the Marquis' arrival at Point Breeze. The distinguished Joseph Bonaparte, now Count of Survilliers, was a magnet for the mighty, and now the two aging Frenchmen regaled themselves in the courtly manner to which the French aristocracy gravitate. Toasts, champagne, flattering compliments, and ovations of all sorts filled the night. I would opine from a distance that never in the history of New Jersey was there so much ego on display!

With a former king, two former princes, and the acclaimed marquis in attendance, there was status enough to go around. Each was secure in a lofty position in life, each had attained their aristocratic status by political manipulations of world class, yet there were rousing speeches to honor the common man and overflowing tributes to democracy. Was there more than a little hypocrisy on display at Point Breeze? Not for me to criticize, but the aroma of too much pomp, circumstance, and exaggeration filled the air.

Abruptly, Achille decided to leave Point Breeze. Perhaps it was abetted by his manic physical tendency. Perhaps he was urged on by the practical availability of money sent by his mother, Caroline, from faraway Austria. Perhaps old angst arose once more between Achille and Uncle Joseph over the failure of marriage between Achille and Charlotte. Perhaps it was the grant of a township of land in middle Florida to his idol, Lafayette, and the desire to further that association. Perhaps it was simply boredom with the insular life at Point Breeze, comfortable but false to the core.

I would vote for some of each.

In any case, the wanderlust, which was to characterize his entire life, overwhelmed what might have been common sense, and Achille journeyed southward to the Florida Territory once more. His dreams, never realistic in the first place, of acquiring riches as the plantation master of Parthenope had failed to materialize. I fear that this child of royalty was accustomed to things going his way and had not well analyzed the consequences of his precipitous action. He had moved somewhere he had never been to do something that he had never done, and his difficulties at Parthenope should have been foreseeable. This was not, however, the way Achille thought. On the heels of failure at St. Augustine, he was headed to Florida once more. Without a second thought that he might be repeating a prior mistake, he booked transport to St. Augustine, placed Parthenope up for sale, and struck out toward Tallahassee on the same Bellamy Road that we had transited.

With wild enthusiasm, he wrote of "dense and towering forests of every foliage, luxuriant over a rolling and picturesque country most verdant with herbage and spotted like the variegated leopard with abrupt and strange marks of richness and sterility."

Reading that in later years, I wondered if he had been on the same road that had nearly driven us to despair. Was he even on the same continent?

So passionate was he about creating a new life in America to atone for the loss of the Napoleonic kingdom and so determined to prove himself worthy that I came to know an essential characteristic of my Achille. He was a dreamer who never let harsh reality color his thinking. He was the Don Quixote of Florida, slaying windmills and preserving the honor of his Dulcinea, the role into which I was about to be thrust.

In later firelight chats, lubricated with some of the wilderness homebrew for which he had acquired a taste, he would disclose confidentially that he too was shocked at the completely primitive nature of North Florida. It was desolate. It was dangerous. It was devoid of social stimulation or intellectual challenge. And what on earth, one must wonder, did a background of royalty and luxurious indulgence in Europe have to do with his present endeavor? Forced to live off the land, eating what game he and his slaves could kill, house arrest at Frohsdorf must have looked so comforting as to have made him wonder about his choices, if not his sanity. Not my Achille! With his slaves and a hundred head of cattle, the prince and his not-so-merry band lumbered along the infamous Bellamy Road as weeks stretched into a month until finally he too arrived at Tallahassee.

At length, Achille met up with a would-be business partner, James Gadsden, who had spent the better part of six years surveying the central Florida backwoods. He and Gadsden would create a plantation venture not far from the huge acreage conferred by the Congress of the United States on Achille's idol, Lafayette in 1825. It was the first of many Murat-Gadsden partnerships.

Of his lands in north central Florida, Lafayette spoke of a new dreamworld, gentle in climate, remote from war, fertile in fields, abundantly blessed by nature and congenial in all respects. Occupying territory between the Suwanee and Apalachicola Rivers, the elder French statesman touted his Vine and Olive Colony as a paradise in the New World and attracted disaffected French to come and share the work and presumably the wealth. In a harbinger of Achille's fate, the Lafayette venture soon failed, and most of its French settlers drifted to a more congenial New Orleans.

Though he never spoke of it overtly, I have always surmised that the admiring Achille sought to emulate his idol in every detail as he developed his new plantation. In naming it, he evoked once more the wistful mystique of bygone years, Lipona, anagram for

Napoli and a nod to his mother's assumed title, the Countess of Lipona. Unfortunately for both, Achille and Lafayette, both of the transplanted French noblemen would be defeated by a reality that could never match their high-flown dreams. Both were as quirky as the pet owl that perched on Achille's shoulders during moments of leisure.

But moments of leisure were few and far between. He pushed his slaves hard and purchased a few more to help clear the virgin forest land, which comprised "Lipona in the rough." Achille himself turned to manual labor for the first time in all of his twenty-six years. Down, down, down the rungs of life he plummeted. The nephew of the world's most powerful man, son of a king and queen, raised in the ultimate luxury of Paris's Elysée Palace, himself a prince with all of the trappings, was now a field hand.

Achille's notoriety as a dignitary spread like wildfire in what passed for society in central Florida. The speculators, desperados, and slave traders were offset by an equal population of legitimate fortune seekers, public officials, and businessmen, and they all were hungry for something exciting to gossip about.

Though they didn't know what to make of him, soon people began to call at the tiny log cabin on the hill, which was Achille's plantation house. It was at the best of times rustic, but neighbors came to call anyway bringing welcome news, dinners, a potent clear homemade whiskey they called shinny, and an alcoholic libation he developed a real frontiersman craving for; applejack.

A frequent visitor, much to the ego satisfaction of Achille, was none other than the territorial governor, the witty William Pope Duval. Duval was as impressed with his new neighbor, the deposed prince, as Murat was with him. The two struck up a most cordial relationship built around political gossip and applejack. Duval promoted Achille as a statesman of sorts, which led him to be chosen as an alderman of young Tallahassee.

Of course, the would-be political commentator of the American scene gloried in conversation with the governor. It gave him ample opportunity to expound upon the foibles of government as practiced in Europe and to debate his observations of American-style democracy, at least as practiced in the piney woods of Florida at a time before statehood. It was, for both men, a pleasant intellectual diversion from the unbearable boredom that characterized the wilderness they called home. Achille needed that.

It didn't hurt either that sometimes Governor Duval would bring his ravishing red-haired daughter, Marcia, who I am told was underwhelmed by the eccentric Murat, clad in buckskin pants, muddy boots, and a shirt ripe from weeks of perspiring under the North Florida sun. (Perhaps it was only Achille trying to reassure me that she was disinterested, for he was surely not!) He had, by this time, also acquired the frontiersman habit of chewing tobacco and spit the vile mess frequently to the dismay of the vivacious Miss Duval. Mother and I would come to despise this ugly habit too, but if it helped turn Miss Duval's head away from the man who would soon become my prince, so much the better! In any case, the combination of Achille's volatile personality, aromatic shirts, and chewing tobacco may have staved off a romantic attraction not to my advantage!

The Stage is Set. The Florida Territory, 1825

OUR ARRIVAL IN Tallahassee was less than spectacular. William, Bessie, and Bucky had gone on ahead, and we were surprised to find Bucky sitting on an old tree stump about three miles outside of town. Shaking his head, he reported the bitter truth of frontier Tallahassee. "Sho ain't much dere. We gonna be wishin' we was back home on de hill in Va-ginn-ya."

"Oh, Bucky, it can't be that bad," said Mother, half to hide her own qualms and half to make us feel better. "We'll be fine once we get settled."

As at the decrepit boarding house on the trail, once again we got a rude shock upon arrival at the log house inn where we were to stay at for a month or two. Florida inns and Virginia inns surely had nothing in common! As Bucky fed and watered the horses, we explored, with a sort of morbid curiosity, the rough-hewn log house inn we would call home for a time. It was larger than that awful place on the trail, and there were twenty rooms, and a more developed dining room with some rather nice-looking furniture that may have been imported. Things were looking up! The rooms, nonetheless, were tiny, and the heat oppressive in those that didn't have windows. In a selfless gesture, Mother and Father took one of these, a mere closet, still rank from the last woodsmen who had stayed there. Empty applejack bottles still decorated the pine chest of drawers. Pine, pine, everywhere pine!

The innkeepers were rough people who had fled south from North Carolina with creditors baying at their heels. They spoke with that strange accent of the Carolina hill people and rudely dismissed Father's request that William, Bessie, and Bucky be allowed to share a room at the back of the property. "Them blacks ain't gonna stay under my roof," said the woman as she took our money for the first week of our stay.

Graciously, Bessie spoke up for them and said, "Ain't no mind to us, missus, we be fine stayin' in one of de wagons soon as we gets it unloaded." And there they stayed for the duration of our time at the inn. Welcome to Tallahassee.

Scrambled eggs and some stringy ham with homemade biscuits greeted us the next morning as we arose to reconnoiter our new hometown. That breakfast wasn't like Willis Hill, but after brutal weeks along the trail from St. Augustine, it was a gourmet feast. It fortified us for our first day as citizens of the new capital city of the Florida Territory.

With the new capital a beehive of building activity, the inn master directed us to some new log houses being built near the capitol building. I saw Father wince as he was shown the capitol—THE CAPITOL!—which itself was no more than a larger log house. If that was the capitol, a private home would surely disappoint, especially after our venerated mansion in Fredericksburg, which we had lost to fire. With a sigh, we trekked along the streets, roughly paved with the oyster shells, which seemed to be ubiquitous to Florida. The sounds of saws and hammers echoed over the piney woods as Florida energetically sought to emerge from the green wilderness that surrounded us.

The same motley people we had observed in St. Augustine were here, but there were some better-dressed folks as well. I saw signs for land offices everywhere, and a banner announcing auction of five townships of land hung at the intersection of Monroe and Madison streets. At the opposite corner, another banner announced a livestock auction. A dapper man, dressed in a suit with a bowler hat, was pushing a small cart. He had attracted a group of Indians to pitch his wares, mirrors, combs, and brushes, and I wondered about the residences these treasures would be taken to out in the bush somewhere. Curious

Indian women gazed in the mirrors, probably seeing themselves for the first time other than in a stream's reflection.

Funny how these first impressions tend to be the ones that last.

Father had been carrying five rolls of banknotes in a bag hung around his neck, and it hadn't been off his person since we left Fredericksburg. That afternoon with Bucky beside him to guard against thieves, he worked out a private credit arrangement at the local bank, also housed in a log cabin, and bought a house on Monroe Street. William, Bessie, and Bucky would have their own cabin to the rear of ours. We were Floridians!

As the days wore on and we had time to wander the streets and byways, we began to break down the overall impression of Tallahassee into a series of little vignettes to better understand our situation. In this case, the whole seemed less than the sum of the parts, not more. A few of our vignettes will suffice to serve to describe the physical environment in which we were to spend the next phase of our lives.

In Virginia, much of our life was dominated by horses. Not just horses, but magnificent thoroughbreds. We bought horses, sold horses, traded horses, rode horses, hunted on horses, harnessed horses, and wagered on horses. To pay off debts before leaving Virginia, Father sold one of my favorites, a bay mare named Maid of the Oaks for $15,000, a very tidy sum and an indication of the horseflesh I was accustomed to. So central to our lives were our magnificent animals that Father even had our fields plowed with thoroughbreds and attained a certain notoriety from that.

As I looked about our little enclave in the Florida wilderness, what I saw instead were mules. Mules pulling wagons, mules hauling logs from the forests that surrounded us, even folks riding sloe-eyed mules. In Virginia, we, of course, saw them occasionally but disparaged them as the lower animals, slow of pace and mind.

On our fourth day in town, my brother Lewis and I were tasked by Mother to search out a good butcher shop. As it turned out, there was but one, and we went straightaway to find it. Without a sign, our only clue that we had arrived was the carcass of a magnificent twelve-point buck hanging from the limb of a large oak tree out front.

Unfortunately for my queasy stomach, we arrived just in time for the butcher's knife to slit the animal's belly cavity, and its entrails came slithering out in a steaming mass. I felt my own stomach do flip-flops at the sight, and coupled with the aroma, it was all I could do to keep down my lunch, which had been one of venison. So much for my helping Mother that day! I made my way alone back to the inn down muddy little side streets I had not seen before. Hens with their scrawny pullets in tow clucked and pecked through the gutters, and bony pigs roamed freely, unaware that the butcher might have his eye on them next.

Without realizing it, tears welled up in my eyes, and I ran the last hundred feet back to the comforts of the rustic inn. As though it could protect me from the alien world outside its doors! I flew to Mother, and we had a long and silent hug. Words would have been superfluous, and when we at last broke, tears streamed down her face as well.

It had been two months since we last were able to have our hair trimmed and groomed, and all eight members of the Willis clan all looked a bit shaggy, like the forest creatures we had so recently been. Sister Mary Byrd and I made it our personal challenge to remedy that. We collected from our cases, still in the wagons, a proper pair of shears, and with much fanfare, after a bath in a large tin tub, set about to cut each other's hair. In a moment, we knew that was a mistake. Snippets of my black hair fell to the floor amidst tears, this time not silent. We had reached our wits' end, and it was then that we decided that we would resort to our personal pocket money and treat the family to proper haircuts as a morale builder, and did we need one!

We were referred to a lovely older lady from New York, at least seventy, who agreed to come to the inn to repair the disastrous coifs we all had by then. She had, we learned, operated a ladies' hair salon at a tony address on Manhattan Island. For the eight of us, it took the entire day, but when we repaired to the dining room that night, every one of us walked a little taller. Compliments flew from the other guests as if to confirm the wisdom of our investment in family well-being. Mary Byrd and I smiled secret smiles of satisfaction. The ever jocular Father even resorted to his familiar steady stream of puns with the Carolina innkeepers, who mostly feigned polite laughter. That reaction, along with some of their blank stares, confirmed for me what I suspected from the beginning, their wit was not on a level of sophistication to match the fun-loving Byrd Charles Willis, Virginia's best loved man about town!

I had been widowed for seven years, was childless, lonely, and, in the course of nature, set my heart upon marriage and family. In Tallahassee, my prospects looked quite dim. I might marry an auctioneer, my mother said. Or one of the salesmen who drifted in and out. A few of the politicians who hung around the government house were not bad looking, but they seemed to be drunk most of the time and seemed to argue all the time. Or a preacher man. Maybe a cattle driver, said Ann. Oh my! The field of eligibles was depressing. With tongue in cheek, Brother John suggested one of the fishermen who came each week with mullet and oysters from Apalachicola. Since you could still smell them long after they'd gone, that didn't seem too promising either. Against this backdrop, it was with excitement that we received invitation to a big social event at the grounds of the old Spanish mission at Fort San Luis.

My dark hair and creamy white skin often led to compliments from admiring men, but here in the piney woods where there was no real competition, I let them fall where they would. Flat. Today would be different, I told myself. There would be political speeches, a picnic, games, watermelons chilled in the spring, and for the men, the ubiquitous applejack. Mostly there would be a different crop of men from the outlying plantations, though I knew most of them already, and all were married. Their wives, who thought me flirtatious anyway and I am sure gossiped behind my back, would be sure to maintain a safe buffer zone. Nonetheless, I would primp myself more than usual, use some of my best dusting powder, some French perfume, a little rouge, and more heavy black eyebrow pencil than usual. Dressed in one of my finest dresses from Virginia, with a new bonnet Father had given me, I thought I looked quite nice as I twirled in front of the mirror. I flashed back the ten-year-old girl twirling in the mirror in Fredericksburg, sighing, dreaming of princes, and causing scores of handsome men to fawn over her at the palace. "Please," I thought, "princes may be hard to come by, but let this at least be a day to meet a gentleman not of the same mold as the rest of Tallahassee."

We had been there not an hour when a most handsome gentlemen arrived riding a dapple gray mare, which reminded me of my Lizzie, the constant companion of my youth on Willis Hill. A few covert glances later, I realized with a rush that it was not the horse I was looking at. I overheard him making conversation with some of our neighbors, who brought him over to meet me in the shade of a hoary old live oak festooned with Spanish moss.

It has never been revealed to me whether it was he or the neighbors who broke the ice with that introduction, but no matter. There at Fort San Luis, I met Charles Louis Napoléon Achille Murat, deposed crown prince of Naples, son of King and Queen Murat, and nephew of the most powerful man in the world. My father is much given to exaggeration, but that is not a characteristic I share with him. When I tell you Prince Murat made me nearly faint with excitement, I pray you not think it overstated. I blushed so that my rouge was completely unnecessary.

Prince Murat took my breath away.

I spoke a little French and knew a few words of Spanish and Latin, but I could not quite place his accent. Little wonder. Part Corsican, having grown up in France, Italy, and the German-speaking area of Austria, he was indeed a man of the world. As a nearby political candidate droned on about fighting the new taxes proposed by the territorial legislature, Prince Murat and I drifted away from the crowd toward the spring below the hill. Our conversation was, at first, strained, for each of us feared, I believe, breaking the spell of the moment with an ill-chosen word. This was exaggerated by my difficulty in understanding his heavily accented manner of speech, but as the day wore on, that only added a layer of mystery to the prince. There may have been no waltzes and no palaces, but here was the real, live prince of my dreams!

As the shadows lengthened and a light breeze sprung up, we found ourselves on a narrow path down to a secluded glen where the creek had carved an impressive little amphitheater over the years. The leaves of the sweet gum tree, which dominated the scene, were beginning to turn, and it appeared to me a stage set straight from God. We sat upon a fallen log, and as our shoulders brushed, I got that tingling feeling up the back of my neck so long absent. Mindlessly, we watched the first orange leaves of fall dance on the lazy current, and there was that mental image from childhood once again twirling with my prince. I closed my eyes and inhaled deeply. Palaces. Fallen leaves.

Princes. Distant sounds of music, not waltzes but a march played up on the picnic grounds above. Dashing uniforms. Lizzie. Struggles along the road from St. Augustine. Now an orchestra was playing in my mind, and this time it did seem a waltz. In that ethereal moment, it was all a beautiful jumble; the past, the present, and the future stirred by the unseen hand of God into a potpourri of, dare I say it, love. Goosebumps chilled my skin, and the reverie was a beautiful complement to the already-beautiful reality of our moment. What was real? What was fantasy? Did it matter?

Without warning, Achille startled me by grabbing one of my feet. "What is this?" I thought. Mother's warnings about brusque Frenchmen with dishonorable intent rang in my head, yet here I was, unafraid and yielding. In a flash, he had slipped off one of my flat shoes and was pouring wine in it from the bottle of muscatel we had brought from the picnic above. Toasting my beauty as only a romantic Frenchman might, in a scene straight from a love-struck poem, he drank from the slipper. It was a Sir Galahad moment; old-world gallantry meets girl of the Florida frontier. If Achille sought to dazzle me with his Gallic gallantry, he was successful beyond his dreams!

"Kate," rang out father's booming voice. "Oh, Kate, where are you?" Thus shaken from our private dreamworld, with some amusement, I slipped the damp slipper back on, and we returned to the main picnic site where the banners were being taken down and carriages brought up by servants to take these frontier Floridians back to their scattered farms and fields. So new were the Willises to the area that we had not yet purchased a proper coach. It was with mild embarrassment that I bade farewell to Prince Murat and mounted our secondhand buckboard wagon, the working man's friend, with brothers and sisters to return to the log home on Monroe Street. As Achille swung into the saddle of his dapple-gray, his voice quietly reached into my soul with a foretaste of fate, "I shall see you again, Mademoiselle Kate, au revoir." I am sure I muttered some inane pleasantry, but now, in hindsight, wonder if it actually came out of an otherwise speechless mouth.

Brother George drove the wagon along the shell-lined roadway back to our cabin home. Sisters Attie and Mary Byrd plied me with nattering questions about the handsome stranger. Mother and Father, unceremoniously leaning against the backboard, took in the scene with the quiet wisdom that comes with age. Lewis, much into his studies, ignored the moment and read one of his books of medicine. John, the image of Father in build and temperament, teased the entire way home. "Allooohhhh, mon cher, 'ow are yew tew-day. Ah, your shoes smell so sweetly, I shall drink from theem I theenk. Oh, dear lovely Kate, what 'ave I done! You must get some dry shoes now!"

"John!"

Surrounded by the love of family, haunted in the inner reaches of my mind by the vision of Prince Murat, and still tingling from the experience of it all, Tallahassee took on a much more convivial air. If I were to choose a single word with which to describe the moment, it would be *joy*.

As I lay beside Ann in the bed which we shared until the new bedroom was finished, I turned away from her and turned inward to my own whirling thoughts. I knew not what they all were, much less what they meant, but I knew I had never had them before or since. I told myself I needed time to think, to process the blur of images and emotions of the day. As sleep overcame me, I finally gave in to the realization that it was not time to think which I needed. I needed time to feel.

The next morning brought reality. This wasn't some foreign fiefdom with turreted castles; this was crude Tallahassee. I wasn't a princess, I was an uprooted Virginia girl. Maybe I had imagined it all. Maybe there had been no prince after all; he certainly didn't dress like one. Maybe he was just another planter trying to scratch out a living from the soil of North Florida. And so, deflated, I turned to my chores helping Mother put away the silver serving pieces we had brought, yet my mind would not allow me to discard that tingling feeling when we had touched ever so innocently.

Lewis, dear supremely practical big brother Lewis, returned from town with gossip. As only a big brother can, with a studious frown he confided that many townspeople reported Murat to be a little daft. If not crazy per se, people commented on his eccentric dress, speech, and manner. Some even rumored of his dalliances with slave girls. I love Lewis for his sincerity of purpose, but if my prince (as I had already come to call him) was a little eccentric, what did it matter? Already Cupid's arrow worked closer to my heart. Then I allowed myself a naughty thought. As to slave girls, I was sure I could improve on his love life.

The days of fall in Tallahassee were not quite like the days of fall in Virginia. In fact, fall rather slipped up on you in Tallahassee with few signs that the seasons were changing. Oppressive, muggy heat happily gave way to lower humidity and some beautiful deeper blue days that were most welcome. Not so welcome were blue days when it was I who was blue. The brief flirtation at San Luis last month seemed an improbable dream, and the man, who for a brief moment held my heart (and my shoe!), only an illusion.

Without warning, one early November day when I returned from the market with Bucky dragging behind him a heavy sack of Apalachicola oysters, there at our hitching post was the dapple-gray, saddled, to my dismay, with a western-type saddle. As anyone knew, only the working class rode Western. As a proper Virginian, I had grown up in an English saddle. My beloved saddle was still packed somewhere in a wagon along with the rest of the tack we had brought, unused since I had nothing worth riding.

When I burst anxiously into the house, that fluttery feeling from San Luis returned in an instant.

"Mademoiselle Kate!"

"Prince Murat," I replied with the tiniest of curtsies. "I had thought you long gone."

"Indeed, I have been, securing at Savannah a dozen new slaves to work the fields of Lipona. You must come and visit someday if your father would permit. It is only fifteen miles, in a district they call Wacissa after the Indian name. Perhaps one of your brothers could accompany you, no?"

With scarcely concealed understatement, I replied, "I shall look forward to it one day." His absence after San Luis, I was happy to learn, had been one of necessity rather than disinterest.

There followed a pas de deux of increasing interest tempered with the polite niceties necessitated by being surrounded in our living room by family. When it was done, I had overcome the anxieties and questions about how exactly one communicated with a royal. Virginia manners were one thing, but royal protocols another entirely. The breaking down of that social barrier along with his urgings to call him Achille rather than prince led to a relaxation that would get only more comfortable with time.

Mother served us a splendid sherry she had been hoarding then discreetly disappeared shooing little Ellen, age ten, before her. I cannot tell you what we talked about for two hours. The subject was completely unimportant compared to the fact that we were together and talking. Brother George returned from hunting, and I made proper introductions.

"George," I announced proudly, "is to attend the United States Military Academy at West Point next year."

"Congratulations, monsieur. That is a great honor. I have some military background myself. And perhaps you would like to hear of my father's military history. He was zee great *Maréchal* Murat, Napoléon's favorite, and you will no doubt study him at West Point next year."

Gasping with disbelief at such an opportunity, George jumped at the moment. "That would be excellent!" said George, adopting a military posture and horning in on my precious time alone with my prince. I saw in that instant though, an aspect of Achille that I had not seen before. He was proud. Yes. He was royal. Yes. But he was desperately lonely and needed a sympathetic ear.

Letting him revisit his past, see proudly again in his mind's eye his own family, and revel once again in his father's fame was our simple way of saying, "Come. Be at ease. Be yourself. Here you are not judged, you are welcomed." I wanted above all things for him to not shy away so allowed the conversation to drift where he steered it, to the exciting yet tragic world of his youth. It would, I was sure, make him more comfortable and likely to seek out my company again. There is, as Mother had taught me so well, a reason for gracious southern hospitality.

It was clear that recollections of his beloved father were highly placed in the hierarchy of his mind and that he relished an audience with whom to share these bejeweled memories of the Murats' finest hours. He had been alone since Frohsdorf. We were not only his audience, we were for a moment his family, and our support gave him a nostalgic bridge back to a better time.

Learning that Achille was to tell of Napoleonic conquests, other members of the family drifted in and arranged themselves around our inconspicuous visitor who was still, in Europe, greeted as Prince Murat.

"Zere ees so much, I hardly know where to start."

"Perhaps you know of zee famous 'whiff of grapeshot, no?'". As his eyes glazed over, we could see him transported on the magic carpet of the mind away from our simple living room to fields of glory where his father's reputation had been made."First swordsman of Europe," the greatest leader of all of Napoléon's famous marshals and eventually a king. Joachim's storied life reminded us that we all make our own lives; that everyone's life is blended from variable parts of luck, opportunity, and skill. If a son of an innkeeper could become a king, what might any of us become? Joachim Murat may have ended ignominiously, but with Achille's help, I saw his many dimensions that afternoon, from unimaginable bravery, to glittering glamour, to the tragic hubris, which sullied his reputation and ultimately ended his life.

Achille regaled us for more than an hour with tales of his illustrious father's battlefield exploits, leading Napoléon's cavalry in battles where the names were familiar from newspaper accounts but sterile without personal connection. On Willis Hill, Father had read aloud the report of his succeeding Joseph Bonaparte as king of Naples. It was a moment of awe that we were in the presence of a man who could tell of such glories in the first person. History was so close, you could touch it, and I wanted to.

Achille told his stories that afternoon with such passion that we were right there, seeing with him the dusty fields of thundering charges in faraway lands. The clip-clop of passersby on horseback added to the mood of the moment, and a distant Tallahassee church bell recalled the bells of Borodino. We were spellbound.

Achille Murat's father, Marshal Joachim Murat, led Napoleon's cavalry at the decisive Battle of Borodino in the ill-fated Russian Campaign. Tchaikowsky's famous "1812 Overture" celebrates his impetuous cavalry charge in one of it's most memorable passages.

He finished the tale of his father's death by firing squad and rose slowly with a note of sadness. With a Gallic shrug he announced, "I must go now. In an hour it will be dusk, and I must ring the bell to call my slaves in from their work, or they shall think me a tyrant for driving them after dark. I must ride hard and be sure they are fed on time." I liked that sentiment and thought it foretold a man of more consideration than those who ran their slaves until exhaustion.

It was obvious that day that Achille had been carrying the monumental weight of his father's death for more than a decade and needed someone to tell it to. I was glad it could be me. His anguish was palpable and felt by every Willis in the room. Even my gregarious father, not easily impressed, silently hung onto every word, knowing that anything he might say about his own service would be overwhelmed by comparison. Of our family, only the great Washington could compare to the legendary Joachim Murat, Napoléon's right-hand man.

I walked Achille out to the hitching post where for the first time in my life there was something erotic about the smell of saddle leather.

I watched him mount and ride away as I stood in my best pose of the demure Virginia lady when all I really wanted to do was for him to pull me close so that I might feel that tingle again.

I would not have to wait long. The following day, he rode in again, and we strolled around the wooden sidewalks of town. Each time he took my arm to cross a street, I would feel a blush of warmth such that I felt that everyone would notice. As he left to ride the fifteen miles back to Lipona, he took both of my hands in his, and we gazed without comment into each other's dark eyes.

It was probably no more than ten beautiful seconds, but in that instant, so much was said, yet no words were spoken. Behind those dark Mediterranean eyes lay all of the pain of the ages, a hurt so deep that I could almost feel it myself. As he opened them widely and arched his eyebrows for a playful second, I could see the child scampering about the Elysée Palace. But just as suddenly, a cloud rolled over the eyes again as though he had inadvertently let me see behind a curtain he wasn't ready to share. Was it ten seconds or ten years? Whatever it was, it wasn't enough.

I brashly touched his lips with mine but quickly pulled away lest I forget myself. The magic of the moment vanished on the breeze, and once again there was no prince, just a deeply hurt man standing in the street and holding my hand.

This became his habit at least twice a week for the next five months. It was now February, and as winter settled in on our friends and family in Virginia, we came to revel in the mild and moderate climate of our adopted home. In March, Achille invited us all to dine with him at his plantation. He had warned us that it was quite rustic, but nothing had prepared us for the cluster of Achille's tiny log cabins arrayed helter-skelter atop a hillock outside Wacissa.

He tried, oh bless his heart he tried. With much pomp and circumstance, he stood over a beautiful roast bird, which we assumed to be a turkey and struggled to lift off a few slices. We were treated to the first, last, and only roast buzzard of my life, and if I never taste another one, it will be too soon. With oysters, some fried chicken, doves, fried mullet, sweet potatoes, corn a neighbor had put away last summer, some pickled peaches bought in town, and fresh pumpkin pie, it was all accompanied by six bottles of fine French wines. To all who witnessed Achille's feast, as we labeled it, it was obvious that he had given this much thought. The country meal under his arbor was incongruously brought to table by slaves in Napoleonic livery and served on Picard plates from France, bearing the laurel crowned *J* for King Joachim. It was probably the first time the plates had been used since the days of royalty in Naples, for they contained a serving of sadness as well as buzzard and corn. The beauty was not in the plates, it was in the moment.

It was altogether an endearing moment as we sat under his arbor on the hill. After a late lunch, the men went off to smoke, and Mother smiled a knowing smile. Upon their return, Achille brought out from his humble cabin a beautiful marble bust by Canova of his mother, Queen Caroline, and one of Napoléon. He delicately displayed, on outstretched hands, his father's diamond-encrusted sword in a manner suggesting that he felt unworthy to so much as touch it. Then came a procession of lovely jewelry from the days of empire. Each item came with a reverently told personal story of the item and its significance in the Murat-Bonaparte saga. The telling brought a faraway look to Achille's eyes, which we all found touching.

By the end of the day, we had decided that he was not so much eccentric as misunderstood by the crackers of North Florida. He was more than a gentleman. He was a gentle man.

The rumors were flying about Tallahassee, the Florida Territory, Virginia, and back in Washington. A Bonaparte descendant was courting a Washington descendant, and it was news of international significance, especially to the gossipy crowd! Except for me, no one, including my mother, knew that it was the female Washington descendant courting, in her own subtle way, the male Bonaparte descendant. This was a man of substance, a man who knew his way around the world, and I was determined to keep it that way and to let him think that the chase d'amour was all his idea.

Even Queen Caroline, now the Countess of Lipona and Achille's mother across the Atlantic, was told of the match by letters from Achille, which took at least six weeks each way. Predictably, the royal reaction was one of disapproval. Who, she fretted, had their eye on her firstborn son? The Bonaparte resistance was dropped, however, like the proverbial hot potato once it was learned that my great-granduncle was George Washington. Thank you, Uncle George! Family, as I have always said, is everything.

Since this was not an arranged match of the sort normally cooked up by the Bonapartes, Caroline could not have stopped the march of our love anyway, but it was preferable to have her blessings as we became more and more serious. In springtime in Tallahassee, everything was blooming, especially our love for each other. We were Tristan and Isolde, Lancelot and Guinevere, Oberon and Titania, and every other love match ever created! In a moment of overflowing Mediterranean emotion, Achille spontaneously burst out that he could not live without me. I felt the same but had been constrained to let the relationship play out its own way, and let him take the lead. I had known other Virginia ladies who had overplayed their hand and learned my lesson from them. Now that the dam was burst, however, flush with excitement, we went straightaway to Father, who in his best patrician Virginia manner and with love and a bear hug for his little girl, gave his tentative assent. He hoped for some reassurances that the Bonapartes would approve the match, a rational request given their status. Achille assured him that his mother, Queen Caroline, would heartily approve, and she did.

My older brother Lewis and Achille's partner James Gadsden filed a marriage bond for us. Though lavish weddings were the custom in both of our families, there was no way to dress up Tallahassee for such an event, and besides, except for my immediate family, well-wishers from both sides lived too far away to share the event. Achille knew nothing of American marital protocols, and I had made a dog's dinner of my first one, so I let mother plan a small, understated ceremony in the best southern tradition.

A small wedding was all right with us; our love needed no embellishment.

On a steamy afternoon, Tuesday, July 12, 1826, we appeared quietly before Justice of the Peace Ed van Evans. With magnolias on a small altar and Mother playing the piano softly in the background, we tied the historic knot, which bound together for the only time in history the houses of Bonaparte and Washington. For our honeymoon, Achille had rented a proper coach for the drive out to his small cabin at Lipona where we were welcomed by his slaves chanting an old hymn in African dialect. It was the most beautiful place and the most beautiful moment of my life. And it hardly registered on me at all that in marrying the prince, I had become a princess.

Newlyweds, 1826

*W*HO KNEW THAT paradise would fit into a twelve-by-eighteen-foot log cabin?

My first weeks with Achille were a combination of incomparable joy and learning some interesting and, shall I say, strange habits of his. He could not have been more different from my first husband, the late Atchison Gray. (He was the one who insisted that I call him Mr. Gray and was so cold and unemotional that it is a wonder we had a child at all!) The poor baby died in infancy so was of no consequence other than to burden my heart for the poor dear now strumming a harp in heaven.

Achille was anything but cold. In fact, he was the personification of the passionate Mediterranean male. Part French, part Corsican, with a touch of Italian upbringing in the mix, he was a lover beyond imagining, and we spent many pleasant moments (or was it hours?) those first months. Mother would have been shocked!

He was most attentive as well and always inquired about my well-being. I sincerely appreciated this as we were quite literally stuck in the middle of nowhere with few creature comforts and no social interaction save a sporadic visit from a neighbor. I marveled at his near-manic pace of life. Always he rose several hours before dawn and read for an hour or so by candlelight. He was a voracious reader because in the wilderness he lacked a stimulating intellectual environment with his peers. He forever read and reread all that he could get his hands on. Sometimes

Achille preferred to plow his fertile mind rather than his fields and spent days penning letters to his friend, Count Thibeaudeau.

With morning reading or writing cast aside, by dawn had seen to it that a frontiersman's breakfast was ready. Coffee was hard to come by and reserved for special occasion, but we started each day with tea, cakes of wheat or corn meal with molasses, salt pork fried up crispy, mush or grits, and eggs from the recently constructed henhouse out back. All told, that meal was quite similar to what I was accustomed to. Other meals were an altogether different story. Achille loved experimenting with the various creatures of the forest that surrounded us. I would politely taste them but didn't share his relish for delicacies such as rattlesnake or the sausages he made up from whatever meat was available. (I stopped eating sausage entirely when I found several raccoon skins discarded on our trash heap.)

Our slaves—we never used that word—were also very attentive and forever bringing to our door something unique they had found. These gentle blacks beamed with excitement and happiness to show their new "missus" a treasure from their labors. After a month, I must have had at least thirty beautifully fashioned arrowheads, which our hands had turned from the soil of our fields. They once brought up to the house an unusual animal I had never seen before, and it appeared to me at first they had found a small dinosaur down in the slough behind the pasture. Achille didn't know its name either as they had no such creature in Europe. Neighbors later explained that it was a species known only by its Spanish name, armadillo. The one I remember most distinctly was when they brought up to my door a small alligator with a rope around its neck. I was a bit intimidated as their reputation was akin to that of a snake. Achille thanked them profusely for their gift and, to my shock, proceeded to make a stew of the poor thing!

Compared to the mansion in Fredericksburg, or even the caretaker's cottage at Wakefield plantation where I had lived for a time with Atchison Gray, I felt more like a desperate pioneer than like a plantation mistress. If the truth be told, we lived a very meager existence most days during our first few months at Lipona.

Achille and I determined to remedy that. He sketched out plans for expanding the plantation house, such as it were, and diverted ten men from their labors in the field to selecting and cutting the best trees and to creating a U-shaped complex, which quadrupled our living area. Hammers and saws became our companions as the new Lipona was born. Fine it was not, and it surely could not be called a plantation in comparison to those of my Virginia upbringing, but it was how everyone lived on the Florida frontier. Three of our most intelligent hands were assigned to me to help with the house, and soon its interior began to look downright civilized in contrast with the spartan hovel of Achille's bachelor days. I pleaded with Achille for a closet in which to hang my magnificent dresses brought from Virginia, as they had been stuffed into trunks for over a year now. Knowing the esteem in which I held my wardrobe, I got my closet though it was minute. The logs of the exterior walls were rechinked, interior walls were plastered and whitewashed, and in two of the cabins, Achille oversaw flooring and shelving of the ubiquitous pine. Next we added glass windows and a real bathing tub, though Achille never used it. Furniture was purchased from an emporium in town, and we gave up the Spanish moss mattress on the floor for a real bed. Lipona was forever a work in progress over which the marble bust of Queen Caroline presided.

Creature comforts gradually overtook the rustic harshness of our first days at Lipona, and we began entertaining neighbors at least once a month. I contributed some heirloom Willis silver serving pieces, over a hundred years old, and Achille's past had left him in possession of some beautiful tableware from France and elegant linens embroidered with the Neapolitan coat of arms. Though the setting was somewhat primitive, like everyone else's on the southern frontier, we had all of the accoutrements with which to dazzle guests, and we did. Though it came more from his status as a European noble than anything we overtly did, Prince Murat and I, his princess, quickly achieved a well-known spot in the pecking order of Tallahassee society.

Achille sometimes reminded me of a flea. Hop here, hop there, never really alight. I have never known anyone so subject to whims and hasty action based on the latest idea du jour. Some were amusing; some were serious and had consequences that should have been better thought out and thoroughly considered. An example of the latter was when he spontaneously responded to comments by his friend and mentor Richard Keith Call that there was a new threat from Seminoles outraged by the white man's incursions. Some outlying plantations had actually been attacked. Without a thought that joining Call's military expedition to deal with the Indian threat would leave me alone, vulnerable, and subject to attack myself, Achille impulsively headed into the forest as Call's aide-de-camp. With no military background save some operatic moments as a child in Italy, I feared that we were both being exposed to danger unnecessarily. While he might have believed he was displaying courage, from my perspective all he displayed was his impetuous Mediterranean tendency to lurch into action without thinking. It was one of the few times I felt it necessary to confront him with my concerns. He would be surrounded by armed colleagues I pointed out while I would be left alone at Lipona except for the slaves, whom we did not allow to keep guns. I had acquaintances who had seen the results of an Indian raid and don't mind telling you that I was afraid. Despite this, with stubborn determination he would not be dissuaded, and this became our first open disagreement. I dropped my eyes and went silent until giving him a perfunctory kiss as he left on the dapple gray with a pistol in his belt, holstered rifle hung from his saddle, and four bony hunting dogs baying. As if to punctuate the tense atmosphere of the moment, he spurred up to a gallop as he whirled the gray around with a jerk. I watched until he hit the main road toward Wacissa and didn't so much as wave good-bye. Men!

Born to the Mediterranean temperament and always having his way as a child, the ardent Achille, I have always been convinced, joined this ragtag force out of misplaced notions of glory fueled by his father's reputation as a cavalry leader. Though he never needed to prove himself to me, Achille, in his insecurity, had never quite measured up, and I think he saw this moment as an opportunity to prove himself.

To whom? General Call? The Bonaparte family? Townspeople? Me? None of those. With an old friend challenging him to "join up" and a new wife to impress, he impetuously rode to the sound of the guns and was awarded the title of colonel. He undertook the entire charade only to prove himself to himself. Meanwhile, with Indians prowling about, I was alone at Lipona. I would show him what Virginia women are made of and made plans to ride out his absence in safety. I posted one of the field hands in a corn crib where he could see the house and gave him a both a rifle and orders to shoot anyone who looked suspicious after dark.

For six weeks, the newly appointed Colonel Murat tilted at windmills in the forests of North Florida venting some kind of masculine yearning for adventure, combat, and fame. Like so many of his endeavors, it didn't last long. The threat abated when it was learned that it was just a few outlaws not the local Seminoles, and Achille quit the mission in disgust calling it "a parody of war." When he returned, I surprised myself with the ease with which I forgave him his rash foray into the wilderness. The tension of his departure was forgotten in the delight of a long soulful hug. I then sent him in to use the new bathing tub and, shortly thereafter, joined him for a more intimate welcome.

As we lay side by side in the warm afterglow, he trotted out his next adventure. Once again, the flea was jumping to new pursuits. Having never had a proper honeymoon, Achille announced with all of the energies of his frenetic personality a grand plan. First we would immerse ourselves for a week in the culture and pleasures of Charleston. When traveling south with my family, I had thought Charleston a delightful, convivial city, but now, after time in the wilderness, it seemed a veritable cornucopia of culture. From Charleston, we were to journey on northward so that Achille might introduce me to the Bonaparte relatives who ebbed and flowed around Joseph's luxurious manor at Point Breeze, New Jersey. We would also visit New York and Philadelphia. How exciting! I had never been north of Washington DC, so that was a thrill in itself, and the opportunity to see and be seen in Bonaparte society was enticing.

It was also a bit intimidating. Joseph, after all, had been a king. I had never met a king! Would this Virginia girl be welcomed, or did they see me as some sort of pariah who would pollute their bloodline? Was I really a princess in their eyes? Did they consider it legitimate that an American could hold such a title, even if my husband, the prince, had been so rudely deposed? In Tallahassee, people called him Prince Murat, and on occasion, some had deferentially called me princess. Would that hold up to Bonaparte scrutiny?

As I came to know the Bonapartes vicariously, I could not help but marvel at the tenacity with which they promoted themselves and the iron-clad integrity with which they rallied around the family against outside threats. At first it was natural for me to perceive them as mere in-laws, for Caroline Bonaparte was indeed my mother-in-law. Further knowledge of the Bonapartes, strengthened when I met Joseph Bonaparte and his family, prompted me to see them as a tribe with their own internal rituals, codes, and strictures which governed their every move. Though I never met Achille's uncle, the great Napoleon himself, his exploits elevated the family to an altogether rarified level which could only be described as a dynasty. And not just any dynasty either. My in-laws were quite likely the most famous dynasty of the age, perhaps in all of history and it was this realization which took my breath away.

Would they look at me in the same light as the unfortunate Betsy Patterson, the other American girl who had married a Bonaparte—she had married Napoléon's brother Jérôme—but lost him when Napoléon demanded her ouster, and the compliant Jérôme abandoned her? Embittered, she had been openly critical of the Bonapartes, and I feared I might be tarred with her brush. My mind buzzed with questions, and as usual, Mother's quiet wisdom put it all into a sane perspective for me. "Kate, you are of good Virginia breeding," she said, "just be yourself and remember to treat them as you would your Willis elders." That meant treat them graciously and with the aristocratic manners she had drummed into me since I was six. Good advice.

Excitedly, I began to plan for this respite from the wearying place I now called home, Lipona. I must pack carefully, for the impressions to be made at Point Breeze were crucial. What dresses shall I take? Do I curtsy before Joseph? How deeply? Do we kiss on both cheeks? When a princess has to go to the bathroom in the night, does she slink out to the privy inconspicuously or just go, knowing full well that everyone else does too. In a tizzy, I fretted with Achille about all of this only to have him provide the same advice as Mother. When would I learn I was as good as they?

Our belated honeymoon sounded glorious though I cringed at the prospects of repeating the trek to and from St. Augustine over the dreaded Bellamy Road. If we were to go by sea, there was no other way to do it, so I summoned up my courage for the slog across the wilderness to the coast.

In March 1827, with luggage loaded onto a wagon, our field hands, together with their wives and children lined up along our little road and with kerchiefs waving, bade farewell to Prince and Princess Murat. Though we were unquestionably the master and mistress of Lipona, and these were our slaves not our peers, it almost felt like we were a little tribe, an extended family eking out days together. I was moved by their display of affection.

In town, we spent the night with Mother and Father, took them to a new inn for dinner, which had opened in Tallahassee, and caught up with family news. The next morning with trunks and cases lashed on top, we boarded a stage and set off on the first of many travels I would have with my prince.

The Bellamy Road hadn't improved. Stumps, ruts, and unbridged streams slowed progress to no more than twenty-five or thirty miles a day, and we were exhausted when we arrived at St. Augustine to await the boat that would carry us northward.

St. Augustine didn't look much different than it had last year. And no wonder. It had been here for more than two centuries, and the ravages of time and shifting ownership had taken their toll. With Achille sporting more money than Father, and with fewer in the traveling party than my last time here, we were booked into a very comfortable boarding house on St. George Street near the plaza. Still, this was the rudimentary St. Augustine, and with several of the windows of our room broken out, we were serenaded each night by bloodthirsty mosquitoes from the swamp. Luxury St. Augustine style was not luxurious. The start of our honeymoon was thus not especially auspicious, but as always, my sweet Achille tried his best to assure my comfort. I had already forgiven him for the madness of his foray into the supposed Indian Wars with General Call and was ready for the luxury that awaited us at Charleston and beyond. For now, we had only to while away the days until the arrival of the ship that would bear us on the first leg of our overdue honeymoon.

Delayed Honeymoon, 1827

*F*OR ACHILLE ESPECIALLY, one of the pleasant diversions as we waited was to make the acquaintance of a scrawny and sickly young New England minister. This would not have ordinarily been an event to remark on, but this one was named Ralph Waldo Emerson. Instantly he and Achille fell into deep conversation over arcane philosophical matters, which I frankly chose not to delve into. Emerson, the Unitarian, and Murat, the atheist, harangued for hours over the perceived foibles and fallacies of religion. No target was spared. Frontier Protestants were blasted, and the Roman Catholic Church excoriated. During these heated rants, this little Episcopal girl from Virginia napped or did needlepoint. There was no way to win in an argument between two opinionated men.

Achille Murat, husband of Catherine Willis Murat, befriended Ralph Waldo Emerson and the two sparred intellectually over a wide range of topics.

The experience did set me to thinking about Achille's religious beliefs, or lack thereof. Quietly over dinner one night, I waded into these delicate waters. Though he had few in person experiences with the Protestant faiths which flourished in the territory he was quick to lambaste them.

"They have nothing to do with man and his relationship with God," he fumed, "and poison the poor and the ignorant with absurd services built on emotion and the need of their pastors to earn a living. They spout nonsense and people chant it back to them with 'amens' and 'hallelujahs.'"

"But what about Roman Catholicism?" I inquired discreetly, knowing he had been raised Catholic.

Obliquely, he rambled off into a diatribe about how the pope had excommunicated Uncle Napoléon, and in return, Napoléon had imprisoned Pope Pius VII for many years. I thought it smacked more of politics than religion and found a convenient excuse to terminate the conversation. Religion was a touchy subject best left alone.

On March 29, 1827, we boarded our little sloop, the *William*, for Charleston with twenty-three others. Packed aboard, we hoped for a favorable wind and pleasant journey, not aware that in sailing the waters of the Atlantic on the cusp of winter, we were courting disaster.

It hit. A journey that should have lasted no more than two days became instead ten wet days of retching in our tiny cabin or over the side. Gale-force winds and hunger, the *William* had run out of provisions, combined to sear this experience into my mind as a most unpleasant start to our honeymoon.

Finally, Charleston and terra firma. Parting with the sea, the now-smelly *William*, and with the brilliant but shrewish Ralph Waldo Emerson could not come soon enough for me. I did not share the latter observation of Mr. Emerson with Achille lest he think me a narrow-minded provincial.

A storm of a different sort awaited us in Charleston. Though we enjoyed several days of social intercourse with cultured citizens befriended on prior trips, while there we learned of serious political discussions sweeping the land that would alter our lifestyle.

The institution of slavery was on the political chopping block, and rumbles of abolition sounded a warning for the plantation economies of the South, ours included. In a private moment, I reflected on how they would fare if freed. We had so deprived them of education and culture that we had created a total dependence on the largesse of their plantation owners. If suddenly told, "Go, you are free," they would be cast adrift in a white man's world without the knowledge needed to survive, and it worried me. From my own standpoint, I could not envision life without the gentle, hardworking souls whose presence was as integral to my life as my own family's.

It was clear though that this was the predominant social issue of the times and would have to be dealt with. My ancestors, who participated in the founding of the republic, had deferred the slavery controversy to my generation. Because it was my own kin who had left it unresolved, I felt especially duty bound to at least resolve it in my own mind. It was vexing, and my views on it flip-flopped a dozen times a day.

After the nightmarish voyage of the *William* from St. Augustine, I was never so happy as when Achille agreed that the rest of our honeymoon travels would be overland via stagecoach. After my pleadings and one particularly good pout, the sweet man said he would do it just for me, but secretly, I think he was glad to proceed by land as well. Either that or he couldn't stand the thought of a week in a small rolling cabin with a sulking wife!

In the bargain, I had also suggested that we might go the more inland route so that I could show him my old homestead at Fredericksburg and introduce my prince to family and friends. This route took us through the North Carolina town named for Sir Walter Raleigh and through Richmond before arrival at Fredericksburg. This was an unplanned diversion of our trip, and we had less time than I would have liked, but I proudly walked Achille up Willis Hill, so soaked with nostalgia. Scratching around in the tall grass, we located the foundations of the old family mansion, Brompton, and a few charred timbers. I picked up a piece of one of Mother's favorite teacups and clutched it close to my breast, carried away on transports of memory. I knew that Mother was gamely trying to make the best of things in a log cabin in Tallahassee but also knew that her home and her heart were here. Unable to control my emotions, I wept as Achille held me in his arms atop the hill which held so many memories.

It was here on Willis Hill that I had pretended dancing with a prince, and now here I stood with one, a handsome one at that, and he was mine. I had ridden my dear dapple gray Lizzie on this hill then. He rode one now in Tallahassee, Ulysses. Before our Fredericksburg time was over, we would feast on even bigger parallels.

We were feted by dear friends for three days before moving on. On the day of our departure, I took Achille by Mother's ancestral home on Washington Street, the lovely Kenmore house, the home built by Colonel Fielding Lewis for his bride Betty Washington. It was here that my great-granduncle George Washington had visited his sister Betty and planned some of the strategies of the American Revolution. As we stood before the elegant Georgian brick home, it was as though lightning struck us at the same instant, and with the same thoughts of historic proportion.

I was niece of Washington, founder of our great republic and one of the most famous people in all of history.

He was nephew of Napoléon, who at his zenith was indisputably the most powerful man in the world and founder of a mighty empire.

Together, we alone represented the convergence of two of the most powerful family dynasties in history.

We alone.

We wracked our brains to come up with other examples, but there were none quite comparable, certainly not in recent history. Perhaps, we opined, Henry II and Eleanor of Aquitaine. Further back, we drew tentative comparisons to Julius Caesar's marriage to Cleopatra of the Ptolemy dynasty. Potent company! Our historic connections were, for both of us, more a matter of quiet pride not overblown ego. We vowed to not let it go to our heads.

We had chatted about this before but here at Kenmore, where the great Washington had trod, where his sister had lived, it was not necessary to talk about it. We felt it. In the swirl of thoughts, emotions, and genes we each brought to our match, we knew we were heirs to something that no one could take from us. Something noble. Something grand. Something unique. This was our moment, and we were transfixed in the silence and awe bestowed by this near-sacred knowledge. We would discuss it many times in the future, in public and in private, but never in the transcendental manner of this moment. It was close to holy for us both.

Soon our coachman summoned us and asked if there was anything more for today. How could there be?

We went on to dinner at the vintage Long Ordinary on Caroline Street nearby, one of Father's favorites. Over a bottle of champagne, we pursued quiet conversation, which invariably led us both down paths of family. I inquired about surviving members of the Bonaparte family. I was particularly curious about Napoléon's mother, Madame Mere, whom I knew was still alive but at an advanced age. If memory served me correctly, so were Napoléon's brothers, Lucien and the improvident Jérôme, as well as Joseph, whom we were headed to visit. And of course, we toasted the other Bonaparte sibling, Achille's mother, Caroline, now styled the Duchess of Lipona. Caroline was still biding time in Austria with her companion General Francesco MacDonald. MacDonald was a holdover from Caroline's glory days having served as her late husband's secretary of war for the kingdom of Naples.

The Bonapartes represented a dynasty in the truest sense of the word, and Achille was glad to fill in the details as we chatted quietly over coffee.

When it was his turn to inquire, Achille asked about my Washington ancestors. George Washington, of course, had had no issue, but his sister Betty did, and with humility and pride, I could claim her as my great-grandmother. He next inquired if my grandparents George Lewis and his wife, my namesake, Catherine were still healthy enough to receive guests, and I sadly replied that they had died before we migrated South. They would have been proud to meet my Achille, and he them. My grandfather George Lewis had commanded George Washington's lifeguard during the Revolution and was a true hero of the American Revolution revered by all. Tragically, now we were able to commune only with their spirits.

Achille, a devout student of history, stood in awe of the success that the American Revolution had attained while France's Revolution had sputtered to a bloody and inconclusive close. Ever the sentimentalist,

Achille raised his glass and ended the night with a simple toast, "To family!"

Fredericksburg was a proud moment for me and burnished my bona fides in preparation to meet the Bonapartes at Point Breeze. I realized that my own family's achievements rivaled those of the Bonapartes and Murats and no longer felt intimidated. We left my birthplace on a good note, and I stood a little taller. Although I was destined to never return, Willis Hill and Fredericksburg would always be revered as home with a capital *H*.

The next morning, the stage left at 6:00 AM, and we were well on the other side of Washington DC by nightfall. The Washington DC name now resonated differently for Achille since he had now visited a property built for one of my Washington ancestors, Betty Washington of "Kenmore."

Roadside stage stops were now at proper inns, and we both felt more comfortable to be back to the civilized environs of America's cradle after some of the downtrodden places where we had been forced to stay in territorial Florida. The next day, we entered and reveled in historic Philadelphia. A brief visit to Independence Hall energized Achille to write further treatises on American democracy. In keeping with his enthusiasm and impatient nature, he started that very night and was still writing when I awoke the next morning. I never ceased being amazed that his mind, and sometimes his body, never rested. Having tarried in Fredericksburg, we were forced to press on without proper rest and soon Philadelphia fell in our dust as we hurried to meet our scheduled arrival at Point Breeze. I felt somehow that I had an appointment with destiny.

A Bonaparte King. Point Breeze, New Jersey, 1827

*T*HERE WERE BONAPARTES aplenty waiting as we closed in on Point Breeze. Not wanting to arrive looking down on our luck, in Philadelphia Achille had hired a fine coach with footmen and two outriders and sent an outrider ahead to alert Joseph to our impending arrival. It was a little pretentious, but these were the Bonapartes, and image mattered.

Once through the impressive gates, we entered a realm of dreams. Joseph had spared no expense to transform his one thousand acres of America into an English country estate, complete with winding carriage drives of pea gravel that crunched sweetly under our wheels, lavish plantings interspersed with the finest marble sculptures, fountains, and a large man-made lake with landscaped islands and, of course, more sculpture. Its grandeur recalled for me visits to family properties in Virginia, notably the Washington's Mount Vernon, William Byrd's Westover, the Warner's Warner Hall, Carter's Nomini Hall, and the Page's Rosewell. Those posh family-connected plantation homes were a way of life for me in my youth, but after the brutalizing experiences of the Florida wilderness, they now seemed a world away. Though the Bible exhorts us not to covet, I must say that it was a most pleasing feeling to be returning to the unmistakably elegant feel of a moneyed estate.

I felt deeply humbled when our coach pulled up to the front of the mansion to be greeted by the former king of Spain, in full formal uniform and regalia as though this were a visit of state. His daughter Zenaide stood in her finest gown and jewels accompanied by her husband Prince Charles Lucien. Achille's brother, also named Lucien, stood deferentially a pace behind. (I would have no trouble remembering the men's names at least!) Further behind this entourage of Bonaparte nobility was the household staff of twenty, all turned out in the full formal livery of Napoléon. The empire and the emperor might be gone from across the Atlantic, but my first impression was that it was alive and well in Bordentown, New Jersey.

BONAPARTE HOUSE
The late residence of
JOSEPH NAPOLEON BONAPARTE EX KING OF SPAIN

Achille Murat, husband of Catherine Willis Murat, frequented the New Jersey residence of his uncle, the former King of Spain, Joseph Bonaparte.
Catherine's family, the Willises of Virginia and Florida, also visited the estate on the Delaware River which was named Point Breeze.

I did my well-practiced and deepest curtsy for King Joseph, who performed the classic European kiss on both cheeks in welcome. I was less formally greeted by his Zenaide and the two Luciens and got the impression that they were determined to take the measure of this new family member without delay and cut directly to the chase.

It was immediately evident that language barriers were going to inhibit a full interchange, but we smiled and struggled through initial pleasantries as we were tendered flutes of champagne by an adorable blond serving girl of about twenty, who curtsied to me as I took the glass from the most magnificent silver-and-gold tray I have ever seen. I wondered if she had other functions in the household as well.

This little enclave of Bonapartes on the Delaware River was a distinctly American version of the royal European estate. Joseph's original mansion there had suffered the same fate as our home atop Willis Hill, leaving only ashes and charred timbers. Father had never recovered from that blow, but the well-heeled Joseph, financed by the crown jewels of Spain with which he had absconded, rebuilt in short order. Starting with the building, which had originally served as his stables, Point Breeze had undergone such renaissance that I found it breathtaking. Its facade was of white plaster over brick, but it was the interior that dazzled. As Achille and his uncle Joseph drifted away deep in Francophile conversation, Zenaide led me through the grand hall, the library, and the gallery. Feeling somewhat deprived and a bit provincial, I admitted that I had never been to Europe, but my imagination took me there now. Never had I seen such a collection of magnificent tapestries and art masterpieces! Deep within, I vowed that I would one day experience all of the glories of Europe but, even in my wildest dreams, could not have forecast just how glorious that time of my life was to be.

Another uncle by marriage of Catherine Willis Murat (Princess Kate) was Joseph Bonaparte, seen here in his lavish coronation robes as King of Spain. Joseph has a vastly different, some would say less manic, personality than his imperial brother the Emperor Napoleon I. Catherine Willis Murat and her family (the Willis's of Virginia and Florida) visited Joseph at his American estate, "Point Breeze" in Bordentown, New Jersey.

Point Breeze proved to be as idyllic as its setting. Days drifted into nights of gourmet feasts and musical splendors. Zenaide and her Lucien were charming. If she were like this, it made me wonder about her sister Charlotte and her little fling with Achille! Ah well, that was a chapter long buried, and Charlotte was now ensconced in Paris with her arranged husband, Napoléon Louis Bonaparte, and indulging her love of art with her lover Louis-Leopold Robert. These Bonapartes and their morals, I never ceased to be amazed!

Although she affected the formal title Zénaïde Laetitia Julie Bonaparte, Princess of Canino and Musignano, I found Zenaide to be unassuming and quite Americanized. She and Lucien (I began calling him by his other name, Charles, to prevent confusion.) were devoted to the study of ornithology and spent much time with John James Audubon. Much sport was made about their birds and my Byrds!

As for Achille's brother Lucien, his reputation as a bon vivant appeared to be well-deserved. He was argumentative, usually inebriated by noon, and had become an embarrassment to the Bonaparte name in town where his exploits were well-known. Quite handsome, I noted that the young blonde beauty, who had served us champagne upon our arrival, paid special attentions to him, and I drew the conclusion I believe anyone would. Achille, in private moments, complained of his younger brother's decadent lifestyle and wrote his mother back in Austria, whose personal pension supported her prodigal New Jersey son. With Achille's nudging, Lucien would fly the comfortable nest at Point Breeze and travel into the relatively unsettled part of the United States recently acquired from Uncle Napoléon under the Louisiana Purchase. Joseph was glad to see him go.

After a most pleasant stay of over two weeks, it was our turn to go too. Before we set out for the return to Florida and our humble home there, an effusive Joseph insisted that we return soon and bring all of my family so that he might shower Bonaparte hospitality on the entire Willis clan about whom he had heard so much. It was evident that he took seriously our close relationship to the Washingtons, and there seemed no status difference whatsoever. For a king, and a Bonaparte one at that, Joseph had shown he possessed a more calm and unpretentious manner than his now-deceased brother the emperor, who had been hard-driving and almost maniacal in his pursuit of power. It was good to see the human side of the Bonapartes. While I could never use the word *warm* to describe Joseph, he was surely of a gentler persuasion than that his brother and a host par excellence.

As we prepared for the arduous trip back to Lipona, Achille, who had been assiduously working on his essays on democracy begun in Philadelphia, suffered an attack of the sort that I had seen afflict him on occasion at home. His normally energetic manner would escalate into an even more excitable and near-frenzied state, and on occasion, his nerves would wear so thin as to cause collapse into a coma-like state. Upon awakening, he would complain of a tingling sensation in his hands and arms and, for a time, lack full use of them. It was a worrisome thing to see my brilliant husband fall victim to what was evidently some kind of dread mental disorder, which no one seemed to understand. There were many in the family, his mother included, who lay blame for these episodes on the trauma of the attempted assassination and explosion that preceded his birth. I was no expert but had my doubts. Our honeymoon was like so many Murat expeditions, begun in a blaze of glory only to fizzle at the end.

In contrast to the leisurely delights of Charleston, Fredericksburg, and Philadelphia on our trip north, we hastened home in October 1827 so that Achille could recuperate properly. No sloop *William* adventures on the briny this time, it was by stagecoach all the way to Tallahassee, passing through the spectacular fall scenery of my native Virginia and the Carolinas, where the gaudy display of turning leaves also turned our heads. The scenery and cooler, less humid air seemed a good tonic for Achille, who suffered no more seizures during our journey.

Back in Tallahassee, we quickly conveyed to Mother and Father Joseph's gracious invitation for the family to visit Point Breeze en masse. I wondered if that trip would ever take place as my beloved mother, with one of those late-life surprises, was very pregnant at age forty-five. Father poured Achille one of his new favorites, a mint julep, and had a good belly laugh at Zenaide's "birds and Byrds" puns. Two mint juleps later, I prodded Achille to set out for Lipona before darkness overcame us. Mother had warned that there had been a few Indian attacks during our absence, and frankly, we had both forgotten that latent threat. Thus reminded, the primitive nature of life on the Florida frontier closed in fast. In haste, we sought out transport to our outlying farm and hugged the family good-bye, uncertain of Achille's health or the next steps in our uncertain lives. Before setting out, he retrieved the double-barreled derringer he had stashed away in his trunk to have it at the ready if needed.

In lengthening shadows, as we clattered up the drive to Lipona in a tacky old rented buckboard drawn by one scrawny mule covered with scabs and horseflies, I suddenly felt smothered by desolation and despair. When I first saw our little cluster of cabins in the wilderness,

I couldn't stifle my sigh of resignation, and a tear was not far behind. Compared to Point Breeze, it was a study in contrasts.

The brightest spot of our return was the flurry of excitement when our hands and a few of their rawboned hounds came rushing up to greet us from the south forty where they were picking the last cotton from the brown stalks. We always let them have the late-crop remnants for their own use, and their expressions of appreciation for the simple gesture were so genuine it almost hurt. Already some of the wives were spinning to create clothes for the chill of winter just around the corner. I felt very maternal about our servants and field hands—we never called them slaves—who now numbered in the seventies. It was my duty and my pleasure to assume a protective role over them whenever we heard of neighboring slave masters who resorted to the lash to exact work from theirs. Philosophically, such mistreatment of fellow human beings, whatever their color, rankled against my Christian upbringing. Achille was less bothered by this than I, but then he was not burdened by the deeply rooted Christian code of ethics into which I was raised. Too, as a purely practical matter, we needed our hands, and they needed us. It was better to have them on our side when it came to both work output and to potential Indian attack. Was I too soft? Probably. Would I do it the same way all over again? Definitely.

All told, our return to Lipona was a far cry from our royal champagne welcome at Point Breeze. It wasn't much, we told ourselves, but it was home.

As the first chill of late fall settled over our little home, Achille sent the house help away to spend the evening with their own families after they had built a fire for us. Gazing wistfully into the crackling flames, we sipped a glass of port and waxed philosophical about the Point Breeze experience and our simple, soulful homecoming. Something had to change, we concluded, as our conversation took on a gloomier edge. Achille and I had both hailed from better. I from highly placed Virginia gentry, he from European royalty, we had both grown up with finery and wealth. No doubt, the mood of the moment was accentuated because we so recently luxuriated at one of America's most celebrated estates.

With his troubling illness and depression, I should probably not have let on to Achille that I too was depressed, but with tears glistening in the firelight, he surmised my mood.

We had made our decisions, and we were doing the best we could. It just wasn't good enough, but I had pinned all of my love and hopes on this marriage and would not let our temporary misfortunes get us down. With love, perseverance, and a little luck, things would get better. I had a goodly streak of Mother's quiet optimism and belief that God takes care of His children. Sometimes His benevolence is difficult to see and comes in mysterious ways, but at that pensive moment, as the embers crackled their last, I could not have imagined the turnabout of fortune just around our corner.

On the long coach ride south from New Jersey, Achille had waxed eloquent about his desire to ease out of the role of plantation master, which had failed him twice at Parthenope and Lipona, and launch into a career that would be more to his natural penchant for thinking, writing, and speaking. In the Florida wilderness, I wondered if this was practical, but practicality had never stopped him before.

Counselor Murat, 1827-28

*A*S FALL OF 1827 drifted into winter, Achille, with all of the impetuous charge of his father's cavalry, attacked the study of law as a new profession. He had been mightily inspired by visiting Independence Hall, home of the U.S. Constitution, and used it as a motivational springboard to prepare for his new career. Of course, he also rubbed elbows with many distinguished members of the bar, Call, Duval, and more, and I suspect he sought to prove himself their equal.

Though Achille remained vague about exactly how he would use this knowledge, he was flailing about as a planter once more and needed a change. I supported him fully. *Lipona* the name was far more satisfying than *Lipona* the reality.

Achille had grown up under the Napoleonic Code but was enamored also of the English common law, and now seemed to forever have his nose in books by Blackstone and other famous figures in jurisprudence. The earnest study of law began to be the dominant characteristic of our lives in the log shanties we called home.

With less time in the fields as an active overseer of the plantation, he was at home more frequently, and our second priority was to spend more time trying to make little Murats. We were both sorely disappointed that I had not become pregnant, and I began to wonder if there was something physically amiss due to the delivery of my firstborn child with Atchison Gray, the one who had died in infancy.

Perhaps too it was Achille, though that topic was never broached for fear of insulting his masculinity. It was de rigueur in such situations to always blame the wife for being barren rather than to infer that the husband had a role in procreation too. Anne Boleyn had learned the hard way to never blame a barren marriage on the husband!

With regard to family and births, we were greeted with the news on October 15, 1827, that while Mother and Father were visiting relatives at Blenheim, Virginia, my mother had given birth to a midlife child. This came as something of a shock. Mother was, by this time, forty-five, and it had been ten years since the birth of her last child, my younger sister Ellen Attoway Willis, Attie. Nonetheless, my unflappable mother took this little midlife surprise in stride as she did the many vicissitudes of life. Having accepted with grace the loss of the family fortune, having survived the arduous move to Florida, she now was a mother again just when she should begin a less strenuous life. My brother Lewis, now a practicing physician, had moved to Pensacola and married in September, so there was a definite generational disconnect with the birth of the newest Willis.

Most fortunately, the birth was without complications when Mother delivered a healthy handsome boy. Partly because both of my parents adored and respected Achille, and partly that we had all become resigned that I was not destined to give birth, at my most fervent request their new son was named in his honor. We were both grateful and flattered. Achille Murat Willis joined the family and, from his crib, announced that he had the lungs of an orator like his namesake. Both Mother and Father doted upon the new son as a gift from God and lavished upon him all the love one could muster. To render his foreign-sounding name easier, Father immediately began a long tradition of calling him Little Mu.

But back to Achille's new venture. There were no formal schools of law in reasonable proximity to Lipona, thus his new endeavor required voluminous reading, sometimes fourteen to sixteen hours a day. Normally given to inconsistency of motivation, his determination to master American law astounded me. When Achille felt properly prepared, he stood for the bar and, as to be expected for one with a brain as prodigious as his, in 1828 was accepted instantly. Proudly, he hung out a shingle at Lipona announcing Colonel Murat, Counselor at Law. The half-cocked expedition against the Indians with General Call had provided him a proper title, and he clung to it proudly. His father had been a marshal of France and hero of the Napoleonic Wars, but for Achille, who had no military leadership credentials save these of questionable veracity, his title colonel was a badge of honor. Now and forever, he was Colonel Murat. For one of royal birth and upbringing, I never fully understood his unquenchable need for little ego supports like this, but it was harmless, thus a point that did not need belaboring.

Colonel Murat, counselor at law, next formed a partnership with an attorney in town, one William Nutall. My prince, now also my colonel and my lawyer, was once again the flea who hopped from one endeavor to another and now became a practicing attorney of the Florida Territory and soon, by act of the Georgia legislature, of Georgia as well. Achieving wealth as a planter had evaded him twice now, once at Parthenope and once at Lipona, so the decision seemed a logical one. The daughter of a failed but proud Virginia planter, I knew something about the vagaries of the plantation economy and about starting over again. Much like my father, Achille's inability to wrest money from the soil had some roots in his fondness for drink. Mind you, neither of them were like the stumbling, brawling drunks we had seen on the streets of St. Augustine, but applejack, the local shinny, and now mint juleps provided much of the fuel for the engine that powered Achille's foray into the legal profession.

Achille declared the law a "very engaging profession," which he liked "monstrous well." I wondered about the frontier justice that he touted when I repeatedly saw defendants chained to fences until their "day in court," which was sometimes in a proper courthouse but equally might be found in a roadhouse or under a tree. The cast of characters who inhabited territorial Florida, along with relatively undeveloped legal standards also meant that many disputes were settled with fists or, even more draconian, by duels. Even my Achille, with his deep-seated need to prove his manhood, was drawn into a duel. I was appalled that he would place so little value on our marriage that he would callously disregard his safety or even his life, but he was determined to prove himself on the so-called field of honor. In this foolish act, I saw clearly the ghost of his father's bravado, now manifest as an act of ego by the son. Fortunately, the event ended with Achille merely losing the tip of a finger rather than more serious injury or death. It may have been painful, but it could have been much, much worse. I hated the code duello and thought it a stupid anachronism of male vanity.

Because of his language skills in at least seven tongues, the Superior Court of Middle Florida engaged Achille to be its official translator/interpreter. With new residents streaming into the territory from many countries, he seemed quite in demand and made a name for himself when he discovered critical documents in the Spanish language, which were crucial to the largest case yet tried in the Territory. It involved dozens of claims against a defunct company, which had operated in Florida under Spanish rule, the Panton Leslie-John Forbes Company, which had started out as an Indian trading company but had amassed millions of acres of land holdings by dubious means. With vague claim on title in the first place, much of the land was now further confused by competing claims of squatters who staked out their own claims however speciously. The so-called Forbes Purchase became front and center in the affairs of the Territory, which was flummoxed by how to settle the matter. Since huge sums of money were involved along with the homesteads of well-intentioned settlers, it was so contentious as to threaten the domestic tranquility of the Florida Territory. Achille, with both his legal skills and language fluency, became a visible force in the resolution of these claims and soon attracted the attention of both United States and foreign government entities. Now in demand by government officials, he became a high-profile wheeler-dealer. I had been raised in a politically savvy household, knew what politics smelled like, and it was rank in the Florida woods and around our dinner table.

Throughout the trials involving the Forbes Company and the exposure to government authorities occasioned by them, Achille learned an essential lesson in American democracy. I suspect it was one he would have preferred to not have to learn, but it was this. More than one's brilliance, more than articulate argument at the bar, more than stirring oration, more than earned reputation, it was personal connections that led to success or failure. This was not a happy lesson for Achille. He bitterly complained that it smacked of the kind of nepotism that he had so vehemently opposed in Europe. It did not seem to bother him that would not be where he was or have the wealth to flit from adventure to adventure if he himself did not have such connections in the Bonaparte power structure.

Once again, he was able to balance conflicting viewpoints without feeling compromised. Was this an inherited trait or a homegrown one? It was just one of his terrible tangle of truths, and I never knew.

While railing against the prevalence of personal connections rather than merit in both government and business, his friend and drinking partner, territorial governor Duval, was always in the background pulling strings. Achille was appointed the postmaster of Lipona (which I thought something of a joke), handled the odd law case, ran unsuccessfully for the legislature, wrote profuse treatises on American government and customs, translated documents for the court, and kept one hand in plantation business. The Mexican government even appointed him as assistant consul for their interests in Florida. The flea was right in his element hopping about frenetically and employing all of the political connections in his repertoire.

In the same winter of 1827-28, pursuant to an invitation by Joseph Bonaparte, a trip was organized for a visit by my family to the Bonaparte clan's de facto American headquarters at Point Breeze. Having only recently returned and reluctant to undertake another strenuous journey myself, the Willis clan, Father, Mother, and my siblings, Lewis, Ann, Jack, George, and little Mary, excitedly trekked up to Point Breeze without me in the early spring of 1828. With Napoléon long since dead and others of the clan out of power and scattered, Joseph appeared as the brightest star in the Bonaparte constellation, and my family was honored with the royal invitation from the former king of Spain. None of my family spoke French, and the Bonapartes' English was at best primitive despite now proclaiming to be Americans. Both sides muddled through.

As with my own visit, our family's Washington connections were sufficient to impress the assembled Bonapartes. Father and Joseph hit it off exceedingly well and regaled one another with haltingly told tales of former glories far into the night over copious quantities of fine French wine from Joseph's cellar. Whatever might have been lost in translation was more than made up in good intentions and the fog of alcohol. As for Mother, the treasures of empire, the park like grounds of Point Breeze, the paintings and tapestries, the baroque French furnishings, the china, crystal, and serving pieces were so overwhelming to cause her to comment upon return to Tallahassee that she found the estate quite like a museum. Virginia elegance was one thing, but Bonaparte excess quite another.

While passing through Washington on the long trip back to Tallahassee, Father, the jovial Byrd Charles Willis of close Washington ancestry, took the opportunity to renew old friendships in the nation's capital. He had worked hard for years for the candidacy of the controversial populist Andrew Jackson. Father called on him during the contentious campaign of 1828, and they reminisced about "the good old days" over some Tennessee sour mash.

Jackson described a goal, if elected, to put teeth into President Monroe's Monroe Doctrine. Monroe had observed the perpetual state of conflict in Europe and determined to use North America's strategic location to avoid such entanglements. This effectively meant fortifying America's ports along the Gulf of Mexico, and one port in particular intrigued Jackson. Pensacola, former capital of the Florida Territory, had one of the finest harbors in the hemisphere. It was there that Jackson had accepted the Florida Territory from Spain in 1821, and he knew it well, having also lived there for a time as acting governor of the territory. All the way back to the era of John Quincy Adams, there had been discussion of fortifying Pensacola Bay and its navy yard was begun in 1826. Jackson, determined to exert more personal control over the project, appointed my father in 1832 as his agent to oversee the contracting and construction.

Since restoration of Father's wealth in Tallahassee had so far eluded him, it was a welcome appointment but would mean yet another move for the Willis family. Despite much posturing around the capitol building in search of opportunity, all he had achieved was appointment by Governor Duval as a colonel of the Florida militia. Much like Achille, he had participated in a few skirmishes against the Indians. Also like Achille, these were mostly, in Shakespeare's words, "full of sound and fury signifying nothing."

With the news that Father and Mother would move to Pensacola, it was agreed that we should hasten into town for Colonel Murat to see Colonel Willis and for both of us to wish the family a fond farewell. With difficulties at Lipona, we too were casting about for a change of locale, and I grieved to think that the closely bonded Willis family might scatter to the winds. When, I wondered, would I see my beloved parents, brothers, and sisters again?

The Grand Dream, 1830

*W*ITH ACHILLE'S POLITICAL and social identity now well established in the Florida Territory, it would seem to the casual onlooker that he had arrived. For my impatient and hyper-energetic husband, however, achieving a certain status in Tallahassee, in the Territory, indeed in the nation, was not enough. Born and bred to bigger things, he could not be contained by Lipona. Rare was the day when he did not complain loudly that his status in Europe remained besmirched and unresolved. The Murat fortune was still impounded, and his father's reputation remained to be avenged. And his own reputation had yet to be made.

Achille's mother, Caroline, still brooded in splendid exile. Her flirtation with Prince Metternich having gotten her nowhere, she now played out her days now at a palace in Florence as a faux countess with new lover Francesco MacDonald, her deceased husband's foreign minister in the heyday of the kingdom of Naples. The hated Metternich, securely at the helm of an aggrandized Austro-Hungarian empire, continued to gloat over any Bonapartes who still remained in Europe to clutch at wisps of former glories. The allies remained near paranoid about anyone with a trace of Bonaparte blood, treating them all with suspicion and hostility. The Bonapartes were the pariahs of Europe, and Metternich took masochistic pleasure in restraining their travel and generally making their lives miserable.

Elsewhere on the Continent, Charles X of France had shut down the freedoms hard earned by the blood of French revolutionaries and ruled with a despotic hand. There was turmoil aplenty in Poland, Germany, Russia, Italy, and Holland where in each there seemed an explosive current of unsatisfied democratic ideals lurking just below the surface. It seemed that all of the nations of Europe walked a political tightwire between old-school monarchists and liberal democrats. The Continent was a bubbling cauldron of discontent and revolution.

To Achille, the repression of freedom in the supposedly advanced nations of Europe was as an old story, which had been told and retold down the centuries, always with the same tragic end. As 1830 dawned over the North Florida piney woods, Achille could take it no longer. My very own Don Quixote, he pulled down the visor of his helmet and determined to challenge the windmills of Europe. I would play the role of his Dulcinea.

Achille was bred to play out his life on a stage grander than the remote Wacissa backwoods. Ever since I first met him, his expansive mind, coupled with boundless enthusiasm, had schemed to redress all of the wrongs of Europe in one fell swoop. In this regard, he was an identical twin to his Uncle Napoléon, and I daresay that it was that imperial legacy that inflamed these ambitious dreams. Napoléon, however, was a brilliant strategist who planned his expeditions in excruciating detail, fully grounded in reality. Achille, also brilliant, had dreams of grand strategy, but was given to flights of fancy, sometimes disconnected from reality by both his enthusiasm and, on occasion, by his highly excitable emotional state and too much applejack.

Partly from unfulfilled ego and partly from genuine idealism, Achille sensed that the moment was ripe for him to play a role. While I worried that he might overreach, there was no dissuading him from his grand plan to ride to the aid of Europe's downtrodden. I wondered how he planned to pull off his one-man conquest and what the end state would be beyond the possibility of recovering millions in impounded family fortune. Both of us having suffered collapse of family wealth, I at least understood that motive.

Throughout 1830, he wrote letters to contacts on the Continent and talked up his glorious mission throughout the community. A small backwoods town such as Tallahassee usually lived in a vacuum of excitement, but by midsummer, it was abuzz that its local son was soon to undertake the rescue of mankind. Achille himself fed these flames with grandiose commentary that "while abroad, such events may take place as would render it, for me, an imperious duty to quit for a number of years my quiet and smug place of retirement and launch again on the busy waters of the world."

In impassioned frontier speeches, he called for the world to rise up in defense of freedom, overthrow tyrants, and seize the mantle of self-government. In the process, his rhetorical self-aggrandizement set us both upon a lofty, if unique, pedestal in the wilderness. Though I was never quite sure whether the small audiences of backwoodsmen comprehended his soaring rhetoric and the finer points of politics, he was flattered by their attentions and enthusiastic huzzahs. Achille, the dreamer and political strategist, became for a time Achille the orator, and I wondered if he was merely rehearsing for the real thing in Europe. It was an era of our lives of grand visions of world-shattering politics but writ small in the tiny theater of North Florida far from the stage where such idealistic dreams would have to be played out.

Achille, I shall freely grant, had achieved a certain notoriety in the social and political structure of our adopted Tallahassee home, and he was much celebrated as he set forth to battle the dragons of European tyranny. I basked in reflected glory, and there were many who flattered me with visions that I might become a queen, or an empress, or I knew not what. Neither did they, but the grandiosity of the moment was for us and for the Florida Territory a welcome diversion.

On the eve of our departure for Europe, Achille's friend and mentor, the distinguished statesman Richard Keith Call, paid tribute to Tallahassee's prince and princess (as I was called more frequently now) by hosting a lavish gala at the Planter's Hotel in November 1830. It was the finest social event in the short history of Tallahassee. We, who had only four years before lived elsewhere, were now celebrated as the territorial capital's favored local son and daughter. It was an amazing event, rustic frontier meets international society.

In this moment as we were hailed by more than a hundred well-wishers, all of the hardships that we had endured to bring us to this pinnacle of honor were forgotten. Gone were the mosquitoes and snakes, gone were the nights sleeping in the open or on floors, the thunderstorms, the dusty rutted roads and broken axles, and the general lack of comforts and provisions for home and hearth. Achille and Kate Murat, now loudly touted as prince and princess, became famous overnight. If it could be said that there was an aristocracy in frontier Florida, we were flattered to stand at its peak. As we prepared to turn the page from frontiersmen to European sophisticate, my normally calm thoughts and restrained manner began to swim wildly at the anticipation of our grand entry into European society. Achille's enthusiasm and idealism had proved contagious, and I fell with great excitement into the wildly optimistic mood of our grand moment.

I had never been to Europe and was not sure how we would be welcomed. Would there be great balls at castles? Parades? Royal ceremonies reviewing troops in elegant uniform? With my halting mastery of French, would I fare any differently from Father's linguistic problem at Point Breeze? Would there be a palace somewhere waiting for the crown prince of Naples and his American princess? How shall I dress? Who will curtsy to me, and who shall I curtsy to? My curiosity raged without ceasing, but of one thing I was sure. We would finally live in comfort if not luxury.

Like visions of sugarplums, my fantasies provided sweet diversion from the hard reality of our last few days at Lipona. With only a vague vision of life in Europe, I allowed myself to dream beautiful dreams. And why not? I had found my prince charming.

The delusions of that ten-year-old girl of Fredericksburg who waltzed in her mirror were soon to become reality.

As frequently happened with Achille's plans, a last-minute snag developed. So suspicious of the Bonapartes were the French and Austrians that we learned that we were to be denied entry onto the Continent. Fuming, Achille smelled in this the hand of his old nemesis Metternich. To me, these were only names, but to him, it was a personal antagonism so deep that I have rarely seen him in such an angry state.

With Louis Philippe now ruling France after the downfall of Charles X, Achille had felt sure that he would liberalize the travel restrictions enforced on the Bonapartes by the prior Bourbon regime. It was not to be. Though of a liberalized branch of the family, Louis Philippe was still a Bourbon after all. And Europe was still schizophrenic at the thought of Bonapartes afoot in the land.

Our plans were so far along by this point that Achille brushed off this apparent impediment with a Mediterranean shrug. If the implacably hostile French won't have us, he announced, the British will, so we would sail not for France but for London. It deferred rather than solved the problem of accessing the impounded Murat fortune, but he opined that it would at least put us a few thousand miles closer to it. And so we left.

After yet another sojourn upon the stump-ridden Bellamy Road from Tallahassee to St. Augustine, we had a blessedly easy sail up the coast to Charleston. There Achille was to assemble financing for our big adventure. It was not a first choice, but he was forced to mortgage our plantation and our seventy-four slaves.

Slaves—I hated that word and grumbled softly to Achille that they little knew that they had once more been put on the white man's auction block like so many cattle.

From Charleston, we sailed for New York and awaited passage to Europe. After a few days of big-city comforts, the dust of Lipona finally washed away, and we departed in mid-December aboard the mail ship *Ontario*. Having had earlier bad experiences in the Atlantic even when sailing coastwise, I confess I was a bit nervous about a transatlantic crossing in winter. Achille assured me that the *Ontario* had done the crossing many times without incident, thus we embarked from New York January 13, 1831.

Fine, I thought, but given the fickle whims of Mother Nature, that is no guarantee. Mother Nature did not disappoint. In retrospect, waiting until more clement weather would have been the wiser choice, but patience was a word foreign to Achille's vocabulary.

The North Atlantic in winter lived up to its reputation, and our storm-tossed voyage lasted a damp and frigid month, pitching in swells the size of New York buildings. I could not believe the size of the North Atlantic waves and came to regard the rough oilskins provided as a shield against the wind and spray as my best friends. We rolled and pitched for weeks on end. Only the anticipation of a clean, comfortable bed that didn't move and a warm bath in a proper hotel kept me going.

London, 1831

OUR ARRIVAL AT Liverpool on February 14 was not met with speeches and marching bands. In fact, we were not greeted by anyone at all; my first indication that the protocols for a deposed prince and his American-born princess were less than suggested in Florida by Achille. I don't know what I expected, but I had thought someone would be there to at least assist with our trunks. Under classic English drizzle and gloom, we put a good face on the lack of an arrival ceremony, hired a coach, and were shown straightaway to our hotel near London's Hyde Park.

We were finally in Europe, we were excited, and we would not allow disappointment to color the day. The thrill of the landmarks of London was exceeded only by the anticipation of thrills to come!

We had tense confrontations with the French and Austrian embassies over Achille's persona non grata status on the Continent. No one, it appeared, wanted a loose Bonaparte cannon crashing about, and they seemed to take pleasure in flaunting their authority over a prince. Their denial was final however, and rolling with the punches, we created an alternate plan. As it turned out, the travel restrictions that confined us to England became a blessing in disguise.

Thus snubbed once more by the anti-Bonaparte cabal under his old nemesis Prince Metternich, Achille determined to make London the base for his campaign. It made sense. Franco-phobic London was a hotbed of anti-French sentiment as it had been over the centuries.

Today, however, the buzz about town was not about conquest, it was a dangerous political gambit to overthrow King Louis Philippe of France, a goal that Achille loudly espoused. Louis Philippe, it must be remembered, held Achille's family's purse strings, so support for his demise was a natural calling. The ancient rivalry between France and England was so old its roots disappeared into the mists of time but so new that it dominated the news and gossip of the day.

Neck-deep in this environment, I began to see for the first time the Bonaparte political instincts up close and personal. As we settled into London, Achille adroitly began to apply lessons of political navigation learned from his royal parents. As he leveraged his way into the upper social and political echelons of London, he was not shy to trade on his famous name. If Murat wouldn't work, Bonaparte would. Immodestly, I must say that my Washington ancestry also proved useful.

Stymied in England for the short term at least, Achille began a series of polite visits to England's upper crust. This rewarded us both socially and politically, and soon we were entertained regularly in London's highest society. To these lords and ladies of sophistication, it mattered not a whit that Achille's famous Uncle Napoléon had harbored designs of empire that a few years before threatened their sovereignty. (We were, however, tactfully reminded on occasion that Uncle Napoléon's final defeat had been at the hands of one of England's favorite sons, Lord Wellington!)

I especially came to appreciate the wry sense of British wit as we bantered back and forth. They seemed to make special sport of welcoming me to "the mother country" and teased unmercifully about my hailing from "the colonies." I could give as well as I could get however, and found many an occasion to remind them of Yorktown! My American pride and credentials as a patriot would hold up to lords and ladies any day! Achille took special pride whenever, in the most ladylike fashion, I would stand my ground like a bulldog. Southern belles, I opined to no one in particular, could hold their own in any society.

London society particularly seemed to revel in the unique attributes of my husband. Not only was he nephew of Napoléon, he was the son of a king and queen, a deposed prince in his own right, renegade planter on America's frontier, lawyer, author, postmaster, Indian fighter, naturalist, and more. As we immersed ourselves in London society, Achille's attire at Lipona—rough shirts and trousers, heavy boots, and a hat of twisted palm fronds—gave way to morning coats and top hats. I hardly recognized my husband, for I had only known him in his frontier personification. If he was handsome then, he was a gorgeous man now. And he even bathed!

The Londoners could not get enough of the Bonaparte prince by way of America. They were, as Achille remarked in private to me, like moths hovering about a candle. While that was an apt analogy, I wondered if some were more like hungry dogs who hoped for scraps from a revived Bonaparte table. After all, he represented the closest contender to that throne. Whatever their motivations, we were in constant demand at private dinners, balls, the opera, interesting lectures at London's splendid museums, and more. I was accorded the refined protocols of England's centuries of royal tradition, treated for the first time as a true princess, and swept up into the giddy milieu of London society.

We were honored to be seated among the nobility at the coronation of William IV. With that special combination of pomp and pageantry as only the British can muster, and set in historic Westminster Abbey, it was a memorable experience for this American girl. All I could think of was how my mother would have loved it. I was thrilled by Europe and stunned at the honors we were paid by society but sometimes wondered if I would forever feel a stranger in a strange land. When I let myself, I could slip into homesickness for America and for my family bravely struggling to fashion a new life in the Florida wilderness. Particularly for my parents who had fallen so far, I wondered if the Tallahassee experiment was working out.

Amidst our lofty London social circle, I was always welcomed as an equal. In this historic land, which boasted royalty and titles galore, I was unfailingly addressed as princess. For this daughter of Virginia, it was a flattering confidence builder and pleasant surprise that I was quite sought after in our newfound social stratosphere.

If only they could have seen me just a few months previous, perspiring in a log cabin in the wilderness, dining on alligator stew! The contrasts of my life never ceased to amaze me.

London's insatiable upper crust had swept us into its inner sanctum, and we were in no hurry to move on. France, the "greater job in Italy," and even the Murat fortune would have to wait as we pampered ourselves amid the sweet life of London society. To present a proper image among the elites, with whom we hobnobbed, we took a splendid town house on fashionable Curzon Street in Mayfair, near Hyde Park, Green Park, and Buckingham Palace.

That all of this had begun with a chance meeting at a picnic in Tallahassee of the Florida Territory fairly boggled the mind!

Faraway Lipona where daily life was a struggle seemed a distant dream. Amid scattered reports of Indian attacks in Florida, when I had the rare moment alone in my thoughts, I worried about our friends and neighbors. For the longest time, I also fretted that the overseer Achille had hired for Lipona would mistreat our servants. In some almost-maternal way, I regarded them as extended family. These concerns receded over time as we were overwhelmed by the lavish luxury of London, but my concerns about our plantation, our slaves, and my still-struggling family at home were never far from mind.

Our frequent company in these heady days included the Lady Dudley Stuart, the Duchess of Bedford, the Duke of Essex, Duke of St. Albans, and other peers of the realm. Even a deposed prince, it seems, held status in the eyes of London's elites. I believe that even Achille was pleasantly surprised at our reception in England, but he took it all in stride. His royal upbringing and my Washington family connections paved the way quite nicely, and we cut a dashing figure.

A special treat awaited when we were visited by Achille's godmother, the ex-queen of Holland, Hortense, and her son, Louis-Napoléon. With a quick lesson in Bonaparte genealogy and politics, I learned that Hortense was the daughter of Napoléon's wife, Josephine, by her first husband Alexandre de Beauharnais, who was guillotined during the revolution's Reign of Terror. Under strict instructions from Napoléon, Hortense then married Napoléon's brother Louis and enjoyed life at the summit of the empire with other Bonapartes. Now, however, she was, like Achille, merely a fellow victim of Napoléon's demise.

A lovely Hortense de Beauharnais, ex-queen of Holland, enjoyed the hospitality of Achille and Catherine Willis Murat during their years in London. Hortense's son Louis Napoleon, elevated to Emperor Napoleon III, remained a benefactor of "Princess Kate" throughout her life.

When she visited us, Hortense was aging and not in robust health, but her seductive charms were still very much on display. Though her hair had turned to silver, her distinctive violet eyes still twinkled as she regaled us with nostalgic stories of days as schoolmate of Achille's mother, Caroline, yet another dispossessed Bonaparte queen. Not having seen Achille for many years, Hortense voiced great pleasure at how he had matured into the role of prince. (It would have been most impolite to point out to her that he never actually served as one.) For this Virginia-born wife who stood in awe, this was obviously most pleasing to my ears and made me proud of my husband and his imperial roots.

Her son Louis-Napoléon and Achille had a long-standing fondness for each other, which reignited with an intensity that frankly concerned me. These two offspring of the Bonaparte dynasty were almost as blood brothers and could cause—or get into—a lot of trouble! Both were committed to the restoration of the empire yet expressed a fervor to free the oppressed, both were given to the sorts of clandestine intrigues that seemed inbred with the Bonapartes, both were deprived of the Bonaparte fortune now held under lock and key in France, both chafed under the allies' travel restrictions, and both had an inordinate craving for adventure. Like Achille, Louis had spent time in America, though his was an exile orchestrated by King Louis Philippe, not a personal choice like Achille's.

Most of all, Achille and his cousin Louis-Napoléon lived in a near-delusional world forever scheming for the restoration of empire and the power and riches that would follow. He sounded so like Achille, it was as though they were each other's alter ego. For me, it was most flattering that Louis-Napoléon accepted me almost as though I was a blood member of the Bonaparte family and forever referred to me as Cousin Kate.

These were halcyon days, textured with the glories of London society and the nostalgia of the Bonaparte past. We drank deeply of our time in London with the lovely Hortense, aging but not at all matronly, and her ambitious son Louis-Napoléon. It was our privilege and honor to cement family bonds and to share poignant nostalgia with Queen Hortense, who proved daily that, at her advanced age, she was every inch still a formidable femme fatale who could compete with the best of them.

I found it interesting that in every conversation the restoration of empire was a subtext that lay just beneath the surface if not openly on the table.

Hortense, older by two decades than I, was a royalist of the old school and not moved by Achille's conversion to liberal democratic principles. Having lived her whole life in the artifice of Bonapartist grandeur, Hortense had no frame of reference whatsoever for understanding our life on the Florida frontier or how the responsibilities of governing could be delegated to the common man. Though she meant nothing antagonistic by it, she chided Achille's vocal disdain for royal privilege and his passion for reforms based on democratic ideals. These, she said over dinner one night, were seditious thoughts he had learned "in a little American hut." As a descendant of the great patriots who founded America, fought our revolution, and followed it up with a government structure envied the world over, I politely sparred with her over sherry almost daily.

I was also the one who had shared that "little American hut" and confess that I sometimes had to bite my tongue. I would have been more charitable in my opinions if I had known then that Hortense was suffering from cancer while she visited us.

Differences aside, she and Achille renewed a fondness for each other, and I too was moved by her aristocratic charms. We formed a sincere and warm friendship with both Hortense and Louis-Napoléon. When it was time to bid adieu, Louis opted to continue residence in London, which was most agreeable to both Achille and me. More than mere friends, Louis and Achille were cousins bound by Bonaparte blood and shared an immediate goal of liberating family assets confiscated after the fall of Napoléon and now held under lock and key by King Louis Philippe.

Thereafter, we saw Louis with increasing frequency and hosted him for dinner weekly with any number of his charming mistresses. (He was quite a ladies' man, and some of his reputation too shocking to repeat.) Nevertheless, the powerful friendship with Louis was a harbinger of the future when he would become a benefactor to my life in ways that no one could anticipate.

If Hortense and Louis had been interesting guests, our next visitor was astonishing. A secretive visitor from Belgium arrived one morning and insisted upon private conversation with Achille in our drawing room. Liberal thought having taken root there, it seems that the gentleman was on a mission from the Belgian National Congress to entice Achille to become a candidate for the crown of Belgium! Belgium at that time was declaring independence from the Netherlands and searching for a leader who could fulfill the promise of liberal government while maintaining a titular chief of state. In these fractious times of the early 1830s, the French-speaking southern states seceded from their government, the nation of Belgium was born, and it was open to liberal leadership. It was to be an intriguing compromise; Belgium was to have a king but one appointed by popular will.

There seemed to be three principal contenders: Louis d'Orléans, duc de Nemours; Prince Leopold of Saxe-Coberg; and my Bonapartist husband, Prince Achille Murat. My husband? The postmaster of Lipona? Colonel Murat of the Florida militia, the one who lost his finger in a duel under Tallahassee's oaks? King of Belgium?

Stunned, the thought trumpeted through my mind that the ladies of Tallahassee, who had sent me off with thoughts that I might become a queen, might actually turn out to be right. The first of many such dichotomies, I, the mistress of a wilderness plantation, offspring of America, was forced to sit lest I faint with disbelief. It was beyond imagination that we might actually trade our shanty at Lipona for the Palais Royal de Bruxelles.

To say the least, our European odyssey was proving more exciting than could have been foretold in the forests of Florida.

I sometimes thought Achille overconfident during our discussions of various possibilities that might evolve if he were to succeed in Europe. He was, after all, a Bonaparte given to grand visions, and I had come to expect that. But here one was laid in our lap, and it was one not even imagined in wildest dreams. Belgium? The crown of a state struggling to declare its independence from Dutch rule?

Why not? The United States had done it sixty years before. In many ways, the American Revolution and the U.S. Constitution that followed had created the model for free men everywhere. Now the same winds of democratic government were sweeping Europe. Like an Atlantic winter, sometimes those winds became stormy before the sunshine of freedom could emerge.

Though an ancient region, the breakaway territory of Belgium was rife with new ideas and a perfect strategic spot on the doorstep of France. It was France, of course, that Achille regarded as the real prize. France itself tottered on the precipice awaiting a leader who would lead it from a confused and bloody past into the light of freedom. After all, Achille's uncle Napoléon had begun his spectacular campaign for world dominance there. Might history repeat itself? So vast were the consequences of this thought that I immediately dismissed it for what it was: a dream. But there was a more immediate and pragmatic reason to eye Belgium as a doorway to France. It was a stepping stone to the impounded Murat fortune. I thus knew Achille's motives, but what were the Belgian's?

Mulling over the prospect, it was he who finally suggested the reason for the offer. The Belgian revolt sought to terminate centuries of monarchy and replace it with liberal democratic rule yet maintain a pro forma chief of state. As the Belgians vetted possible candidates, only Achille, of all of the imperial family, had succumbed to the lure of democracy and the rights of man. He stood alone, the sole contender likely to appeal to Belgium's liberal groups now fanning the flames of freedom. These were the same ideals that had motivated my own ancestors in the founding the nation I called home, my beloved United States of America, and I readily grasped what he was saying and why the Belgians had looked to him.

For all of the differences of our upbringing, the commitment to freedom was a common thread we shared and held most dear.

Achille voiced a deep philosophical kinship with Leopold and had no stomach in opposing a fellow true believer in the rights of man. Perhaps more pragmatically, he observed that if he should accept and become a Belgian Bonaparte, France would likely attack immediately and overwhelm the struggling new nation. In this cauldron of tension in the Benelux nations, Holland was strong and Belgium weak. Achille saw the risk as too high. His kingship might be over as soon as it began, the light of freedom extinguished at its birth. History and countless freedom-loving Belgians would hold him to account.

Though supremely honored to be courted for the position, Achille, in a flash of clarity, declared the situation too precarious to introduce a Bonaparte wild card. I thought this an example of his best strategic thinking. In a confidential moment, however, I learned his true reason.

"A greater job is awaiting me in Italy when France will be really free," he mused. Publicly staking out such a lofty goal left my mind reeling. He had turned down the near certainty of the crown of Belgium in order to chase the chimera of "a greater job" in Italy. Like his father, King Joachim, before him, he dreamed of a unified Italy, and in choosing the words "a greater job," left little doubt whom he envisioned as its leader.

My suspicions were confirmed when he wrote to an old friend, Godfrey Caviagnac, that "I am the only one who could unite Italy and make her free . . . I feel the importance and sublimity of this role, and I am vain enough to believe myself capable of filling it." While I loved my husband with a love of the ages, it seemed a bit melancholy to me that his Murat ego had so gotten the better of him that he truly believed that Italy, if not Europe, awaited his enlightened leadership. His belief that he was "the only one who could unite Italy" stood in such stark contrast to our log houses in the Florida wilderness that it was as though he had, like his uncle and father before him, succumbed to his own propaganda.

It was thus that the ghost of Achille's late father, King Joachim, hovered over him as he danced along a philosophical tightrope. On the one hand, he was a most ardent champion of government by the people; on the other, stood the mesmerizing allure of the throne, which his father had so coveted: a unified Italy. Deep in his heart, I know he was conflicted and, at varying times, motivated by both. His belief in democracy was rooted in ideology, but I wondered if his deep yearning to rule Italy was his personal way of vindicating his father. One thing was for certain. It was unfinished Murat business.

There was now a certain dynamic tension in our everyday lives as he wrestled with decisions that would not only affect us as a couple, but also could conceivably alter the face of Europe and of world history. I had come so far from Willis Hill in Fredericksburg that it fairly staggered the imagination. Achille, on the other hand, remained stuck to grandeurs long past. As for me, I thought that the Belgian offer had more promise than a fragile hope that Italy would achieve the unification that had always eluded it. A unified Italy was the final unfinished work of his father however, and Achille was manically driven by an unspoken compact with him to finish the job.

From an outsider's viewpoint, Belgium appeared a bird in the hand while reigning over a unified Italy nothing more than a will-o-the-wisp dream. Neither Belgium nor I could compete with the unfinished Murat legacy, so the tangible Belgian offer was dismissed in favor of the Italian fantasy.

In our discussions, I caught shadows of his thought process but never saw it definitively laid out. In classic Bonaparte fashion, these were cards played very close to the vest, even with a trusted spouse. I did not know all of the most intimate details, but I knew that somehow we were holding hands with history.

Now left fairly in the dark, the one thing I did know was that the firsthand discussions with Belgian officials, which started this ball rolling in the first place, intrigued Achille. His move on Italy would have to await a more propitious time, and Achille's cockles were aroused now. My husband, if nothing else, was a man of action. Against this backdrop, he confided that the Belgian revolution intrigued him to the point where, having spurned their Belgian offer clearing the way for Leopold to be king, he would once more roll the dice of fate.

Leopold did accept the proposal of the Belgian National Congress, was appointed king, and crowned at the ancient palace of Coudenburgh on July 21, 1831. In accepting the crown of Belgium, Leopold became a new kind of king, not just a warmed-over autocrat whose interests lay in concentrating power in the crown. He swore allegiance to the very constitution that would limit his power, effectively becoming a power-sharing king with representatives of the people. Intellectually, this was the tantalizing prize for Achille, a constitutional monarchy akin to England's. He vociferously claimed that in turning down the Belgian monarchy, he saw even greater opportunity hiding in the wings. Was it Italy? Was it France? Was it a Bonaparte renaissance of continental proportion?

While he claimed to see opportunity, as his wife, what I saw for the first time was the more devious, oblique side of his persona.

Here was the grand strategist playing for advantage. Here was the same Murat blood that led to Joachim and Caroline's double-cross. I wondered—feared is more like it—if he was getting in over his head. I had seen this behavior before. He was again the Lipona planter riding to the guns with General Call, a sincere but impetuous amateur flying off without considering the consequences. Perhaps without realizing it, he was mimicking his father's headlong battle charges. I loved him for the passion he brought to his plans but prayed that those plans would be realistically grounded before he set them in motion.

We were not allowed free movement on the Continent, so our next steps would need to be taken sub rosa. Cloaked in secrecy, Achille suggested that we might infiltrate secretly into Belgium and see for ourselves and, in the process, take a fatal step toward France and the Murat millions for which he fought tooth and nail.

Of course, he was still denied travel on the Continent, but it slowed him not at all. With the abandon of his father's cavalry, he would plunge into the fray. Perhaps he could have his cake and eat it too.

The Would-Be King, 1832

*T*HIS WAS THE adventuresome Achille at his finest most grandiose hour, not unlike riding off to battle the Seminoles but played on a grander stage. He was now, in his own mind, a Bonaparte contesting for the world. Throwing caution to the winds, he set us on a course to leave London forthwith. He had high hopes that we would arrive triumphantly on the Continent as the current-day incarnation of his imperial uncle Napoléon. I was not as optimistic and worried that it might be more like our unheralded arrival in the rain on a deserted dock in Liverpool. Or worse. He might be arrested.

Seeing his Bonaparte ego in reckless action, I became convinced that had Achille preceded rather than followed Shakespeare, I was sure that a play would have been written about him!

But of course, I was biased.

In less than a month and in blatant defiance of the edict that he not enter the Continent, we set boldly out for Belgium where we chose lodging at Brussels elegant Hotel Belle Vue. I was pleased that Achille immediately received audience with King Leopold, courtesy of the emissary who had visited us in London. In short order, Achille and Leopold formed a strong bond of mutual affection built of a shared belief that an unstoppable wave of democracy was about to crash upon the shores of Europe. Each paid homage to the other's ego by pronouncements that the two would surely lead this transnational trend, saving Europe's millions from a future under the heavy boot of monarchists.

*King Leopold I of Belgium, colleague and friend of Prince Achille and Princess
Catherine Willis Murat. At his invitation, Prince Murat commanded a regiment
of Leopold's foreign legion at a time when Belgium was establishing independence
from Holland. In Brussels "Princess Kate" and her princely husband were frequent
companions of Leopold and his young queen Louise Marie.*

I took it all less seriously and decided to avail myself of the many
cosmopolitan pleasures of Brussels. I was new to the ancient continent
of Europe, and while Achille and Leopold schemed, I gloried in the
cultured attentions of Belgian high society, ever under the patronage
of Leopold's young queen, Louise-Marie, with whom I quickly formed
a close friendship.

On one particularly beautiful summer's day, the queen and I
accompanied the family of a British diplomat to the countryside for a
ride. I considered myself an accomplished rider and was determined
to show these European ladies a thing or two about American
horsemanship. Our mounts for the day were brought out, and I was
assigned a sleek but huge chestnut Hanoverian stallion, which must
have stood over seventeen hands. This breed was renowned for its
robust strength and, I thought, perfect for me to demonstrate my

ability in the saddle. As we turned into the park, my horse immediately decided to challenge for who was in control. I quickly lost. The giant Hanoverian thundered up to a gallop, which he maintained for at least three miles. It felt like fifty! My companions, the teenage British girls, were hard pressed to keep pace but gamely followed, politely calling out to me to slow the pace. Try as I might, I could not wrestle the Hanoverian stallion down to a manageable gait until we reached the barn from which we had departed. Breathlessly, both girls arrived disheveled by their own gallop and commented to me that I was a superb rider. "But," they said, "do all Americans ride so fast?" I, proud American horsewoman and under the international microscope, dared not let on that I myself had been on the verge of terror. It was a proud but humorous moment for this daughter of Virginia who had ridden since age two.

Queen Louise Marie of Belgium was a friend of Prince and Princess Murat during their time in Belgium, when Prince Murat commanded a regiment of King Leopold I's foreign legion.

Brussels was marvelous. For me, a refined most sophisticated social life, and for Achille, participation in the Belgian revolution. It was not all simply abstract politics and social graces. With the hostile Dutch government skirmishing on his doorstep, Leopold's leadership was threatened early in his reign. King Leopold invited Achille into his closest circle of advisors where the military and political strategies of the new nation were hatched. Prodded and emboldened by my husband, Leopold took the assertive step of charging his new friend Achille Murat with the establishment of a foreign legion to aid his defense. Colonel Murat of the Florida militia became, by royal decree, Colonel Murat of the Belgian army and given the mission of recruiting and training his legion, which was garrisoned at the Fortress of Ath, hard on the French border. He was living a dream, fulfilling a commitment to his late father, burnishing military credentials, scaring the French, and helping to midwife a new democratic nation.

Surely both Leopold and Achille knew that this was rubbing salt into old Bonaparte wounds. The scars and legacy of the Napoleonic era were still fresh. The odd cabal of a Belgian king and a cracker planter of Bonaparte ancestry must have known that their defiance would be opposed by the Continent's anti-Bonaparte factions, which nervously watched every move from the sidelines. Achille, emboldened by success and by his first military command, was not dissuaded by the political peril of the moment, seeing instead the opportunity as a foot in the door of revenge.

I took all of these manipulations in stride recognizing them as Achille intended them, a means to an end and salve for his fragile ego. A military force under his command would provide his first real leverage against the French, who continued to deny him access to the impounded Murat fortune. While Achille rejoiced in his newfound status, I recognized the symptoms. The scent of power was in the air, and as a military commander, he would at long last be able to walk in his famous father's footsteps.

Many commented that Colonel Murat of the Belgian Foreign Legion looked for all the world like his famous uncle. This provided an unforeseen strategic advantage in recruiting and leading his regiment, which was assembled in short order, filled largely with battle-seasoned veterans who had fought under the banner of Uncle Napoléon. Soon there was a veritable flood of recruits overcome with nostalgia for the fallen empire and eager to serve under the heir apparent, none other than my husband. Never having believed that he measured up to his illustrious father, he now swelled with pride remembering that his famous Uncle Napoléon had predicted when he was a child that "Achille will make a good soldier."

As Achille stepped boldly from frontier colonel in buckskins to colonel of his Belgian regiment in full regalia, his duties demanded more and more of his time. Pressure mounted daily as William of Orange led his troops south toward Ath. Military confrontation with Achille's regiment was avoided, but there were clashes at Leuven and Hasselt as the Dutch force invaded.

As he trained his polyglot force from many nations, I spent lonely weeks without him but knew this was something he had to do to fulfill his destiny. Achille's old insecurities melted away as he vicariously stepped across the ages into his father's world of leading soldiers, and for one brief shining moment, it gave him a confidence not seen before or since. How he would have fared in actual warfare, I could not say, but as a politically astute leader, he excelled. My guess is that he would have led from the front in an effort to prove himself equal to his father's reputation for bravery.

One could not avoid seeing the parallels to his father, Joachim, and his uncle, Napoléon. To this day, I don't know if I was flattered or terrified by this comparison. Probably some of each. But whatever I thought was irrelevant. It was certain that nervous heads of state saw the comparison reviving the old paranoia of a resurgent Bonaparte empire. And it all focused on Achille.

Who among Europe's leaders was enraged at the upstart young king of Belgium appointing a Bonaparte descendant to command a military force at their doorstep? Which among them opposed this threat on the Continent when Achille wasn't supposed to be on the Continent at all? Who was vulnerable to the democracy movement? Everybody!

Led by the French, on whose very border his regiment was garrisoned, the furious allies, who earlier had set the terms of the Bonaparte surrender, demanded that the new and unsure King Leopold straightaway disband the Murat foreign legion. One can hardly blame them. Leopold, still uneasy on his throne, and Achille, unlawfully in Europe, had poked their fingers in the eyes of Europe's established order and lost their bluff.

Achille had halfway expected it. In fact, I think he was mildly surprised that the edict came as a verbal demand and not an attack on his regiment. He knew that he had been playing with fire and sulked that "it forms a part of my existence that I am accustomed to it . . . These delicate attentions with which these worthies pursue, with all their power, a young man who has never been distinguished for anything whatsoever, who has still done nothing for history . . . reveal my resources to me."

Responding to the explosive reaction from Europe's leaders, Leopold's foreign legion was forced to disband. Perhaps it was a stillborn venture by two who should have known better. I saw it in its larger context. Achille's military command was a defining period in his evolution from exiled boy prince to self-confident manhood.

As the day for furling the colors approached, he received a touching poem from his men. It was, to all who read it, an elegant testimony of the esprit de corps Achille had helped to generate during his tenure as their commander. These battle-hardened veterans of the Napoleonic Wars honored their commander with accolades declaring him to be cherished in their hearts forever.

It was a poignant moment. Achille and I shared a tear over their overflowing sentiment, and I proudly saw between the lines of those stanzas that my husband's leadership had stirred in them the same sort of passions for which both his father and uncle were famous.

As his wife, I knew how important that was to him. Never again would he feel a need to hide insecurely in his father's shadow. I was proud to accompany Colonel Murat to the soulful ceremony at Ath at which his regiment was disbanded and listened with watery eyes as he thanked and extolled his men in seven languages, a prodigious feat in its own right.

In our brief Belgian sojourn of 1831-32, the Belgians loved him. Shortly after our foray there, a gentleman by the name of Maurice Arnould wrote a book to commemorate his respect for my beloved husband, *Achille Murat in Belgium: An American Citizen in Service to our Revolution*. While this was flattering after the fact, it was clear that Achille's play to simultaneously support his friend Leopold while pressuring France to release his inheritance had not met with success.

It was thus that we closed the Belgian chapter of life without result and with mixed feelings.

The "young man who had done nothing whatsoever" had once more lost at the wheel of fate.

But perhaps the "greater job in Italy" still awaited.

Collapse of the Dream, 1832

*W*ITH A HEAVY heart Achille fell into depression that his self-financed one man venture to free the Europeans from tyranny was on the verge of collapse. To his dismay, he was reminded again and again that his Bonaparte ancestry was now a liability rather than an asset. Worse yet, even other Bonapartes had offered no support for his one-man assault on the ills of Europe. Privately . . . very privately . . . family loyalty appeared to me a scarce commodity among the Bonapartes, but of course I could not say so for fear of insulting him.

Not only were his loftier goals unfulfilled, but on a pragmatic level the confiscated Murat millions for which he contended remained untouchable, securely under France's lock and key.

When we retreated from Belgium back to London, I wondered what our next chapter would bring. The answer was not long in coming for the man who craved above all else to ascend the throne of a unified Italy. In this exaggerated goal, he was the successor to his ambitious father. It would have been unseemly to point out to Achille that his father had failed even with an army at his beck and call and the unlimited resources of his kingdom at hand. Achille had only himself and a few thousand dollars remaining from our mortgaged plantation and the obvious was, well, obvious. The extent of his disconnect from reality began to reveal itself and it saddened me. In the sobering wake of the Belgian experience a mood of melancholy reassessment of his goals overwhelmed our lives for several months.

Just when I thought he was about to give up, he was again struck with a bolt of inspiration. He now talked once more of an entrée to the throne of Italy. I thought this a mere pipe dream and could scarcely stand the wishful thinking which lay behind the scenes. I nevertheless had to give him credit for perseverance. Even when his optimism seemed unfounded and the reality appeared harsh, the man never gave up.

When it looked like a French force under his cousin Louis Napoleon (Hortense's son) might succeed with a French thrust into Italy, it was exactly the kind of news to renew Achille's passionate quest. Louis had been our guest in London only the year before so Achille arrogated a role for himself and planned to rush to his aid.

With a force of one.

With no weapons save the little over-and-under derringer which was always on his person.

By this time I was thoroughly wrung out with strategies and intrigues and plots created from thin air. I was weary of fog, drizzle, and arcane European politics and I missed my home. The clarity and simplicity of life in America called strong and in a perverse sort of way, I even missed the primitive little log cabin complex at Wacissa and the good people who worked it for us. Forever grateful for our time in Europe, I formed a premonition that it would be futile to remain further while Achille awaited a royal opening which in my private opinion would never come. It was time to close the book on Europe.

As if to punctuate my decision, Louis Napoleon's Italian gambit collapsed in defeat at Strasbourg before he could even slip southward toward Romagna which was his goal. For me it was the final hapless stirring of the Bonapartist pot. I could take no more. After long discussions, Achille and I agreed that it would be best for him to remain in London without me to wrap up his unfinished business while I returned to take up plantation business in Florida.

Our years in Europe had been an enriching experience for me and had given me a sense of the sweep of its history which I would take to my grave. Unfortunately that same sense of history had revealed the ancient games of power politics still played on the continent, one giant chess board where the kings and queens still manipulated the pawns and the occasional knight or bishop.

More than ever I was convinced beyond question that I had been correct about Achille's European adventure. It had started out with noble goals which may have been unrealistic in the first place. The attentions of royalty and nobility in England and Belgium were flattering, but offered no tangible support for a campaign to introduce democratic government to the ancient monarchies of Europe. It was thus that I came reluctantly to admit the fallacy of Achille's grand adventure. It had been a close first cousin to Don Quijote's attacks on the windmills of Spain — a beautiful but impossible dream.

And so in February 1832, in the company of my friend Mary Pringle, fiancee of the politically connected American Joel Poinsett, the curtain descended on my three year stint in Europe. It had been grand for me, Achille had had his day in the sun, but for this proud Virginia-born patriot the lure of the stars and stripes was never stronger. At Southampton, I kissed Achille good-bye and turned toward my homeland with memories of Europe and gratitude that I was an American. I had experienced first hand the convolutions of European politics and, with all of its shortcomings, I longed for the unvarnished simplicity of my homeland.

The North Atlantic in winter was once more a challenge, but I was so ready for home that it scarce affected me at all. Mary and I delighted in the pleasures of New York for a few days, and while there I learned that yet another Bonaparte had plunged back into the political fray. There must have been something genetic about their need to stir the pot! While I was making my return passage, Joseph, like Achille, flaunted the travel restrictions imposed on the Bonapartes and set out for Europe.

Ostensibly his reason was to take Napoleon's 21 year old son, the so-called "eaglet" and "Emperor of the French", under his wing during an illness. By now I had learned though that with Bonaparte adventures, nothing was as it seemed. I suspected that Joseph's maneuver actually had to do with dreams of a grand restoration of power. However expansive, his Point Breeze mansion on the Delaware River was too small to hold his ego.

The young Bonaparte, Napoléon François Joseph Charles, styled Napoleon II, was anything but the Emperor of the French. That title, which had been conveyed in a moment of delusion by his father, was in fact nothing more than a classic exercise in Bonapartist self-deception. The Orleans monarchy was securely in power in France, the heavy hand of Austrian Emperor Metternich was still in play, and the entire family remained ostracized and under the yoke of the allies. How, one wonders, was there room for an "Emperor of the French"?

When Napoleon II (aka, The King of Rome, "the eaglet", and the Duke of Reichstadt) fell ill with tuberculosis, Joseph Bonaparte, now living in New Jersey under the assumed title of Count of Survilliers, returned to Europe seeking to aid his ailing nephew. The effort was in vain and the young Napoleon died in Austria in 1832. He was a cousin of Prince and Princess Achille Murat.

Common sense suggested that the allies who had vanquished the powerful First French Empire might have had something serious to say about the "eaglet's" claim as "Emperor of France".

As Joseph hastened to Europe, fate once again crushed Bonaparte ambition. The "eaglet" died suddenly, and Joseph's excuse for return to France died with him. Chastened, Joseph diverted his itinerary to Florence where his sister and my mother-in-law, Caroline, had settled. There Joseph would remain until death. I was never quite sure how either of them had wormed their way past their travel restrictions, but by now I had several years of close-up experience with the Bonapartes and I knew they always had a sleeve full of tricks.

When I learned of this latest drama, it made me all the happier that I was back on *terra firma* in the United States. Bonaparte intrigues had worn me out. Even Achille, schemer and dreamer that he was, was aghast at the fallacy of Joseph's wild and unlawful incursion. For Achille, this was a dark brooding admission which he came to only after acknowledging the obvious. The Bonaparte era was over.

He was now able to fume aloud that even he, nephew of the great Napoleon, was an outsider to the family. Bonaparte plans never included him and he was insulted. The Bonapartes, to use a crude expression from the animal world, were famous for eating their young. Even the famous Talleyrand had said of Achille's mother Caroline that she carried "The head of Cromwell on the shoulders of a beautiful woman." If it had been my family, I would have felt angry and ostracized also, but when it came to Bonaparte family politics I had long ago learned to hold my tongue.

Achille, by his own admission, was now backed into an untenable corner of suffering the restrictions of Bonaparte exile while being treated as an outsider by his own family. The magic was gone.

Back in the United States in 1832 after an exhilarating but exhausting time in Europe, I arrived just in time to see my parents as they left Tallahassee to move to Pensacola, the original capital of the Florida Territory. Father's long-time effort to aid Andrew Jackson's bid for the presidency had paid off with a patronage appointment as the president's agent at the growing Pensacola Navy Yard situated on one of the hemisphere's finest harbors. I was sad to see them leave Tallahassee just as I was returning, but it was a good move for Father who had, like Achille, been unsuccessful in his political ambitions. He had likewise failed to recover his lost fortune. This uncanny parallel between our families would hover over us forever.

My homecoming at Lipona was a subdued one. I spent the first few months reviewing accounts and refreshing my memory with land boundaries, crop plantings, markets, and so on. Achille had always tended to these things, and as I examined the few records we had, I came to better understand why we had not been more successful. The prince was not a planter! Our plantation manager Nat Turner had let the place go to ruin in my three years away, and it was disappointing to see just how run down our beloved home had become. I was alone with no one to help me get Lipona back on its feet.

My greatest satisfaction came from renewing my acquaintance with our hands. There had been some deaths, and twelve new babies had become citizens of Lipona. They seemed glad that I was back on the plantation, and I was happy to see these shining black faces. The juxtaposition of this simple life at Lipona against the political intrigues and lofty social forays of my years in Europe was breathtaking. What a study in contrasts.

Reminiscing over almost three years in Europe, from the depths of my heart I had a transformative insight. Though deeply grateful for my recent experiences with royalty and nobility and forever enriched by new friends and old histories, through and through I was a girl of the American south. Though I would visit Europe again, the depth of my love for the United States of America never waned. I could never trade the privilege of being an American for all of the pomp and privilege of nobility.

As I experienced these private revelations at our humble home in Florida, in London Achille recalibrated his life once more. He had not achieved any degree of political power, but his views on governance had been sharpened by the same machinations of power which had driven me home to Florida. With the passions of unfulfilled political destiny as a backdrop, he turned once more to his very substantial literary talents. If he could not personally and directly recast European society into a democratic mold, he would do it indirectly. With his characteristic flurry of excitement and energy he turned to the next best thing to governing: writing about governing.

First came the publication of *Lettres sur les Etate-Unis*, which he soon expanded and published as *Esquisse Morale et Politique des Etats-Unis de 'lAmerique du Nord*. From Europe he extolled his experiences in the United States and held himself out as a sort of world-expert on the socio-political scene. With some aggrandizement he predicted that American style democracy would "spread throughout the world." By 1833 his two publications in French were translated into English and received glowing commentary in many important journals of public opinion.

He sent me a copy of the Windsor *Express* which hailed his writings with much fanfare. I was thrilled and knew he was in his element when I read their critique of my husband. Achille was described as "an enlightened statesman who takes in at one view the whole scheme—moral, political, and historical—of his adopted country." England, it seems, accepted him as an authority on governance even though he had no experience in governing. Unlike other Bonapartes who ceaselessly craved political power, his niche in the world was firmly established as that of an outside observer and pundit. The world needs both.

With populist President Andrew Jackson in the White House, Achille's writings took the perfect tone for the times. His humanist tendencies were fully fleshed out now in critical blasts at the very power structure which had elevated him to his princely title. Among the remaining Bonapartes he was now *persona non grata* for challenging the very basis of their exalted status in the world.

Stirring the continental pot once more, he speculated that France might succumb to a cabal of Germany, Italy, and Spain. Using the United States Constitution as a model, he challenged not only France but all of the ancient orders of Europe. I once again felt he was overreaching, but he was an unstoppable juggernaut turning out political commentary at a furious pace. In 1833 he published in French his *Exposition des Principles dy Gouvernment Republicain tel qu'il a ete Perfectionne en Amerique* and in the same year, in German, *Daretellung der Grundsatze der Republikanischen Regierung*. My flea was hopping frenetically once more. I had mixed feelings of admiration for the high regard he was garnering for his writings but a bit of relief that I was securely back home and not riding the European whirlwind alongside him.

Achilles Return, 1833

I HAD BEEN LIVING alone at Lipona for a year and a half, guarded at night by field hands whom I entrusted with a rifle. Indian attacks necessitated it. Since President Jackson's "Indian Removal" policy, the local tribes, especially the Seminoles had become even more embittered at the white man's land grab. Rampages though central Florida from time to time were usually associated with a whiskey binge while they awaited relocation to the Indian Territory known as Oklahoma. One could hardly blame the Seminoles for their anger as these were ancestral lands on which they roamed freely for generations. The entire notion of private land ownership was an alien concept. The treatment of the tribes in our area was shameful to me and seemed paradoxical for a nation founded upon the equality of man.

Across the Atlantic, Achille's surge into the literary spotlight dimmed. A final burst of effort to force France to restore the confiscated Murat fortune likewise met with no success. Of the $10,000 we had taken to Europe from mortgaging our plantation and slaves, the bottom of the barrel was now visible. No meaningful change had come to most governing structures of Europe, and there was not even an inkling of a chance at the crown of Italy. His military command had been disbanded out from under him, and the prospects of power were nil. Even to the optimistic Achille, the failure of his European gambit was now obvious, and our marriage was separated by an ocean. A despondent Achille sadly began tidying up affairs in London and without fanfare sailed for New York and his adopted home. Tail between his legs, Achille booked passage for New York.

With great excitement and relief Achille arrived in New York August 1833. I was glad that he did not tarry there for I missed him terribly. Shunning the pleasures of the city he set out straightaway, making his way southward by steamer, stage, and rented horseback. At length he arrived in Tallahassee and hired a coach for the fifteen mile trip to Lipona.

His sudden appearance caught me by surprise on a steamy August afternoon as I brushed gnats from my face and pulled weeds from the small vegetable garden out back. I was surprised at how much weight he had gained, but oh how dashing he looked in the formal clothing which he had adopted in Europe.

Here once again was an example of the stark contrasts which characterized our lives; Achille entered our log cabin complex in morning coat carrying a hatbox with his top hat!

Lipona was experiencing a heat wave which overlaid our reunion with humidity and abundant perspiration. By three each afternoon great thunderheads boiled out of blackening skies, and for an hour or two all one could hear was the rasping of the cicadas in the pines which surrounded us. Then the skies, no longer able to contain the moist air from the Gulf of Mexico to our south would let go with a torrent. We relished the torrential rains which dribbled through our roof. Experience had taught us that they would cool things down for a few hours.

When I approached Achille about the plantation's woeful finances I got in return even more woeful news. All of the $10,000 we had received from mortgaging Lipona and our slaves was gone and the bank was demanding repayment. We had no income from Lipona at this time and were reduced to reliance on the small stipend provided to Achille by his mother and a few francs yearly from funds entrusted to Madame Mere for Bonaparte descendants. Together the prince and princess stared into an abyss of financial hardship as rain drummed on our leaky roof.

Bleak as our reunion was, it became even more challenging when Achille's stipend from his mother Queen Caroline stopped. By this time they had the greatest difficulties maintaining a cordial relationship for they had both eschewed the chance to see each other during Achille's years in Europe. Achille fretted that she was spending the last Murat money for a palace and a life of artificial grandeur in

Florence as the Countess of Lipona. In return she fumed at him as her prodigal son.

If Europe had rejected Achille he was warmly remembered and his re-immersion celebrated by our neighbors and peers in Jefferson County, Florida. Old friends came to call and to offer support to our renewed plunge into the Florida Territory. In mere months the frustrations, schemes, political intrigues, and failures of London and Brussels vanished into the mists of memory as we set about resurrecting a profitable life in Florida.

Having felt down on himself after disappointment in Europe, Achille's peers helped him strengthen his battered sense of self by insisting that he accept a position as judge of Jefferson County; all properly done by petition to Governor DuVal. With only minimal self-effacing hesitation that he felt unqualified, he accepted. By 1834 the man who had so recently been tendered the crown of Belgium was seated as a county judge in a remote backwater of America.

Just as our lives began to stabilize, I received a personal blow of staggering consequence. My beloved mother, having endured the profligacy of my father, depletion of family fortune, and loss of home to fire, who had suffered the hardships of relocating to rustic Tallahassee, who had moved yet again to Pensacola to start anew, and who had buried three of her children, was herself felled by yellow fever. I could scarce comprehend that my dearest mother was gone, yet the scourge of yellow fever was too well known in our Florida home. Achille and I hastened to Pensacola to provide support to my father and siblings. This was the first time I had visited family since my brother John's death in Key West the year before, and our visit was as black as the funeral bier. Though a citizen of Pensacola just a few years, mother was eulogized in the Pensacola *Gazette* thusly. "We have lost a friend and the city has lost one of its brightest ornaments, a lady the center of social attraction, one whose place will not soon be filled. If her life could have been saved by preventive measures, they would have been cheap at thousands of dollars." The scourge of yellow fever had struck and the jovial giant of Fredericksburg, my beloved father Byrd Charles Willis, the social lion of the "Old Dominion" was brought low by the death of his lifelong love and companion.

We remained a few weeks at the family home on Bayou Chico, consoling father and giving him time to renew and strengthen his bond with Achille. It was also a time for Achille to get to know . . . and vice versa . . . his young namesake, my little brother whom I scarcely knew, the young Achille Murat Willis, now seven. "Little Mu" as we called him was stoic in the face of the dreadful loss. Bittersweet days.

Back at Lipona, Judge/Colonel Murat turned his energies to replenishing the monies we had expended in Europe. First he had to overcome the failed cotton crop at Lipona. This he did by leasing a cotton gin and processing cotton for other plantation owners for a fee. Next he received an appointment from President Jackson to serve on a commission to inspect the United States Military Academy at West Point, New York. En route, he spent a number of days renewing his passion for American democracy by attending sessions of the Senate. In the process he acquired a new dedication to the red, white, and blue and departed for West Point with renewed interest in politics and new political supporters.

Despite our unpleasant experience on the continent, Achille's European origins were never far from the surface. Though still under travel edict of the allies, he was suddenly seized with the idea of becoming an emissary of the United States. With support from a number of Florida backers he petitioned President Jackson to be posted as Ambassador to Portugal. Though Achille reported to me that Andrew Jackson was "very friendly to me", he was vehemently opposed by Vice President Martin Van Buren who ultimately blocked the appointment. Thus angered, Achille made political bedfellows with the new Whig Party and was empowered to bring Florida into their fold at the next election. Prince Murat, almost King Murat, now Judge Murat and Colonel Murat was now to become a regional leader of the Whigs.

When he returned from West Point, Achille the new self-appointed Whig had but two weeks to prepare himself for his first plunge into the realities of American politics. It was one thing to write about it but another entirely to endure the exhaustive pace of campaigning, especially with rheumatism now impairing his movement. As candidate of the Whigs for a seat in the Florida Legislature, he proudly wrote his mother of his campaign speeches that "Everywhere I made a great sensation" and that he was "assured of quite a large majority." The propensity of political rallies to become alcoholic brawls stoked his own tendency to imbibe and the frenetic pace of campaigning on horseback in the heat of August proved too much even for Achille's prodigious energies. Shortly before election day, he fell so ill that he was unable to move for days. His political enemies even declared him dead.

On election day he rose from the dead only to be defeated at the polls. American politics, it seems, was more difficult in reality than on the theoretical pages of his treatises. And a lot messier.

Defeat was a crushing blow for the man whose political writings had yielded such accolades in England. In utter disgust he withdrew from political life, yielding the Whig mantle to his friend and mentor Richard Keith Call. Call would at the next election cycle ride the Whig Party to victory as the governor of Florida. Though Achille never opened the secrets of his heart to me on the matter, he was surely hurt that a close friend who rode his political coattails succeeded at elective politics where he had failed. Another failure now lay heavily at his door, but he brushed it off with a politicians indifference. His frail ego defended itself by ranting that it was, after all, the "damned preachers and their dupes" who had cost him the election. That it took it's toll on his enthusiastic spirit made me sad.

The whole experience set me to wondering. Was he good enough to be King of Belgium but not good enough to be a small town legislator?

Achille fell into understandable depression which he medicated with mint juleps until at last he was ready to venture forth into the world and tackle a new venture. All of the disillusionments he had suffered in the last few years began to exact a cumulative toll on him, and his health slipped a few notches with each. People sometimes wondered in private about some of Achille's eccentric tendencies, but if they had walked a few miles in his shoes they would wonder why he was as normal as he was !

Feeling the pinch of financial downturn as were so many Americans in 1832, with a sigh, Achille summoned the internal strength to forge ahead with a way to refill the family coffers. Perhaps, he opined enthusiastically over dinner one night, the investment opportunities of America and the Florida frontier would enable him to restore a level of wealth commensurate with the Murat fortune which still lay under French impound. It would take knowledge. It would take contacts. It would take a certain amount of luck.

And it would take an in with the new Union Bank of Florida.

Despite many financial reversals which had plagued him since the heyday of his royal youth in Naples, Achille never once doubted his destiny of wealth. I too had suffered family financial disaster so I had first-hand experience with the anxiety it could produce. Achille however tended to approach money as an entitlement of his noble birth. As for me, while the country skirted the fringes of financial depression in the 1830's, I worried that the time might not be propitious for him to begin a new career as an investor. Wild speculative land ventures were not limited to Achille, and the entire economy of the nation went through a series of shock waves and rampant inflation.

Though he was no different from other reckless investors, here again was his unbridled optimism, racing far ahead of our precarious situation. I got the sense that for Achille, it was almost as if by wishing it to be so, the sought-after wealth would materialize.

Achille fancied himself a financial wizard, but in retrospect I now see that he had more experience spending money than making money. There was no dissuading him from jumping into the world of finance despite our precarious situation. This tendency to hasty action was one which I could now describe as a pattern and privately it frightened me. Of course rural Tallahassee was not exactly the center of the American financial universe, but as with so many of Achille's ventures, reality was but a minor impediment. He struck out to convince the bank of his financial prowess.

In the process of discussions with the Union Bank, it's board of directors saw in Achille the incisive mind which I had always known lay under the baffle of his European temperament and overly optimistic nature. They also perceived that as a prince he must have both deep pockets and personal connections to enormously wealthy prospects.

With abandon, Achille borrowed $13,266 from the bank with which to purchase shares of stock. In return, he was offered $5,000 a year to serve on their board of directors and presumably expected to attract capital from the wealthy colleagues and relatives he had bragged of. I know for example from correspondence which he shared that he approached his aunt, the aging Letizia, to funnel Bonaparte wealth through Achille to the Union Bank of Florida.

This, I thought privately, was one of his most erratic romps into fantasy. The Bonaparte millions were of course secreted across Europe where there was a powerfully established banking structure which would overwhelm a start-up banking institution on the Florida frontier. I could not criticize my Achille however as he was so excited and enthusiastic about his new path to riches. Any note of caution from me would have been perceived as an attack on his abilities. He had been hurt enough and didn't need another hurt from his wife, so I kept my counsel and remained silent while he jumped in with both feet.

Not all service on the bank's board of directors was so glamorous. Because of his legal training he was assigned by the board to review mountains of documents associated with land titles and financial records of investors. In this endeavor, he applied himself conscientiously, and I could honestly say that it appeared to be the first time of his life in which he worked in the traditional sense of the word. Under the most primitive conditions the conscientious Achille spent weeks inspecting land titles, mortgages, and the credit-worthiness of customers.

The bank's other directors were unfortunately more prone to gambling than to analytical decision-making, and the dark side of politics once more showed itself. Achille's tedious work was summarily set aside in favor of risky lending decisions and sale of questionable bonds issued by the Florida Territory.

Conscientious Achille did not understand the politics of money as practiced by the Union Bank of Florida. His lack of actual banking experience quickly became obvious exposing a philosophical disconnect with other members of the board. What the bank had wanted was his presumed conduit to wealthy investors. What they got was reams of reports. When "the prince" produced no inflow of capital from the supposed horde of wealth he could tap, his position as a director was terminated.

Yet again he returned to Lipona a beaten man. The gloomy pall of failure once more overhung our lives and our little down-and-out plantation.

What does a planter do when his plantation is in shambles and his money drying up? He buys another plantation with borrowed money! I sighed and retreated into my own pleasant world of sewing, needlepoint, and entertaining. Privately I could not fathom his rationale for buying from his friend James Gadsden another 960 acres and 51 slaves when we could scarcely wring a dollar from the plantation we had. At this moment for the first time I worried seriously about our future for all of the optimism in the world would not pay our mounting bills.

*James Gadsden was a neighbor, friend,
and business partner of Prince Achille Murat.*

The tough reality of wresting money from the frontier and the high-strung world of a Napoleonic prince seemed to diverge farther and farther. For all of his intellect, Achille demonstrated daily that reality was not the handmaiden of brilliance.

Despite his failed business venture as a director of the Union Bank, our neighbors and friends John and Robert Gamble next asked Achille to head an ambitious project to join the beautiful blackwater Aucilla and Wacissa Rivers by a canal. I suspected that like the bank, what they really wanted was his perceived money, though we had none. Having failed at agriculture and finance, he now became president of the Wacissa and Aucilla Navigation Company, up to it's neck in engineering and construction. He saw himself as an entrepreneur. I saw him as figurehead being used for self-serving purposes by our supposed friends.

The goal was to dredge and enhance these natural waterways for navigation. This would enable commerce with ports along the Gulf just to our south; cotton from the interior to coastal seaports for transshipment and commodities such as salt from the Gulf to the interior. Territorial roadways were abominable then and the notion of a canal sounded just right to Achille. With his usual enthusiasm re-ignited, he talked up the company to our colleagues as likely to yield a two or three-fold increase in property values.

I have explained for many pages the tendency of my Achille to overreach, and you can guess what transpired next.

How did he maintain his sanity when the venture folded?

Charles Louis Napoleon Achille Murat, the son of a king and nephew of the most powerful man in the world, was reduced to private tears by this latest failure. I alone knew just how fragile he had become. He was a proud man but now felt embarrassed among our friends in the territory and drew a curtain of privacy around our home and lives. All the while his health suffered the degradations of stress and aging while Lipona deteriorated for want of money to rebuild the fences and outbuildings so necessary for a plantation. I desperately wished for a way to console his grief and give him comfort in the depths of his insecurity.

We would, he announced, have to look for opportunity elsewhere. It was 1835 and the mercurial prince, colonel, judge, planter, banker, and engineer looked westward.

Louisiana Interlude, Early 1830s

*T*HOUGH THE FLORIDA Territory was thoroughly American, part of Achille's original fascination with it was its connection with France. The huge tract given to Lafayette was the primary inducement for Achille's move from St. Augustine to the region of north central Florida now known as Jefferson County. He identified with his hero the marquis, though no real relationship of substance existed.

To Achille's mild surprise (but not to mine), no meaningful French atmosphere had developed in the territory. After many agricultural failures and prodded by occasional Indian threats, the French settlers who had come to populate Lafayette's Vine and Olive Colony had moved on to greener pastures. Tallahassee was left culturally isolated, bereft of anything French or even remotely resembling the European ambience we had enjoyed during our years in London and Brussels. It was a rough-and-tumble, uniquely American atmosphere in which we struggled socially, culturally, and economically. In this frontier backwater, we were a misplaced couple, I as a classic daughter of Virginia aristocracy, he as an exiled European prince.

Where would a Frenchman search out a more compatible environment? The answer was instantly obvious.

Achille had visited New Orleans in 1827 and loved the Continental ambience so carefully designed by the city's large cadre of French. After the United States acquisition of the Louisiana Territory from Achille's Uncle Napoléon, French expatriates had flooded into the city, and it now resembled a "Paris on the Mississippi." Though some identified a specific area of New Orleans as a French quarter, to Achille all of New Orleans appeared the best of all worlds, a cosmopolitan French community with the freedoms and safeguards of America.

How would we make the transition from log cabins on the rustic frontier to the cultural oasis of New Orleans, a sophisticated city of sixty thousand?

Suddenly.

Yet again leaving a caretaker in charge, we were gone from Lipona in less than a month from his decision. The slaves were to be allowed to grow their own food on our land and to remain in their rough-hewn cabins, but few other considerations were dealt with when we abruptly left our plantation and set out by coach through Pensacola where we visited family, then onward through the French cities of Mobile, Biloxi, and the small community of Pass Christian, Mississippi, where the wealthy of New Orleans luxuriated in summer. All were squarely in the path of our new destiny.

Upon arrival in New Orleans, we stayed for several weeks with another family of French transplants we had met recently during a visit to my family in Pensacola, the Charles Garnier family. Like Achille, Charles Garnier was a displaced nobleman whose family had been driven from Europe as "the terror" swept France exacting the heads of aristocrats and the well educated. Though not a precisely identical background, this common thread, plus deep-shared disdain for the rule of Charles X, quickly fostered a strong bond of friendship. Deep into the night, the two conversed in French over copious quantities of champagne, which seemed to flow from a bottomless well at the Garnier's home on St. Peter Street. Achille had found a way to be European in America.

When contrasted with our hardscrabble life at Lipona, the sophistication and comfort of the Garnier's life in New Orleans was one that I made no secret of admiring. Instead of leaky log cabins, rutted dirt roads, and prowling Indians, here we found brick-paved streets lined with gas lamps and elegant homes and public buildings of brick construction. Many had charming European-style courtyards, and some even the luxury of indoor plumbing. If there were prowlers about, instead of Indians, they tended to be revelers enjoying the many amusements of New Orleans rather than Seminoles with bloodlust on their minds.

Our host, Charles Garnier, had carved out a life of wealth and ease since immigration to America while the elixir of success remained elusive for Achille. Charles was a profitable commission merchant who supplied necessities and luxuries to support the opulence of affluent planters on their large agricultural tracts upriver. Of interest to Achille, he also had a law practice in the Vieux Carre near his home.

As the two whiled away their evenings in convivial conversation, which virtually floated on champagne, his wife, Lubin, and I got on famously chatting about the theater, the arts, family connections, foods, girl-gossip, and, of course, the latest in women's fashions. With many common interests and a thirst to elevate our lives from the harsh Florida frontier, it was not long before the outlines of our next chapter of life began to take shape.

Achille, of course, had stood to the bar in Florida as both a private attorney and as a judge. Of special interest to Charles was his familiarity with the Napoleonic Code that, alone among all of the states, was practiced in Louisiana. The next step was obvious. Achille and Charles joined in law practice and set up their venture in Exchange Alley near the commercial hub along the riverfront. It would be understatement to say that I was thrilled that we would relocate from the rustic Florida frontier to the cosmopolitan city, which emphasized the joie de vivre of the French and provided culture and creature comforts of a level unknown on the frontier.

While guests of the Garniers, we were invited each Sunday to attend mass with them at the beautiful St. Louis Cathedral, which adjoined the old government building known as the Cabildo and fronted the river. Though not Roman Catholic, I was moved by the spectacle of the building's three spires reaching toward heaven itself. The message of its trinity was not lost on this girl of staunch Episcopal upbringing. Though I found the arcane services themselves unsatisfying, the building itself was one of the most beautiful houses of worship in America, and as guests of deeply religious friends, it was a virtual command performance that we accompany them.

Sundays evoked a grumbling sort of tension among the otherwise convivial group of Garniers and Murats. Though Achille had been raised Catholic and I Episcopal, over time we had drifted away from regular church attendance as there were none within fifteen miles of Lipona. In retrospect and more to the point, there were no churches anywhere that could satisfactorily merge his agnostic views with mine, which hailed straight from the Book of Common Prayer ordered under Henry VIII's split from Roman Catholicism. Moreover, Achille had had horrific quasi-religious experiences at the hands of some rabid fundamentalist country preachers who rode the circuit in backwoods communities of Florida. In disgust, he vowed that he would never pledge his soul to any god, becoming, along the way at least an agnostic if not an outright atheist. Such beliefs, or lack thereof, were the basis for many a row between Achille and his friend Ralph Waldo Emerson, who himself espoused some unconventional beliefs.

But to avoid being rude to our host and hostess, we shined ourselves to a churchly sheen every Sunday and attended mass at the cathedral alongside the pious Garniers, quietly biting our tongues every minute of the experience. It was only polite but set me to wondering as the priests droned on in French, Latin, and English. What God exactly did Achille look to as we faced the crucifix on the high altar? What spiritual underpinnings had he learned as a child accompanying King Joachim and Queen Caroline to services not unlike this one? Did he see a supreme being inside the cathedral? How much Roman Catholic doctrine lurked behind his private protestations of disbelief? What about Jesus Christ? The Virgin Mary? The resurrection? The stations of the cross that lined the walls? The Eucharist? Transubstantiation? All of it. Though raised in a staunch Christian home, I looked at these issues through a gauzy curtain where the answers were troublingly indistinct. Achille's rejection of Christianity made my answers all the more difficult to pin down and caused me to question my own Episcopal upbringing. The rigid formality of services at St. Louis Cathedral, shrouded in mystery and incense, left my spiritual self to starve while the Garnier's busily said their rosaries.

I yearned for answers where there were none.

Achille had no such dilemma, for he ostensibly threw the Christ child out with the bathwater. Deep within, I felt sure that he must have some empty spaces, which needed filling. When I tried to engage him about religion, he was dismissive, and I sensed that his nonchalant attitude would deflect my inquiries off into space without satisfaction. I could not understand God, and I could not understand Achille.

If he could not believe the God that the Garniers worshipped faithfully at St. Louis Cathedral, did he see God in the beauty of sunsets over the lazy bayous? In the clouds? In the tempests we had experienced at sea? Did he see a god, any god, at all? As the son of a king, did he even perceive the need for a god, or was a king a very god on earth? Each Sunday presented awkward moments in church, but they inevitably passed, leaving the spaces still empty and questions unanswered. We would shuffle out onto the plaza, which fronted the cathedral, mutter pleasantries with the bishop, and delay our spiritual fulfillment for one more week.

But not all of New Orleans created such angst; in fact, some events were imminently satisfying. On the heels of Achille's momentous business decision to practice law with Charles, our next task was to find a suitable home, which we did with the Garnier's help. Along the pleasant Esplanade, which ran up from the river along the edge of the Vieux Carre, the Garniers knew of a home owned by the statesman Pierre Soulé that was presently for sale. With the help of a bank, which dared not deny a Bonaparte relative, we purchased it straight away without a second thought. It thrilled me that Achille quickly committed to permanent residence in New Orleans, for frankly, I admit a certain envy of the Garniers and their lives of sophistication and luxury. Years in the wilderness had left me with a craving for a more substantial home affording comforts such as that of my Virginia upbringing and our sweet life in London and Brussels.

Princess Catherine Willis Murat. Painted in New Orleans in the late 1830's by French portrait artist Jacques Amans. Image from the book "Louisiana Painters and Paintings From the Collection of W.E. Groves", Pelican Publishing Company, Gretna, LA, 1998.

$16,000 later and 919 Esplanade was ours. Before occupying our home, we embellished it with a thoroughly modern convenience, indoor plumbing with running water and water closets for one's private functions. Excitedly, we sent immediately for some of our slaves and for the few quality furnishings we had at Lipona. From shops along the balcony-lined streets, we augmented these with purchases of Louis XIV furnishings from France. These pieces in the high French style were bought for a song from disenchanted settlers who returned to

France after the demise of their American dreams. There seemed to be many. When we were done, the town house on the Esplanade and its furnishings were suitable, I felt sure, for a well-connected Napoleonic prince destined for the top of New Orleans legal profession and citizenry. I sighed a deep sigh of relief but continued to look over my shoulder at our shaky finances lurking in the shadows.

Twelve of our best plantation hands made the journey with some of the furnishings from our run-down cabins at Lipona. These selected field hands would be retrained to serve as our gardeners, grooms, housekeepers, and cooks as we preened proudly in our new setting in the Vieux Carre. Of course, William, Achille's faithful valet, headed the group. As was his wont, Achille insisted that when in public, our servants be attired in the livery of Uncle Napoléon. His family connection to the emperor and the imagery of empire set us upon a much-envied pinnacle of social status in New Orleans. If the reality of Napoleonic power no longer existed, its memory spawned a nostalgic outpouring of affection, even awe, for the newly arrived imperial prince and his princess. No matter that our titles of prince and princess presently had no legitimate foundation, image, nostalgia for the lost empire of Napoléon, and a little pretension on our part could go a long way!

To complement (or perhaps to announce!) our arrival, Achille purchased a fine new phaeton and team of matched dapple grays, which reminded me of my beloved Lizzie of my youth. Many evenings, just at dusk, we would have a liveried servant simply drive us along the quaint streets lined with lacy ironwork balconies and nod casually to passersby as a light zephyr from the river stirred the humid air. I smiled to myself as Achille lifted a hand in the grand manner, as though he were a real prince dispensing favor to the hoi polloi. The grand gestures of royalty learned in his youth still lay close to the surface.

How we reveled in our new home, our new status in life, and our new circle of friends! The Bonaparte name, roundly ostracized in Europe, carried a special cachet in New Orleans, for the city remained a hotbed of Napoleonic nostalgia. As the emperor had marked time in exile on Elba, an active cadre of supporters in New Orleans had actually purchased a home for him hoping for the day when he might cross the Atlantic to sprinkle his Bonaparte magic upon the waters of the Mississippi and their lives. Of course, we know this was nothing more than a pipe dream, but the hallowed name of Bonaparte opened doors for us in New Orleans whereas in Europe it had caused them to be slammed in our face.

Even many who had no connection to Napoléon or France were spellbound that a nephew of the great emperor, and a prince to boot, was to live among them. Much of the wealth of New Orleans and of the American frontier had its origins in Uncle Napoléon's historic transaction with Thomas Jefferson, the fabled Louisiana Purchase. Even if there was no direct nexus, citizens by the thousands owed their livelihoods to Uncle Napoléon, thus Prince and Princess Murat, heirs to the blood of the emperor if not the wealth, basked in reflected glory.

In no other city of the Americas was the good life so celebrated. Soon we became a central fixture in the gaiety of social life in New Orleans. Parties, balls, the opera, card games, intellectual salons, and exquisite restaurants decorated our lives, and annually there were riotous festivities associated with the pre-Lenten celebration known as Mardi Gras. Can you imagine a more stark contrast to Lipona?

Even our friends here were more glamorous and, in contrast to the homespun of the Florida backwoods, dressed to the nines. I had come to love the French zest for life and their silken language that trilled off the tongue like petitions to heaven. Virtually all of them carried old and proud French surnames similar to those I had learned to pronounce—almost to sing—while in Belgium. Among our new friends, there were the Thibodauxs, the Landrieus, the Marquettes, the Villeres, the Levasseurs, the Barrineaus, the Petitjeans, and more—Francophile, sophisticated, rich, and devoted to the enjoyment of life.

Like drunken seamen signing on for the excitement and riches of a clipper passage around the horn, we signed on for the giddy life of New Orleans socialites. There was an other-worldly quality as we danced and drank our days and nights away in an escapist fantasy world far from Lipona and the stumps of the Bellamy Road. Like Mardi Gras, life itself became a carnival detached from reality, and we slid, without so much as realizing it, into the illusory world of pleasure without responsibility, floating like so many others on the dreamworld of hoped-for riches to be borne from the muddy waters of the mighty Mississippi. Paying for the good life in the crescent city could wait, yet in the distance, I had a sense of storm clouds gathering like a thunderstorm off the Gulf.

My father, having come down from Parnassus and Willis Hill when his wealth vanished in Virginia, was now solidly ensconced as President Andrew Jackson's agent in Pensacola and proprietor of a prosperous brickyard contracted to build forts for the government. Despite the aura of success, which finally arose from the ashes of his collapse in Virginia, he was still under a pall of gloom due to Mother's death. I grieved that the joy he always brought to life seemed smothered. At our insistence, he came to visit our dreamworld in New Orleans bringing three of my siblings including the eight-year-old Achille Murat Willis, Little Mu. That name, of course, honored the sadness that I was not destined to bear children and paid tribute to my renowned husband.

Colonel Byrd Charles Willis, father of Princess Catherine Willis Murat ("Princess Kate") and his son, a late-in-life child named Achille Murat Willis, "Little Mu", in honor of Kate's husband Prince Achille Murat. With no children of their own, the Prince and Princess were honored to welcome a family member whose name memorialized the life of Prince Achille Murat. Image painted by Emmanuel Leutze, most famous for his "Washington Crossing the Delaware".

My god. Though my much-younger brother was all Willis with not an ounce of Murat blood in him, he appeared to me a miniature Achille. I was fine that this was simply wishful thinking, and I relished the role of the doting big sister. The happiness I experienced with Little Mu was momentary though, never quite lasting long enough to fill the empty spot in my heart where my own child should be. When Mu's laughter died away, my eyes filled with tears knowing that I would end my life without my own children, barren and unfulfilled.

Sighing, I realized I could be nothing more than a surrogate and part-time mother to my precious little brother, Achille Murat Willis, "Little Mu." During the family visit to New Orleans, these few days encapsulated for me all of the joy and sorrow I would have felt if young Achille Murat Willis had been my son rather than my little brother. As much as I gloried in the warm affections and childhood chatter of Little Mu, Achille seemed stilted and emotionally distant from it all. I chalked it up as an echo of his childhood amid the pretensions of life as the son of a king and queen. He was raised not as a son to be cherished for that and that alone, but as the dauphin to assume the crown.

To distract from the pain of Mother's death and brighten their lives, we took my family via paddle wheeler steamboat up the coffee-brown Mississippi all the way to Natchez, enjoying the somewhat rowdy life aboard a showboat.

This, opined Achille as the paddle wheel churned the muddy waters, was what America was all about. I agreed.

Aboard the *Memphis Belle,* Achille had many occasions to drink with fellow passengers who had earned handsome fortunes as sugar plantation owners. This, he was certain, was a crop that would surely set us upon our pathway to wealth and the entrepreneurial satisfactions of making it on our own. I listened to these fanciful discussions with a skepticism borne of Achille's many prior forays into the financial unknown. Surely, I privately reassured myself, since we were already deeply in debt for two failed plantations, he would exercise some caution and not act rashly. But then I remembered, his legendary father Joachim was renowned for rashness and, indeed, had made his reputation by casting caution to the wind and brazenly riding into the mouth of the cannon.

The son had not fallen far from the family tree.

Within a week of our return from Natchez and soon after Father's departure, Achille announced that he would be gone for a few days and took the phaeton upriver to Baton Rouge. On the day of his departure, I stood beside him sweeping in the image of Prince and Princess Murat in the gilded full-length mirror that graced our center hall. Somehow we didn't quite look like the couple whose reflections we had caught in the waters of a stream near the old Mission San Luis in Tallahassee. I adjusted his collar stud, arranged his tie, and kissed him passionately, full on the mouth as if to confirm for us both that this was indeed my husband. I stood on the porch to the rear of the house and watched him awkwardly struggle to climb into the phaeton. *His gout must be bothering him,* I mused.

Faithful old William, the valet, and Walter, the groomsman, had prepared the team and carriage. Acting as driver and footman, both were turned out in full Napoleonic livery in order to impress Baton Rouge with the ghost of glories past.

I had experienced Achille's little vanishing acts before and glossed over the event as I lunched with Lubin Garnier at a sidewalk café of the sort I had loved in Europe. We should plan to attend a performance at the St. Charles Theatre together while he is away, we decided. It would be a distraction. It would provide a few hours of joy while our bills mounted. It would be as a carnival mask, shielding my aging face and figure from view. It would stave off the unpleasantries of our desperate finances if only for those few hours.

Daily I was becoming more nervous about how Achille held our creditors at bay. His cavalier manner in brushing off my questions left me with a malaise that prickled my skin like summer heat. With an air of confidence, he assured me all was well, so I tried gamely to bury my anxiety with the insouciant air of all the rest of the socialites who lived on credit.

Perhaps the piper would play on for a few more hours before demanding payment.

Four days later, Achille returned in the same clothes that he had worn as I sent him off. There was no tie now, and he had lost the diamond stickpin I had given him in Belgium. He had not shaved since he left and appeared bloated. I suspected that Baton Rouge had drawn him into its own cocoon of decadence in its resplendent plantation life, a Potemkin replica of grandiose society on the banks of the Mississippi and thoroughly walled off from reality.

I worried that the entire scene of wealth that they, and we, enjoyed was precariously balanced on the easy credit and laissez faire risk taking that fueled a bubble of prosperity in much of the country. Money was now a mere plaything, but I had seen this effect before, right before the financial collapse of my own family in Virginia. Parties. Gambling. Alcohol aplenty. Easy money. Easy fun. Easy come. Easy go.

Indeed, I was right. Achille rushed breathlessly up the stairs to announce that we would soon spend part of the year at Baton Rouge at our new plantation, Magnolia Mound, a sugar plantation acquired over mint juleps and self-delusion. How much, I inquired, had he spent to acquire a third plantation? "Only a hundred thousand," he replied with a big grin on his face, "but it came with another thirty-one slaves."

As though it were a gift from the gods, he proudly added, "And the bank will finance it all." He was born to royalty, and royalty, I shuddered, never worried about such mundane things as repaying loans.

Alice, I realized, had walked through the looking glass and fallen down the rabbit hole. We had crushing obligations in Florida supporting two decrepit plantations, which now grew nothing. We had just acquired a new one in Louisiana with enough debt to flatten a flounder. Florida voters had rejected him in politics, and he had walked away from a judgeship there. He was persona non grata with the Bonapartes. European leaders had driven us from the Continent, and the Murat fortunes remained under lock and key of the French government. However enjoyable it had been, chasing the ghosts of the past in Europe had squandered all of the money from mortgaging Lipona and our slaves. We occupied a town house along the Esplanade that was actually owned by the bank.

For all of his intellect and political brilliance, I grieved that Achille had now amassed a litany of failed businesses including his new law practice, which languished for want of attention. The creditors were baying, answered only by vague alcohol-fueled promises of recovering the impounded Murat fortune from France. How could this go on?

To complete the insane picture, my thoughts were interrupted by a groomsman wearing the laurel-crowned *N* of Napoleonic livery at our door inquiring if "massah" was through with the carriage. Alice had not only walked through the looking glass but was now consorting with March Hares and Mad Hatters.

In tears, I excused myself and closed our bedroom door wondering where the king of Belgium had gone.

Feigning illness, I stayed in bed the rest of the day, tried not to think too crassly, and exhausted myself trying to make some sense of it. Answers were hard to come by. When answers came, what they delivered instead was more worry. Another plantation? Another hundred thousand dollars of debt? Try as I might, that afternoon in bed, I could not think it away. Hearing him on the stairs, I pulled a pillow over my head.

Always searching, never finding, Achille had at long last gone too far. Our lives had become a parody of themselves, a prince and princess of naught. In trying to live out his father's life vicariously, to prove he was a real prince, this son of the outlandishly gallant King Murat of Napoleonic fame had, with each failed venture, slipped away little by little until I wondered if there was anything left of him. I knew with certainty that he always measured himself against his famous father and had forever driven himself to try to create a parity with his privileged birth and upbringing. Headlong charges into iffy business ventures were false echoes of headlong cavalry charges, a phantom world where Achille tried vainly to establish enough self-esteem to justify in his own mind the storied name of Murat.

When I arose and went downstairs at dusk, I looked again in the full-length mirror and saw nothing.

Of Sugar and Slaves, Mid-1830s

*I*F OUR FINANCES were a shambles, we were not alone. America's false prosperity of the last decade came undone by a combination of factors including policies of Andrew Jackson, inflation, bank failures, falling prices, and most especially, irrationally speculative real estate investments, ours among them. Many actually called this the Panic of 1837. If the country itself was in panic, it was multiplied manyfold in the Murat household. In fact, I thought fleetingly that Achille's wildly enthusiastic investments in land ventures an apt metaphor for what had transpired throughout the country. Perhaps he was the face of the Panic of 1837.

Our plantations, now numbering three, were especially hard hit when the price of cotton fell below ten cents a pound. Under the drumbeat of abolitionist politicians, some of our slaves simply slipped away into the night, leaving sullen attitudes among those who remained. Though I was sublimely happy in Louisiana, we were so deeply in debt that I could not imagine how we would sustain the house of cards that Achille's financial decisions had created. Was there a way out? If so, I couldn't yet see it. Oh well, Magnolia Mound was ours as long as the bank indulged our shaky credit. Tenuous though it was, we put on our happy faces and leapt gaily into the sugar planter's life ignoring the press of indebtedness which lurked just below the surface.

Achille and I spent several months getting to know Magnolia Mound, where he shamelessly exploited the social value of the Bonaparte name. Though neither of us had a moment's experience as sugar planters, we were instantly accepted and lavishly entertained by our well-heeled neighbors. Like New Orleans, most of our associates were French. Even our home had been previously owned by the Duplantier and Villar families.

Magnolia Mound plantation was the sugar plantation of
Prince and Princess Murat near Baton Rouge, Louisiana.

Never far from the surface in Florida, the subject of slavery was at a boil along the Mississippi. The very river itself was a symbol of the divisions which the slavery controversy stirred in America. The mighty Mississippi flowed southward from the Free States surrounding its headwaters through states like Missouri, which didn't know what to make of slavery, and down through the slave states of the South. The whole milieu of problems which slavery embodied flowed along with the commerce of the river until it was finally regurgitated into the Gulf of Mexico.

The issue was as muddy as the Mississippi itself. The plantation owners of our social circle could not survive without the slave labor that worked their fields and tended their homes. The blacks, who had been uprooted from Africa and brought in servitude to America, along with their white apologists in the abolition movement, of course, saw it differently. It was a familiar dilemma that had followed my life since birth. I had never known life without scores of blacks working the fields, and from my privileged station in life, it was taught to me as almost a birthright, yet it never failed to stir controversy. The country was changing, and we were swept up in the tide of social change despite, or perhaps because of, Achille's many political writings on the subject. From my family's home in Virginia to the homes I shared with Achille in Florida, New Orleans, and Baton Rouge, slavery gnawed at the fabric of life and remained a pox on the American scene.

My family had always had slaves in Fredericksburg at Willis Hill, and Achille and I used slaves at Lipona, slaves on the Esplanade, and slaves at Magnolia Mound. My brother George and my father had even followed some escaped slaves all the way from Pensacola to the waters off Key West, so the stain of slavery cast a shadow over our lives as it did the entire country. Though I was involved, I was uninvolved. I felt a helpless bystander to the hurricane of sentiment that surrounded the slavery question. All of America was subsumed by an issue as large as mankind itself.

Try as I might, I could not envision a solution to the slavery question. It was on everyone's tongue. Since the tongues we listened to were all slave owners, the conversations in which we indulged were totally one-sided. I heard it all, participated in most, yet all the words of all the parties did nothing but amplify the divisions that tore at America.

I felt unable to encompass so vast an issue and typically took the same stand taken by America since her founding. I ignored it.

Most of the late-night rants of plantation masters were liberally laced with alcohol, and it brought out the worst. The genteel wealthy people, from whom I expected polite debate, grew irrationally vicious when the slavery issue was well oiled with wine. One dare not even imply a sympathy for black mothers separated from their children by the auction block. Achille seemed oblivious to the moral dimension of all of this, and it made me again question, in the depths of my heart, his sincerity in the principles of freedom. Unspoken, the issue of "freedom for whom" remained a disquieting and unanswered question within the Murat home and homes all across America. Even as a member of a slave-owning family, it made me so uncomfortable that I began making excuses rather than attending social events along the river.

Achille was vocal in his defense of slavery. He wrote that "at the time of the revolution, a portion of the United States had already got rid of their slaves, since then their example has been imitated by others, and at a future time, more will probably imitate it, but some are so situated as to make it absolutely impossible for them to do without slaves, and these states will probably continue to have them for a long time." He followed this observation thusly: "Any attempt to make laws respecting our slaves would compel the Southern states to separate themselves from the union. This is an obligation founded upon the right which every man has to defend his life and property. Would you believe that there are people so foolish as to not be sensible to this, and so shortsighted as to be willing to run this risk?"

My ancestors, who had laid the cornerstone of America, tossed fitfully in their graves at the mention of fracturing the Union. That Americans would tear apart this precious experiment in democracy was testimony to the depth of feeling that haunted the slavery question.

Plainly, Achille was "not so foolish" and championed slavery as loudly as any plantation master who whipped the hide from his blacks under the Louisiana sun. And when all of his eloquence was exhausted, he still fell back on the notion of a slave as property. At least he acknowledged that it was an evil, though he defended it as necessary. Like everyone else's mental gyrations in defense of slavery, his most passionate writings tended to go in circles, which failed to address slaves' fundamental rights as fellow human beings. Here once more was an inherent conflict which warred within his prodigious brain. I was deeply conflicted too but not inclined to be as vocal as my husband.

Beyond our Louisiana homes, the racial divide was tearing at the fabric of Florida too, and it was not exclusively about the blacks. Pushed farther and farther away from tribal lands, the Indian population—Creeks, Seminoles, Mikasukis, and Cherokees—were a sad and disenfranchised lot. Human emotions being what they are, I could not blame them for reacting harshly against the white man's laws and actions, which treated them as subhuman. I could and did blame them when it got bloody, however, and was shocked to learn that a child of one of our slaves at Lipona had been kidnapped in a midnight raid a few months ago. His name was Sam, he was just seven, and when I saw him last, he had a toothless grin as big as all outdoors.

Achille frolicked and hunted with the planters along the river, made the acquaintance of famed naturalist and painter John James Audubon, and generally lived the high life for almost a year. During this time, I spent most of my of time at our home in New Orleans partly because I was so conflicted about our slaves, partly because Achille's drinking and gambling had become vociferously unpleasant, and partly to protect our town home on the Esplanade from foreclosure. Not even the avaricious bankers with whom we had taken a mortgage dared seize our property while it was occupied by a princess. Or at least a supposed princess.

As poverty came a knocking, posturing as a princess seemed a farcical role, which I became increasingly reluctant to play. Achille loved the honors and attentions paid to a prince, but I wanted no part of what had become a sham. Though our love remained strong, it was at this moment when Achille and I started to diverge philosophically and physically. With creditors at the door, he retreated more and more into a make-believe world of Bonaparte fantasies where wealth was no object and the world was his to command. I continued to adore him but could no longer occupy that dreamworld with him.

The Panic of 1837 doomed the plantation economies of the South as prices for the commodities they grew collapsed. If Louisiana's economy was bad, it was even worse in the Florida Territory. There, things were so bad that our close friend with whom Achille had partnered in many a venture, James Gadsden, was forced to take back our second foolish Florida plantation venture, leaving Lipona as our only port in the event the financial storm worsened.

By summer of 1838, the wolf was at the Louisiana door also. Unable to make even token payments on Magnolia Mound, and with funding from Bonaparte assets in Europe a thing of the past, the bank foreclosed sending sugar planter Murat, a.k.a. Prince Murat, almost-king Murat, Judge Murat, Colonel Murat, etc., begrudgingly back into town to join me. As you might expect, things had become strained due to his erratic and risky decisions, which threatened the very roof over our head. Child of royalty accustomed to a bottomless well of money, he had gotten in so far over his head that we were drowning in debt without any evident means of repaying creditors or salvaging our comfortable Louisiana lifestyle. Just when it appeared that it could get no worse, his law partnership with Charles Garnier fell apart, and the bank, which had financed our town property at 919 Esplanade, called the loan.

In a flash, our Louisiana adventure was finished. The dance was over, and the piper at last presented himself for payment. We hurriedly sold our furniture, sold the phaeton, sold most of our slaves, even sold our mules and beat a retreat to Lipona, now decrepit from lack of maintenance. This time, we arrived by a rented hay wagon rather than fine coach, and even it broke an axle on the washed-out driveway. We grimaced at the broken-out windows and weathered log siding where the chinks had fallen out.

No one came to help us unpack the wagon; in fact, it was almost as though we were invisible. Perhaps we were.

As Achille handed down the marble bust of Queen Caroline from the battered wagon, the incongruity of the moment seemed a metaphor for the last few years of life. In the heavy air, the smell of summer rain mingled with the earthy smell of red Florida dirt as the first huge drops fell like little bomblets sending up tiny dust clouds. We hurried in as the rain began to fall in earnest and sat on the floor as there was no furniture. A spider crawled over Queen Caroline's marble face, frozen in the royal beauty of youth. Welcome to Lipona.

The small weathered sign "Colonel Murat, Counselor at Law" seemed laughable as it seemed to sneer at us from the wall where it hung at an angle. Only a few scrawny cattle grazed in the south forty where our once-fattened herd had roamed. Some had been rustled away by starving vagrants, some eaten by our slaves, some stolen by Indians, and a few lay dead near the barn. The vultures, which tore at their carcasses, were so hungry they didn't even fly away when Achille shot at them. The corn crib had been broken into, and judging from the whiskey bottles that lay about, it appeared that someone had been living in it. Who? The dried thorns, which bristled from what remained of my prized garden of yellow roses, seemed an apt symbol for the moment. I felt dried up too.

Flies buzzed around my face as I surveyed the scene. I reached deeply within for strength or for something appropriate to say, but as I searched my mind for the Bonaparte princess of old, I could find nothing. Had the princess remained in New Orleans? In London? In Belgium?

Where did I lose her? Or had she ever existed at all?

Perhaps she lurked somewhere, but her happy countenance would not show itself for months to come. Hands thrust into his pockets, the almost-king of Belgium stood mutely looking out of a broken window, and when he turned, tears streaked his dusty cheeks.

Surrounded by the detritus of Lipona, I took stock of just how far we had fallen. Though it was all attributable to rash and ill-considered financial moves by Achille, I realized this was not the moment to heap my confused feelings on my fragile husband. He had quite enough on his plate. Surely I deeply loved the magical man who had given such excitement to my life, but the humbling return to Lipona set me to thinking.

As I have written earlier, Achille was the smartest man I ever knew. Despite the catalog of failures, which now hung like an albatross from his neck, I still believed in his intellectual prowess. But I had now come to conclude in the private recesses of my mind that he was like so many brilliant people, intelligent but at the same time irrational to the very edge of lunacy. I do not mean that my beloved husband was really insane, just that he had difficulty living in a world of harsh realities for which he was unprepared. Perhaps this was the same phenomenon that had afflicted all of the Bonapartes. If one goes back to the unreality of his operatic childhood in Naples, his uncle's maniacal rampage across Europe, pursuing power at all costs, followed by his father's death by firing squad and his mother's duplicitous intrigues, clearly the hand of destiny had long ago written the outcome.

As we closed the rickety door, I hoped that the mental depression, which had plagued our last days in Louisiana, would not find us hiding from the world in the wilderness of Lipona. Clearly it would take some time to lick our wounds and regroup for whatever was to come next. For the moment, the prince and princess felt defeated, demoralized, and absolutely bereft of ideas as to how we might recover or what shape our lives might take as we emerged from the ashes of Louisiana. Sighing, I told myself that surely this was the nadir of life.

If only I could have foreseen what came next.

Hard Times for a Prince, 1838-39

*T*HE NEXT MORNING, we had a rather military-like formation of our slaves. There were ninety-four including twelve we had brought back from Magnolia Mound and the Esplanade. During our absence, seven had disappeared, nine had died, and eleven born.

Though each welcomed us home as we walked together down their lines; I saw a faraway look in their eyes as though the human spirit no longer lived there. We had given them privileges on the property while we were away, but this was as destitute a lot as I have ever seen. Their clothes were threadbare and torn. Iridescent green flies feasted on the ooze of open sores, and their gaunt frames bespoke a hunger of long duration.

Threatening them with the lash, Achille put his face mere inches from their deep-set eyes and savagely demanded information about the seven who had run away. He smacked the coiled whip against his leg, cursed them all, and swore he would have the hides of the runaways. I had never seen him like this, wondered what kind of king he would have become, and shuddered at the angry man posing as Prince Murat. Surely this was an impostor and not my gentle, aristocratic husband, but then I remembered the tales of Uncle Napoléon's cruelty and shivered.

After Achille had passed, I spoke softly to each of the women, taking their bony, leathered hands and expressing our happiness to see them again. Perhaps some saw it as a false gesture, but I sensed that it was sorely needed.

Six times, we learned, the Seminoles had raided the property while we were away. With sobs to equal the pain of the ages, the mother of little Sam described the night he was taken. Drunken warriors wearing white man's clothing but with painted faces attempted to rape her while her family watched, but Sam leapt on them with a fury, his little hands tugging at their long hair, and kicking them in the parts that even little Sam knew to be the most painful place to kick a man. With a grunt and a torrent of profanity, the leader dragged all sixty pounds of little Sam screaming into the night. He has not been seen since.

When the Indians returned, one of them was wearing strips of little Sam's shirt braided into his hair, and they stayed drunk for a week in the corn crib, insulting the men and terrorizing the women.

I could take no more and retreated into the house where I sat in a corner of what had once been the bedroom where youth, passion, and lofty ideals lived. After berating the men for allowing their fellow slaves to escape, Achille calmed down and organized four work parties to make sense of the Lipona property once more. The old well pump behind the arbor screeched rustily as I filled pitchers of tepid water to quench the thirst of the group. In the house, I found a colander and picked scuppernongs, which found the hungry mouths of our work party. One of the four women assigned to work with me in the house began to hum a soulful melody with African undertones. As she hummed, the others seemed to fall into the moment as though mesmerized, and soon the foursome was raising an anthem to God's glory. As we worked side by side, one even picked up the harmony in a hauntingly beautiful soft voice. Where, one wonders, do they find the hand of a loving God in their godforsaken lives?

At dusk, we sat on the benches under the arbor, and they described the nightmare of helplessness they had undergone in our absence, when not only Seminoles but also starving white vagrants foraged the plantation, taking everything but the few skinny cattle, which our hands had defended armed only with tools from the field and their raw courage. Our time in Louisiana had left us destitute in purse and spirit, but they had been through a greater hell. Maybe all men are created equal after all.

During our self-delusional time in Louisiana, our finances had been gobbled up by unwise financial decisions abetted by the nationwide Panic of 1837. The entire Florida Territory, wobbling along with a fragile government and only twenty thousand white settlers, suffered the same fate as we, drained by speculative excess and abandonment of homes and dreams by destitute settlers. Then there were the Indian troubles. From our comfortable homes in New Orleans and Baton Rouge, we had been only vaguely aware of sporadic Seminole raids back in the Florida Territory. When we returned, however, it was to a new and more dire situation prompted by Washington's policy of Indian removal. The scattered white man's outposts of north central Florida, including Lipona, became, at night, like little fortresses in which families banded together for mutual protection. Many of our neighbors actually just walked away from hearth and home rather than face the anxiety of lonely uncertain nights in the wilderness. We had blundered squarely into what was later called the Second Seminole War.

The northern portion of the Florida Territory now fell under the military command of a General Winfield Scott. Appointed by President Van Buren and headquartered in Georgia, Scott was deeply conflicted and troubled by his orders to round up and relocate the Indian population. None other than our long-term friend James Gadsden was his chief of staff. Colonel James Gadsden and his brother Octavius had done many business transactions with Achille as well as occupying a prominent spot in our social lives from their neighboring plantation called simply the Gadsden Place.

Buttressed by Secretary of State John Quincy Adams, General Scott saw Washington's "Indian removal" policy as a political ploy to facilitate a massive land grab. For all I knew, perhaps it was. Scott's orders to ship the Indians off to the Oklahoma Territory stood in stark conflict with his personal beliefs. In the plight of the Indians, I saw a parallel to the slavery matter and tended to have a soft spot for Seminole and Cherokee families forcibly driven from their homes.

I was surprised by Achille's rabidly hard-line views on the subject. I supposed it was his military mentality for it seemed to come straight from Uncle Napoléon's tactics. "Follow orders and do whatever is necessary." It would have been imprudent of me to note that had his father done that, he might still be alive today. Achille publicly lashed out at General Scott, labeling him as a fool, soft on the Cherokees and Seminoles. I held my tongue, for in my eyes, it was the Indians who were wronged by this policy. They had lived here long before we arrived to enforce an alien culture upon them. We knew they had been here for centuries, for we had found many of their arrowheads as our fields were plowed. By this time, however, it was hard for me to discuss either the Indian situation or the slavery issue with Achille, whose mind seemed closed to both. I thought his angry denunciation of both slaves and the Seminoles an irreconcilable contradiction with his writings, which espoused the equality of man, yet I could say nothing for fear of causing an argument or precipitating another of the epileptic seizures, which had become more frequent since we returned from Louisiana.

The Indian question was to have unanticipated consequences for our supposed new start at Lipona. We were not yet on our feet after the disastrous foray into Louisiana, when the Union Bank was spooked by the uncertain environment of the Seminole Wars. Achille and Colonel Gadsden, having got together the mortgage proposition for the bank when we needed money for Europe, sought to hold off a foreclosure, but it was for naught. The bank's inventory of Lipona's assets showed 1,060 acres and 108 slaves. They were all awarded to Colonel Gadsden as it was Achille who had withdrawn the money for our venture to Europe while Gadsden was merely the cosigner and guarantor. We had now been foreclosed at the Esplanade, at Magnolia Mound, and at two plantations in Florida shared with the Gadsden brothers. There was, quite literally, nothing left except our personal fortitude and our families' good names. Given the reputation Achille had acquired for rash decisions, I, for the first time, thought it likely that my Willis name carried more credibility around Tallahassee than that of Murat or Bonaparte. His father, King Joachim, had been shot, his famous uncle had died in exile, and I wondered if a similar fate awaited us.

Mother had always told me I had a strong constitution, and if so, this was surely the time it took over. We had returned from Louisiana broken in finance and in spirit. There was time for sulking later, but a matter of urgency lay at our doorstep and would not allow the indulgence of heavy sighs and wishful thinking. It needed action. We were soon to lose not only our fields and pastures but also, and of more immediacy, the roof over our heads. Something had to be done immediately. "Kate," Achille approached me one day, "what would you think of looking at the smaller place called Econchattie?" We had visited Econchattie for it was on our social circuit, but I had no idea it was for sale. We put pen to paper and discovered that by selling most of our personal possessions and eight of the twelve slaves we had remaining, and with a small personal loan from my father, just eke out the purchase price. It was thus that Murat and Bonaparte jewels, some Achille had given to me and some he retained as family treasure, ended up decorating Florida ladies who had no idea of the amazing history of the pieces or of their even more amazing itinerary. These treasures of royalty had been shepherded from Paris to Naples to Austria to New York to St. Augustine to the rawboned Florida frontier to London, to Brussels, to Louisiana, and finally back to the Florida frontier. Perhaps their roundabout journey was symbolic of our own. Both had begun in grandeur and ended up nigh meaningless, I sighed.

"No point crying over spilt milk or lost jewels," he opined, and in a matter of six weeks, Econchattie became ours. We and our remaining four slaves moved to the property on one of those grand October days where the green pines and hoary oaks stood out against a cloudless fall sky. I took it as a happy omen upon which to start anew once more, yet I was nervous. I had been optimistic before.

Achille had waxed hot and cold over the years concerning the recovery of the Murat fortune impounded by the successors to Uncle Napoléon's empire. With millions at stake and now so down on our luck that we were reduced to eating pork from wild razorback hogs that roamed the forests nearby, for obvious reasons the matter took on renewed urgency. Achille's motivation, and mine too, soared, and he began a series of correspondences with his family, especially his royal mother, now widowed again in Florence. With unctuous prose, he sought to heal any old wounds by writing her that "if the sceptre of power has slipped from you, those of grace, manners, spirit, and intelligence have remained. Nothing can take them away from you. Reign with them and try to fill your dear life as pleasantly as possible and happiness will return to you. Alas, that I myself can contribute nothing to it."

Achille was rarely given to understatement, but "contribute nothing" surely rang true after four foreclosures, the sale of our personal servants and the jewelry of empire. If homage such as Achille's letters to his mother, the deposed queen, would bring us closer to a way out of our poverty, I smiled and applauded his effort. We would have starved but for the tiny stipend doled out annually from the estate of his grandmother Madame Mere and the bounty of the forests and streams that surrounded us.

Now, in genteel poverty in 1838, instead of writing legal briefs or political tomes, he now spent his days preparing a series of arguments and petitions to the government of Louis Philippe (whom he had been unsuccessful in overthrowing). Would they fall on deaf ears? Would his strategy to separate his claim from the remainder of the family alter the outcome? We were so desperate he even offered to settle the claim for a discount. Would that sway the purse keepers, or was the money hostage to a hatred so deep it would never see the light of day?

Impoverished, we needed an answer, and we needed it soon.

A second thrust of effort to rescue us from poverty was pressed onto his uncle Joseph, who continued to live in luxury at Point Breeze. Achille believed, with no documentation to prove it, that prior to the fall of the First Empire, Napoléon had entrusted $400,000 in U.S. currency to his brother in America to be used for the welfare of the long-awaited Napoleonic son, Napoléon François Joseph Charles Bonaparte, the so-called King of Rome. But the King of Rome had been dead for six years now. Where was the money? Achille believed its proper fate to be a distribution to the various surviving members of the family rather than a default to its custodian. Joseph would have none of it, and in truth, it had probably already been spent. Who knows, perhaps it had paid for his New Jersey estate, which we had so enjoyed. Never having enjoyed a particularly cordial relationship since declining marriage to Joseph's daughter, the split between Achille and Joseph the ex-king of Spain was now irreparable, and we settled in to make the best of a bad situation at Econchattie.

There were no resplendent evenings with royalty, no balls in fine gowns, no stirring military reviews, no coronations, no soirees capped with French champagne. There was only the unrelieved wilderness and each other.

Painful Separation, 1830s

$\mathcal{F}$ROM HER LAVISH villa in the cultured city of Florence, Italy, Achille's mother, Queen Caroline, was enjoying a resurgence of former glory funded by the largesse of French king Louis Philippe who, despite his obstinate refusal to relinquish control of the Bonaparte and Murat fortunes, had ceded an annuity of 100,000 francs to Caroline. She played to the hilt the role of faux nobility as the Countess of Lipona, reveling in art, culture, and the fawning attentions of Florentine society.

The Bonaparte name still had a certain cachet, and Louis Philippe sought to appease the powerful Bonapartist political bloc lest he end up as so many figures in France had, under the guillotine. Though she had been an ambitious sister of Napoléon, Queen Caroline by this time was aging, female, and had no overt aspirations beyond la dolce vita in the ancient Etruscan city. Louis Philippe's gift to her was a purely political gesture not connected to the Bonaparte and Murat fortunes that still engorged his treasury. I frankly saw it as an astute ploy to generate sympathy and support from that large portion of the French population which still wallowed in Bonaparte nostalgia.

The self-centered Caroline, now in ill health, put all of Louis Philippe's generosity to use on herself and shared none of her good fortune with her financially strapped son in Florida or any of her other three children.

Rightly or wrongly, Achille and other members of the Bonaparte family considered the residue of Napoléon's vast wealth as their inheritance. The impounded Murat fortune to which Achille held a claim was also substantial. Petitions, talk, and all the maneuvering in the world could not alter this fact however: none of it was coming our way though we were in desperate need.

General Francesco MacDonald was Secretary of War to King Joachim Murat of Naples. After the execution of King Murat in the final days of Napoleon's empire, MacDonald secretly married Murat's widow, Queen Caroline and remained her companion until death at a villa in Florence, Italy.

Achille constantly fumed over his daily applejack that his legendary father had done so much for Napoléon, led the *Grande Armée* to victory after victory, and this was the thanks we got! He conveniently dismissed from his mind King Joachim and Queen Caroline's end-of-empire act of treason. Silently, I also wondered if the precocious peacock King Joachim would have recognized the unshaven Floridian in dirty clothes who cursed the French and drank himself nightly into a stupor at Econchattie. Sometimes I wondered if I recognized him myself. To be sure, there was still love, but it had altered after the series of epic failures culminating in the Louisiana foreclosures, the loss of Lipona, and his retreat into moodiness and drink.

I was never sure that Achille's dream of inheriting Napoléon's wealth was in the realm of reality or if it fell into the category of some of his other far-fetched hopes and illusions. Of course, I was never privy to the actual documents by which these claims were made as they were tied up in international agreements well beyond the reach of a private citizen of a foreign country.

While I did not know the details, what I did know was that for some twenty years, all efforts by Achille and other members of the Bonaparte diaspora had been futile, and the mood of the French government was not likely to change. Louis Philippe sat precariously on the throne of France, and I thought it unrealistic that he would open his treasury to the Bonaparte opposition, which had actively sought his overthrow.

At home outside Tallahassee, we privately sunk deeper into despair while putting on a show of gaiety with parties and dinners at Econchattie. We could scarcely afford it, but it was expected of us. For purposes of image, our servants were still attired in the royal livery of the great Napoléon, but our friends would have been shocked if they could have seen behind our curtain of illusory social graces. Some days when I felt especially blue, our present days struck me as a microcosm of our entire years together, carefully crafted for the perception of the public.

The glorious sendoff to Europe several years ago with all of the fanfare and gala celebrations had effectively been undone when we returned penniless and without result. Achille's reputation as a child of royalty, self-styled world leader, and local sensation were now replaced by oft-told tales of his eccentricities. His fondness for drink fueled the gossipmongers of Tallahassee and probably beyond. I heard the rumors whispered in my social circle and was certain that there were other more damning tales circulating about him, but I was powerless to stop them. As his wife, I was privately hurt for Achille but never brought these slanders to his attention. All I could do was to defend him, not as a world-changing leader but as gentle husband who tried his best. The fall from almost-king of Belgium to erratic alcoholic had been brutal.

The rough-hewn man on the skinny horse had become a parody of his former claim to fame. No one around Tallahassee seemed to bother much about the prince and princess titles anymore, but most still would toss his way the former title of colonel as a polite sop. Perhaps it was only that they were puzzled about how to pronounce "Achille."

It has been my experience that when things seem dark, often an event will occur that helps to place the situation in perspective. This happened when, in 1839, a letter from Florence arrived the day before Tallahassee's annual celebration of American Independence. Achille's mother, Queen Caroline, wife of a king and sister of the most powerful man on earth, was dead. It was a blow for which Achille was totally unprepared and a blunt reminder of our own mortality. My prince, the man who almost followed his father's footsteps to kingship, broke down in my arms, again the helpless little boy propped up by royal regalia but inside a tormented mass of nerves. On and off for three days, he slipped into recurring seizures, and then almost as if he willed it, he took control of himself and the situation, declared a course of action, packed, and planned his departure for Florence where he would oversee the affairs of her estate. During this time, he successfully obtained a waiver of the travel ban that had stymied us on the Continent. This was quickly accomplished by using the new invention called a telegraph to communicate with French ambassador to the United States. How remarkable! Words could flow as if by magic along wires strung out on poles and come out at the other end. I could see much promise for it, and in this case, the telegraph hastened Achille's ability to travel.

Before his departure, we had much conversation about what I should do. I was most willing to make the voyage with him simply to be a good and supportive wife in his hour of need. Though things were sometimes difficult lately due to his moodiness and excessive drink, I felt it the least I could do.

I was stunned when he announced that he would go alone.

What would I do alone on the Florida frontier for what promised to be an extended absence of my husband?

As I watched the raindrops course down my bedroom window, I received my inspiration as though from above. If he was to leave, so would I. Econchattie would have to wait.

Achille was not alone in experience of family deaths. My father, Byrd Charles Willis, had also spent the better part of recent years in grief. First the loss of my mother to yellow fever in 1834, followed by loss of my beloved brother Lewis to drowning in 1835. My sister Ann had died in 1827, brother John in 1833, and an infant lost before their move from Virginia. With four children dead, plus the crushing loss of his beloved wife, Mary Willis Lewis Willis, Father had too many times followed caskets down the aisle of memorial services. In Pensacola, he continued to serve as Andrew Jackson's agent at the navy yard as well as owning a profitable brick factory while shouldering sole responsibility for raising my little brother Achille Murat Willis. If I could help out my beloved father while Achille settled his deceased mother's affairs in Florence, Italy, it seemed a good choice all around. My letter to Father suggesting that I come and stay with him in Pensacola for the duration of Achille's time away was met by enthusiastic response, so I began to make plans for an extended absence from Econchattie.

By this time, my sister Ellen Attoway Willis, or Attie as we called her, had married Samuel Duval, of the family of Florida governor William P. Duval, and they maintained residence in Tallahassee. Like my own family, the Duvals were transplants from Virginia, and we frequently shared stories of the Old Dominion. Samuel and sister Attie were gracious in agreeing to come to live at Econchattie for the duration of my sojourn to Pensacola.

Our last few days were frenetic preparing to go our separate ways for an unknown time. Achille was to set out eastward by stage along the much improved Bellamy Road to the Atlantic coast for his passage to Europe. I would turn westward on the same road for the two-hundred-mile trip to Pensacola. It was an intense time for both of us. We had been under enormous financial stress, scattered Indian attacks continued near our home, Achille's health was not good, his mother's death haunted him, and our beloved Lipona was gone. The entire scenario of recent months was overlaid with a sense of frustration at Achille's inability to achieve the success he felt was his due. Then there was the specter of a lengthy separation with the Atlantic Ocean separating us.

On the day of departure, we had one of our men drive us by wagon down to the stage stop where we chatted nervously until time to depart. All I remember is a good deal of inane conversation since neither of us knew what to say. Of course, we offered each other reassurances of spousal love, but I can't remember the specifics for I was filled with anxiety.

I do remember that despite his pronouncements of undying love at the stage stop, I wondered if I would ever see him again. The Bonapartes' track record for marital fidelity left something to be desired, and we would be continents apart.

As his last bags were secured to the coach, we clung to each other for several precious minutes. When at last we broke our embrace, it seemed not enough, so I pulled him close once more. He gathered my face between his palms and with furrowed brows and a deep sigh said, "Kate, I shall miss you beyond words. I am incomplete without you. If I have not always been easy to understand, I hope you shall forgive me. I have always tried to fulfill your dreams while fulfilling mine. I must now go to my destiny with my mother one last time though it breaks my heart to leave you. Have courage, my love, and be happy until I return."

In those poignant moments, my apprehensions melted away in his arms. He was now and always would be my prince.

"I will be here waiting for you always. Take my last yellow rose as a token of my love until I feel your arms about me once more," I said and mounted the step of my coach.

The magical and varied experiences of the last thirteen years fluttered before my mind as though it were a magic lantern show. Our chance meeting at San Luis in 1825. The delicate dance of our courtship. Our historic marriage linking the houses of Bonaparte and Washington. Perspiring side by side as we carved Lipona from the wilderness. Politics American style with Achille's unique Mediterranean twist. Crouching in the dark during Indian attack. Nostalgia in Fredericksburg at the site of my burned-out childhood home. Washington and the U.S. capitol. Philadelphia and Independence Hall where my ancestors helped bring forth this blessed land. Point Breeze with King Joseph, Zenaide, et al. Charleston. New York. Exciting but treacherous sea journeys. Ralph Waldo Emerson. High society in London. Queen Hortense and Louis-Napoléon. Brussels and the possibility of kingship (I might have been a queen!). European military pomp befitting his father's glory. New Orleans law practice. Magnolia Mound on the banks of America's highway, the Mississippi. And finally, our sad retreat to Florida. Then remembering the humorous days of carved turkey buzzard and pink-dyed dresses, I smiled. Prince Achille Murat was now so woven into the fabric of my life that we comprised a single bolt of cloth with threads both homespun and royal.

As our separate journeys began, mine to Pensacola and his to Europe, my memories were not only numerous, but also they were so varied that it seemed impossible that one lifetime was enough to accommodate it all.

Was there a man on earth who could have afforded such a life of adventure and excitement?

I think you know the answer to that question as well as I.

After pleasantries with fellow passengers aboard the coach, I turned to the window as a tear rolled down my cheek, and in two minutes, I was sound asleep, exhausted.

Bittersweet, 1839-1841

I WAS AWAKENED ABRUPTLY when a large snake in the road frightened the two-horse team so that they reared and led the coach off into a ditch. I had been dreaming frightening dreams as I dozed and was almost grateful to realize that I was not facing painted Seminole warriors as in my wild dream. The coachman announced that we would stop for a while for him to inspect the wheels and axles, and I took the opportunity to step out to stretch and catch some fresh air. Gazing around, I was struck by the sameness of the landscape of north central Florida. There was very little relief to the terrain, and the curtains of pine trees to the very edge of the road seemed smothering in their sameness. The air was humid as well as heavy with the scent of turpentine. My coach mate, Mrs. Brosnaham, and I sought out a thick stand of shrubs for some privacy to attend to personal functions. It reminded me of the moment years ago when Father killed a rattlesnake that was threatening my younger sister Attie on our initial trek from St. Augustine to Tallahassee.

There had been much water under the bridge since then.

As we climbed into the cramped interior of the coach to resume our journey, conversation turned to titillating gossip about Queen Victoria, who had been on the throne less than two years. Mrs. Brosnaham inquired if I had traveled to England, but I demurred, not wishing to brag that I had actually met Victoria when she was a child. With my chatty companions at such close range, it would likely lead to inquisitive personal conversation, which I did not care to pursue. Anonymity would be my friend as the stage rattled its way westward.

Her query prompted me to withdraw into feigned sleep. I had no desire to be Princess Kate on this trip. I just wanted to arrive at Father's house in Pensacola as soon as possible and forget that I had just sent my husband away with a very real possibility that I might never see him again.

As the first stars began to twinkle in the western sky, we stopped for the night at a weathered stage stop. I sat alone in a corner over my simple meal pondering both my life to date and my uncertain future. I had, after all, just sent my husband across the ocean in a return to the cultural and emotional embrace of familiar Europe. Leaving my dinner barely touched, I went upstairs to my tiny room overlooking a big mossy oak tree out back. Dropping my bags, I sat with a flump upon the bed. There, not five feet away, the image of a once-celebrated lady of high society stared back from the mirror. Her face was dusty from the trail, and her hair tousled from the wind. A few gray hairs peeked from under her chignon. Was this the princess?

I was not vain, but tonight, I focused with a special intensity upon the image in the glass. At first, I was so startled that I hardly recognized her, but her image whispered across the years. Was she the happy-go-lucky child of Virginia aristocracy? The near-royal wife of the near-king of Belgium? The much-celebrated socialite over whom British nobility had fawned? Was she the farmwife soaked with perspiration working in the Florida wilderness? The mistress of a now-defunct plantation along the Mississippi? It was frankly dizzying. In my disoriented state, the obvious flooded over me loud and clear. The reflection of the mirror was indeed a reflection.

It was a reflection of my entire life. As the spouse and life partner of one of the most amazing people of the era, nephew of Napoléon and son of a king, I had been all, seen all, done all. But now, only the haggard figure in the mirror with dusty face and disheveled hair remained. Who was this woman? For a moment, sadness overcame the face in the mirror. As I prepared for bed, I was struck with the harshest reality of all. I could not blame the mirror.

Nor could I blame Achille. He had faltered many times, but as the one who knew him best in the world, I knew that his heart was good and that a critical observer might call him just a rash foreigner. As his wife, I would characterize him in gentler terms. I knew Achille's mind, his heart, his dreams, and his demons, and through it all, my admiration for him remained intact. He had set off alone into the unknown when only twenty-one. In America, he encountered linguistic and cultural barriers along with the rude awakening that an upbringing of royalty had not prepared him for the rough-and-tumble of business on the frontier. Achille's frustrations and failures had nothing to do with his heart, which I knew to be in the right place. If the American South was now, in 1841, less tolerant of the eccentric prince, it was abundantly clear to me that what these uneducated (or undereducated) settlers were describing was actually their own intolerant eccentricities.

Achille was simply a misunderstood victim of culture shock.

I also believed that there was something to the notion that his brilliant mind and superior education threatened the self-esteem of the working men who called the southern frontier home. Despite Achille's business failures, his amazing mind continued to astound me. One had only to look at his published treatises to see that. And that he could do all of this in seven languages rendered it all the more alien to the capabilities of the men and women with whom we were surrounded. The cotton planters and shopkeepers of Tallahassee did not read intellectual discourses in German or French and, if they could, would have felt them irrelevant to anything. Thus in a bid to continue feeling worthy themselves, many on the Florida frontier felt in necessary to denigrate Achille as a crazy foreigner. In doing so, they pointed the finger straight at themselves.

He might have some unusual habits, but crazy he was not, and I would defend him to the death.

If anything, surviving the tribulations of the past few years together had made our love more resilient and durable. We had weathered many ups and downs but always with immutable love and optimism. We had stood together at royal coronations in Westminster Abbey and through the depression of losing Lipona to creditors. We had pondered the possibility that he might become a king and I his queen. Yet we had retreated from Louisiana in poverty and failure. I had laughed so heartily with him that I once burst a corset stay, and I had tearfully held him so many times when his cruel epileptic seizures immobilized him. For a couple so young, we had done it all, and I could find no blame in my heart for the many times Achille had tried and failed. Only love.

Sighing, I realized that we had actually lived the meaning of our wedding vows.

For better or for worse, in sickness and in health.

But now, he was gone away to Italy, and I knew well that country's siren hold over him. King Joachim's legacy once more loomed out of the darkness and roosted foursquare in my airless room at the stage stop. I knew that for Achille, his illustrious father had not died under that firing squad at Pizzo but lived in his psyche and prompted his every move. Having been repeatedly thwarted, it would be frighteningly easy for Achille to be seduced by the memory of his royal childhood beside the Bay of Naples, to walk away from the hardships and wife waiting in the Florida Territory, and to search on the Continent for the satisfactions that had painfully eluded him in America. Italy, it must be remembered, was the source of his princely title as well as his revered father's fondest wish to govern. Could I compete with the luxury, art, culture, and history of Italy? Could I survive the attentions that would be lavished on him by whom? Siblings? Cousins? Nostalgic hangers-on to the memory of the Murat kingdom? Noblemen seeking and granting favor? Bonaparte admirers?

Beautifully coiffed ladies schooled in the wiles of courtly life?

I could drive myself mad with this kind of thought! Thankfully, sleep came quickly, as only the deep sleep of stress can. Before it came, I had one of those clarifying moments, which helped me better understand my nervousness.

In the darkness behind my eyelids, a powerful message thundered, the last thought before blessed sleep came.

I was alone in the world for the first time in my life.

In my youth in Fredericksburg, there had always been the constancy of family. At age fifteen, as I stepped timidly across the threshold from childhood to the adult world, my arranged marriage to Atchison Gray had been wholly unsatisfying. But as unfulfilling as it was, I was at least never alone. After Mr. Gray's death, I then fell back into the comfort and security of my family once more, and while it was not easy, my life was girded by love and security. Then in Florida, my life had changed dramatically when I met Achille. Our marriage, for all of its ups and downs, had been most exciting and fulfilling, always keeping me surrounded by love in the secure cocoon of our bliss.

Now I was alone and already missing Achille. Would I ever see him again? Could I cope with the emptiness? On that unanswerable question, sleep came to my rescue.

The next day, we left just after dawn for another day upon the Bellamy Road. The coachman had done this route many times and advised that we would need only one more day to reach Pensacola. I could hardly wait to unwind my nerves at Father's home on the bayou near the beautiful Pensacola Bay where the tranquil waters lapped at a snow-white shore. Despite nearing middle age, I knew that I needed the solace and comfort of family and that it was awaiting me there. I was overcome by a warm feeling of comfort and self-satisfaction. I knew my family roots were important, but now they loomed larger than ever. Family would help me weather my swirling storm of uncertainty.

Without children of my own, and now with my husband upon the Atlantic headed for Europe, I needed to throw off the worries of the last few years. I had been through Achille's foreclosures, my mother's death, and the gracious poverty after Louisiana. (It may have been gracious, but it was still poverty!) I had known the fears of Indian attack and the gnawing insecurity of debt. I had worried my way through Achille's more frequent health problems, and I had tried, of late, to gracefully accommodate the decline in our social stature.

All of these, and more, played out against the backdrop of our unplanned and unpleasant return to the rough-hewn frontier where we lost our beloved Lipona and moved to Econchattie, which I struggled to love. Anxiety had become my middle name.

Now that I was all alone and Achille off to the glories of Florence, I could add loneliness and worry.

As the coach rumbled westward, I tried to fend off my unsettling feelings of isolation by envisioning my life for the next few months while Achille settled Queen Caroline's estate. Though I was thirty-six years of age, I still felt like daddy's little girl who needed the secure feeling of family and the love and support implicit in that. Aside from some much-needed time under Father's roof, where I hoped to both console and help him, I was excited at the prospects of spending time with my precious little brother Achille Murat Willis, now eleven. Having watched Achille the prince's frustrations and fall from glory, I determined that I would do my best as the doting big sister Kate to influence life of Achille the little brother. Perversely, I thought that compared to Prince Achille, young brother Achille would have an easier life because he was *not* born into royalty and had no unrealistic role models to chase.

At about 4:00 PM, we rolled into the stage stop on the outskirts of Pensacola. By letter, Father had told me that he would assure my onward transport from there to his home by the bay but failed to explain. Just then, I caught sight of a familiar and most welcome face. It was Bucky! Bucky the family servant from Fredericksburg. Bucky who had accompanied us southward. Bucky who had endured the hardships of the Bellamy Road with us. Bucky who had always had our night's encampment along that road waiting for us. Bucky who tended our horses. Bucky who cut the firewood. Bucky who had in fact proved indispensable.

My heart leapt with happiness as his grin spread from ear to ear under a tattered old straw hat. I would not have been happier if it had been the president of the United States welcoming me to Pensacola! It may seem inconsequential, but for me, it was a comforting reach back in time, which foretold the simple pleasures of the next few months.

"Oh, Bucky, I am so glad to see you!" I called across the courtyard of the stage stop. "We're here three hours early. How did you know when to come to meet me?"

"Mistah Byrd tole me dat I could be de one to come to get ya so I wasn't gonna take no chances. Ah jes been excited to know you wuz a comin' home for a spell so ah been here fo' two days wid de wagon. Ah jus slep undah it while ah was waitin' fo' yah."

Bucky had been eighteen when we made the trek from Fredericksburg to Tallahassee, and he was now almost middle aged. The sobering thought was that the same thing had happened to me, day by day, moment by moment, and I realized I must look a fright from days on the road.

"You are a sight for sore eyes, Bucky, and I am ready to get home." I sighed with understatement.

"Lemme get yo' trunk, missus," he said, "and we be headin' home. Everbody be glad you gonna be wid us a spell. Bessie gwine fix your favorite fried chicken for yo' homecomin'."

How could any human being with a heart and half a brain see these loyal helpers as mere slaves? How could their essential humanness be hidden by the color of their skin? In a flash of memory, I was reminded that my views on the subject were not shared by Father, who was from a long line of slave owners, or my brother George, who tended to treat them as a commodity. It would be a tender point of disagreement at the Willis home, but one we could work through, I was sure.

Bucky helped me totter up onto the wagon, the final transport to that magical place called home. As he clucked to the bay mare, which stood blinking sleepily, twitching flies away from her ears, we started to roll, the final leg homeward. Bucky could hardly wait to tell me of Father's new role in life and the successes that attended it. Father, I learned, was using brick from his brickyard and leasing his own slaves to the navy as laborers for building forts around the harbor. "Missus, dey's a lots mo' of us now. Mistah Byrd got a big business working fo' da guvmint building forts, and he done bought twenny-fo' mo' folks to help out. Dey works hard settin' brick out at a place called Fort McRee, near where Mistah Lewis done drowned a few years ago."

It seemed sweet to me that though he was among those who did the back-breaking work, Bucky took pride in Father's achievement.

"Mistah Byrd always take care of everbody like he always done, and he even give us off from noon Saddays 'til Monday morning. He give us a dollah a week too."

As President Jackson's personal appointee at the Pensacola Navy Yard, Father was in position to award contracts and evidently saw the opportunity for steering lucrative work to his brickyard. I was never quite sure of the legality of all of this, but evidently, it was the financial success he needed to recover from the Fredericksburg disaster.

"Mistah George work with Mistah Byrd some and now dey shippin' brick way down south to sumwhere called de Keys."

"Mistah George got thirty-fo' hands helping him at de brickyard so de fort building business muss be good. Ah jus stays wid Mistah Byrd 'cause he ain't as hard as Mistah George who still uses de whip some."

I had heard of the Florida Keys, but they were about as remote from Tallahassee as the moon, so I had no idea about what my father and brother George were doing. As the wagon clopped off down the ubiquitous oyster-shell road known as Garden Street, I was interested to learn that George had left his post as customs inspector at Port Charlotte, Florida, in order to work with Father.

Indeed, the fort building business must be good if between Father and George they were employing eighty-eight slaves. I was glad for Father that he was recovering some of his lost fortune, for with that, he was sure to recover some of his lost self-esteem. I hated to hear though that Brother George was still of the old school regarding his slaves. The whip had no place in human affairs.

Bucky and I passed the time with chatter about their lives in Pensacola, their small hot log cabins, the many times that one among them had passed out from the heat at the construction site at Fort McRee, and the terrible day when my brother Lewis drowned while crossing the nearby body of water called Grande Lagoon on his horse. Lewis was of a mind such as I when it came to our servants, whom he also refused to call slaves. Such inconsistencies within families were not uncommon as the unresolved poison of slavery splintered states, regions, and thousands of families. Slavery did violence to the founding principles of America and to many a family of American citizens.

In the case of my beloved brother Lewis, now departed, there was never a doubt where his heart lay. The doctor in the family, Lewis was valiantly trying to reach one of Father's out-leased servants who had had a heat stroke working at Fort McRee. The strong tide swept Lewis's horses feet from under him, and Lewis's feet tangled in the stirrups. Horse and rider, still entangled, washed up on the beach two hours later, tragic testimony to my brother's commitment to the welfare of the gentle people who worked for us.

Soon we turned into the drive to Father's house on the bayou. Could there be a more different environment from our plantation house high on the hill in Fredericksburg? Beside the water? In the Florida Territory? No horses? No cattle? Building forts?

The most dramatic difference was of my shattered family however. Mother was dead. My sister Ann had died at twenty-two. Brother Lewis was dead, drowned in his humanitarian gesture to save the life of a slave. Brother John had died in Key West and was buried there. Sister Attie was married and living in Tallahassee in our small plantation house Econchattie. Sister Mary Byrd had married the commander of the Pensacola Navy Yard but had moved away. Brother George had left both West Point and his job at Charlotte Harbor to work with Father. He had married Martha Fauntleroy of Virginia, but she had also died, so George maintained his separate widower's residence in Pensacola. As a family group, we were devastated.

But then there my precious little brother, now age eleven, Achille Murat Willis—Little Mu. And my father.

As the wagon came to a halt, my beloved father, the social lion of Virginia, came bursting from the house. I hardly recognized him! He had lost much weight and now weighed well under his former three hundred fifty pounds. He was tanned from the Florida sun. His silver hair suited his new leaner appearance, and I instantly knew that my move here would be a good tonic for us both. Father and I hugged beside the hitching post around which twined a flourishing bush of yellow roses, the favorites of my childhood, and the bush brought with loving care all the way from Willis Hill to Tallahassee, then transplanted yet again to Pensacola. Indeed, we had all been transplanted since the days of my youth.

Beside him stood proudly my eleven-year-old brother Achille Murat Willis, lovingly known as Little Mu in honor of my husband. Proudly, he thrust out a hand to shake as though I were a business colleague rather than his sister whose heart he had stolen long ago. "Sister Kate, we are glad you will be visiting with us. I hope you have given my Uncle Achille, the prince, my very best wishes," he offered, half bowing in his best courtly manner.

Mother, I thought, *may be consorting with the angels now, but her influence was still alive and in control at the Willis house.*

"Come to Sister Kate, and you give me a hug!" I teased. At that, he flung himself close against me, and as I held him, he looked up with sparkling eyes. "Do stay a long while, Sister Kate," he implored. "I have missed you. And Father says you will become the lady of our house. I'd like that!"

"I plan to, if you will have me, Mu!" I replied, noting again that young Mu had received the blue Willis eyes. He was a beautiful child, and the thought that he was not mine brought moisture to my eyes.

Mu continued to hold my hand as we walked inside, Father walking behind and gently slapping me on the shoulder as I made my way in. "Kate Willis, we're glad you're home," he offered. Bellowing with that familiar Willis booming voice he added, "And we're going to put you to work, but first, you get some rest."

Without a spoken word, we knew that the Willises of Fredericksburg were still family, but a changed one indeed, fractured, battered, and missing the lady who had held it together. We had been nine Willises when we left Fredericksburg; now we were three. Without Mother, my hopes for a return to the jolly days of my youth were not to be, for the inexorable years had taken their toll. It was a bittersweet homecoming as I was shown to my room by dear old Bessie, now seventy-seven, still in her Willis liveried uniform and still the headmistress of the kitchen. She would have it no other way. As I climbed the stairs and she huffed and puffed beside me, there seemed a comforting continuity to this moment despite all of the tragedies and changes. I was home. However changed our family and despite the fact that I had never lived in this house, it was still home.

When all is said and done, home is where the family is.

Little Mu bombarded me with a thousand questions during that first hour as a spectacular sunset colored the western sky reflecting in the still bay. Old enough now to be fully aware of the Bonaparte legacy, he quizzed me about my interactions with them. He vaguely remembered the family trip to Joseph Bonaparte's estate in New Jersey and had a childhood concept of having met and briefly lived with a real king. Fully cognizant of the Murat name, which he bore in tribute to my husband, he wanted to know if Prince Achille was gone to Italy to be made the king. What a poignant moment. Nothing would have pleased Achille more than to be perceived, even in childhood imagination, as worthy of that station. It was tribute too, in a maudlin sort of way, to my deceased father-in-law, Joachim, who literally died in a vainglorious attempt to become king of a unified Italy. Achille, I dutifully explained to Little Mu, was on a simpler mission to bury the last of Napoléon's immediate family. Astutely he chimed up, "Oh, you mean Queen Caroline?"

"Yes," I replied. "Queen Caroline has passed away, and Prince Achille, even though he is a famous man, is still a grieving son on account of her death. I know he is sorry not to be here with us so that he could tell you some more of his stories of Naples and Capri and Paris after dinner. I even brought one of Achille's swords for you. It is a gift from him as he loves you very much and could not be with us now."

I wondered just how much of a little white lie I had just told my trusting little brother. Was Achille truly sorry to be headed to Italy rather than Pensacola? Would he really rather spend the next few months with my family in Pensacola than with the courtiers of Italy, who would seize upon him in search of favors from Queen Caroline's estate? How would Pensacola stack up against Florence, the fabled center of the Renaissance and art center of the world? And just where did I fit into all of this?

Exuberantly, Little Mu's childhood enthusiasm gushed. "Splendid, Sister! A real sword!" he exclaimed, jumping up and down and making fencing slashes at the mirror.

Age eleven. I wistfully remembered the young girl of ten dancing with her make-believe prince in the mirror in Fredericksburg. How the years slip away like quicksilver. Princes and princesses come and go, but family, I silently concluded, is forever.

From downstairs, the familiar voice of Bessie, which I had known all of my life, called up. "Dinner be ready, Miss Kate. Ah fixed your favorites. Dese Flahda chickens sho' am scrawny compared to de ones we usta get in Fredericksburg, but ah done de best ah could."

Decorously, Father, Mu, and I were seated by the three liveried servants who attended my homecoming. One I noted with special pleasure was Jefferson, who had been with Father for more than thirty years and had grown quite sophisticated in his manner. Sometimes I thought it was Jefferson who kept Father on his toes with proper decorum rather than the other way around.

Achille and I had dined with kings and queens in many a palace and in the finest restaurants of Europe, but nothing ever tasted as good as Bessie's fried chicken, sweet potatoes, black-eyed peas, and biscuits. After the glories of my travels with Achille, I was a Southern girl after all.

Little Mu, 1839-1841.

*I*T WAS FOUR lonely months before I heard from Achille. When finally a letter arrived from Achille just before Christmas of 1839, it was so crumpled and water stained as to be almost illegible. I nevertheless drew from the partial contents, which were vaguely legible, that his brother Lucien and two sisters Letizia and Louise Julie Caroline had also descended on the saddened villa of their mother, the late Queen Caroline. In the wake of his mother's death, there was, as expected, a melancholy tone to Achille's letter, devoid of the Murat bravado of old. I thought he sounded defeated, at least despairing. It was a turn of his personality with which anyone who has experienced the death of a beloved parent could identify. I knew it all too well.

In this and subsequent letters, Achille mentioned several approaches to King Louis Philippe of France concerning the Murat assets still under impound twenty-five years after the death of King Joachim. Since Achille had exhausted his credibility to deal with Louis Philippe directly, he pleaded that these were wrongs done to an American citizen and turned for assistance to the U.S. ambassador to France, Lewis Cass. What a tangled web. The crown prince of the defunct kingdom of Naples used an American diplomat to appeal to a French king for help freeing assets garnered by a long-dead emperor and king whose territories no longer existed.

Though I had to give Achille credit for perseverance, I continued to feel that in the end his decades of effort would be in vain. Tilting at windmills was a well-established characteristic of the Murats, so I took this news of his latest effort with a grain of salt. Achille and the other Bonaparte descendants had tried openly to overthrow Louis Philippe, and I thought it unlikely that the king would open France's purse strings to any member of the Bonaparte clan still considered threatening. My Achille stood at the top of that list.

As the months wore on, I received a letter every three or four weeks. While he was solicitous about my welfare, it was clear, as I read between the lines, that he was in no hurry to leave the luxuries of a royal villa in one of the world's most celebrated cities. Achille's enthusiastic descriptions of life in Florence belied his statements about missing Econchattie, Florida, the United States, and me. Today, an art lecture at the Uffizi Gallery. Tomorrow, dinner in the hills above Florence with friends at a villa in Fiesole. Last week, a visit by a duchess. (With or without her husband, I never knew.) My love for him remained strong however, and I wished for a magic carpet with which to whisk him away from the temptations of Italy. I never doubted that we belonged together, however, and through many a lonely month of his absence, I desperately hoped he felt the same.

The most worrisome part of my correspondence from Achille was that he was always silent about the matter of his return. Months and seasons passed without a word. Out of self-preservation, I began to steel myself for the worst case, which might lay before me. Occasional concerns morphed into serious worry. Many a night during my stay at Father's house in Pensacola, soft tears moistened my pillow as sleep stubbornly refused to black out my worried mind. Sometimes during his long absence, I would cry out in my fitful sleep, but there was no one to hear, no head on his pillow.

Mostly I could not erase from memory a worrisome pronouncement Achille had made during our recent years in London. He had famously told me and anyone who would listen that "a greater job is awaiting me in Italy." On the heels of that, he had even written his friend Count Thibodeau that he was sure that he alone held the credentials to rule a unified Italy. Given Achille's past of leaping impetuously into new ventures without evaluating the likely outcomes, that terrified me. What schemes might that prompt? What pathways might he be led down by his starved ego? What would the memory of King Joachim lead him to undertake to avenge the unfulfilled Murat legacy? I tried vainly to convince myself that Achille had outgrown all of that. But had he?

As the one year anniversary of Achille's departure approached in summer of 1840, several large packages and trunks were delivered to Father's house by the bay by a special messenger hired in Italy to accompany the shipment safely to Florida. What a trove of items! Here was Achille's share of Queen Caroline's household goods, and a royal mixture it was. Little Mu, now a curious twelve, took special pleasure in helping me lift each item up for public inspection and comment. Among the treasures were three magnificent tapestries, eight old world masters fit to hang in a palace, lovely rugs from Persia, at least twelve pieces of jewelry of the late queen, and many of her exquisite court dresses.

The latter would be so out of place in rustic Pensacola that I fairly giggled as I held them up in a charade of dressing for a royal ball. Mu joined in the fun and bowed deeply to me in his best imitation of a royal courtier. Splendid china, silver, satins, silks, and crystal glittered in the Florida sunlight as we unpacked Caroline's royal treasures.

An elegant marble bust of Uncle Napoléon went down to the sideboard in Father's dining room for its unlikely place of honor. Henceforth, we speculated over meals that the world's most powerful man might be puzzled at having wound up in such an improbable place watching mullet jump in the bayou. Some nights, Little Mu wore his Uncle Achille's sword down to dinner. Clearly fascinated with the military connections of the family, Mu sometimes performed saber salutes to the long-dead emperor who stared back in marble silence and presided over the Willis dinner table.

The incongruity that this man, who had come close to ruling the entire Western world and who was responsible for the deaths of some five million people, was my uncle by marriage was intimidating to say the least. Napoléon had been dead long enough now to have become a sort of cult figure, so his presence in Father's Pensacola dining room spawned many an interesting discussion. His inscrutable stone visage offered no clue as to how he felt about life on Bayou Chico.

From the depths of Queen Caroline's trunks came further more practical treasures. My clothing had taken quite a beating over the past few years, and there were few mercantiles in Pensacola, other than Mr. Barkley's, where I might replenish my wardrobe. I put to good use the sheets of fine Egyptian cotton and fashioned a dozen practical dresses appropriate for Pensacola's muggy climate. More unusual, however, from the bottom of Caroline's trunks came embroidered cook's aprons. And more cook's aprons. And more cook's aprons. A hundred of them! Perhaps Queen Caroline needed cook's aprons in such quantity, but between Father, our one cook Bessie, and me, we had a good laugh at the aprons!

I was learning to live without Achille. Without my beloved husband, at least it was gratifying being a part of Little Mu's upbringing. As he approached puberty and little peach fuzz appeared on his chin, I walked with him every afternoon down to the edge of the water where we would sit under the big oak tree and converse about every topic under the sun. Though he had lost his mother when he was not quite seven, he seemed not to mind that I had stepped into her shoes. It was almost as though he knew the depths of my sorrow at not having my own child, and the bond between us grew with the passing days. Mu needed me; I needed him.

I gloried in the role of surrogate mother to my precious little brother. It seemed an odd turn of fate that my husband Achille had given way to my young brother Achille, who almost felt now like my son Achille. I fended off gloomy thoughts that I might someday lose my husband to the seductions of Europe with comforting thoughts that I was now firmly ensconced as a sort of surrogate mother in the life of his namesake, my young brother. It was hard for me to not want to take over entirely. I was grateful that Father leniently allowed me to play an increasing role in his young Mu's life. I hoped they all found me worthy.

We saw my brother George every week or so when he was in town, but he was seldom home, alternating between the brickyard at Gulf Point and markets in both Louisiana and the southern wilderness of the Florida Territory, which he knew well having spent time both at Charlotte Harbor and in the Keys, those mysterious islands far to the south I heard so much about. George lay under a pall of sadness that his lovely Virginia-born wife, Martha, had died in Pensacola in September 1839. I had barely met her when she was struck down.

George was a great business help to Father, whose gout bothered him exceedingly by 1841. Brother George had become a stiffer, sterner man since the loss of his beloved Martha. Of course, we were bound

by family loyalty, but we had since youth been of different beliefs and
temperament while close in blood. He enjoyed traveling as a means
to fill otherwise empty days, seeking out the comforts of the Old
Dominion, our familiar Virginia of old, at every opportunity. Lonely
and having acquired enough fortune to acquire property in Virginia,
he returned to the Virginia of his youth, purchased a great plantation
known as Wood Park in Orange County not far from where Father
and Mother had started their marriage so many years ago.

I passed the time pleasantly at Father's house, but news from Achille
became less and less frequent as the months paraded by. With a lapse
of at least two months between his posting a letter until it reached
Pensacola, it could hardly be considered news anyway. A lonely wife, I
eagerly awaited each precious communiqué from my prince. I missed
my faraway husband so dearly that I read each letter so many times
that the worn and folded paper would become almost illegible.

My prince, questing after the so-called "greater job in Italy," had
fallen into his familiar role as a fantasist. I could sense it from certain
phrases he used in his infrequent letters. Of course the Murats all
had a penchant for intrigues and irrational dreams of grandeur but
Achille topped them all. His dreaming had expanded in relation to
his disappointments. What he could not achieve in the physical world,
he projected grandly into the world of imagination. I felt absolutely
certain that maintaining the illusion of royalty was how he dealt with
the rejections and failures of recent years in both the Florida Territory
and in Louisiana. If he were not to occupy the castles of a king, then
he would occupy castles in the air. And did. Realizing the depths of
his detachment from reality was a poignant moment for me but in no
way diminished my love for him.

Sometime about the one year anniversary of his flight to Italy, Achille
disappeared into oblivion. His letters stopped, and I had no way of
knowing what was behind this ominous trend. Had the Bonaparte
genes prodded him into yet another foray into politics? Was he deeply
into a clandestine plot? Was he in prison? Or was he simply deeply
mired in the hedonism of Florence's many pleasures, all funded with
his inheritance from Queen Caroline?

I never knew. Though I wondered, I never asked, and he never told.
Such a conversation might have opened a Pandora's box better left
alone. As long as he planned to come back to me, I need not be a

party to his personal life in Italy. It was not an easy choice for me, but it was imminently practical.

After some eighteen lonely months without him however, I had no choice but to contemplate a future without my prince. As I fell into a mode of thinking that I might well live out my days alone, I felt the ground shift beneath my feet. I had become so totally integrated into life with him that a future without him seemed an incomprehensible nightmare. There being nothing I could do about it, in order to protect myself, I began to plan for life in the American South alone. Through it all, I felt solidly grounded in my Southern heritage and the comforting reassurance of both Father's steadfast love and particularly my role as surrogate mother to Master Achille Murat Willis.

Fleetingly, I wondered if Achille and I became divorced or if I was simply abandoned, if I would still be considered a princess. It really didn't matter. Few used that honorific much anymore especially in the Florida Territory, but I had been flattered with the protocols of royalty in Europe. I suppose that American culture was and always would be opposed to the notion of royals in their midst. We had, after all, fought a revolution to rid ourselves of that. It was, I decided, not something to be concerned with as I had no voice in the matter. I surely didn't feel much like a princess anymore.

On a bright October day in 1841, when the humidity of summer had largely dissipated, Father took Mu and me by boat out to one of the forts he had built under orders from the national government in Washington. Fort McRee was situated at Foster's Bank on the eastern tip of the island known as Perdido Key just southwest of Pensacola. The odd three-tiered fort, occupied by a company of artillery and a company of infantry, was part of the defense of Pensacola Bay. It was not quite clear to me what threat existed, but millions of Father's bricks had been consumed here, and his slaves had been leased to the government for its construction. Contracts to build Fort McRee had provided the backbone of Father's financial recovery, though it was clearly a far cry from the golden days of Fredericksburg with its lavish balls, prominent social life, and the Jockey Club.

Fort McRee held tragic memories for all of the Willises, for it was here that my brother Lewis lost his life by drowning while trying to attend to one of Father's laborers. On that day when I visited the fort with Father and Little Mu, Mu insisted on wearing Achille's sword and proudly paraded himself before the soldiers. He was the same age at which Achille had scaled the cliffs of Capri with his father in an assault on the British. I could scarcely comprehend it for Mu was such a child. Tragically, he was not *my* child!

An Ocean Between Us, 1840-1841

CHRISTMAS OF 1840 slinked into the Willis household almost unnoticed. But for the excitement of Little Mu, it might not have happened at all. Achille had been gone for over a year and a half, his letters had stopped, and I had been sliding further down the hill of despair by the day. On Christmas Day, father insisted that we all attend traditional services at the pretty Christ Church on Seville Square in the old Spanish section of Pensacola. I had been lost in the wilderness of Achille's atheism and out of touch with the God of my youth; a subject of immense concern to father. When I allowed my denial of God to peek out of the dark corners of my mind, it troubled me too.

Father knew best. Attending services at Christmas proved a comforting re-immersion into the solace of familiar Episcopal liturgy; a re-connection with God I desperately needed. I hoped He would welcome me back into His flock.

Aside from spiritual renewal, I especially enjoyed that father was on one arm and Little Mu on the other when we entered the sanctuary. Without my husband for so long my widowed father and my young brother Mu had become the men in my life. It was they who filled my days, but the long nights remained disconsolately empty without Achille.

Catherine Willis Murat (Princess Kate) attended church services at Pensacola's Christ Church with her father, Pensacola businessman Byrd Charles Willis. Willis also served as agent of President Andrew Jackson at the Pensacola Navy Yard and helped construct forts around the harbor. Princess Murat made her home in Pensacola in 1839-41 while her husband settled the affairs of his deceased mother in Florence, Italy. Photo by the author.

As I knelt at the communion rail, I prayed that God would help me navigate the byways of loneliness which I had been experiencing while Achille pursued his goals . . . whatever they might be . . . in Italy. By this time one part of me almost didn't care. The other part however longed for the man I loved. I ached for his familiar smile, his gentle embrace, his ready wit, and the quirky but fulfilling dimension he had brought to my life. I was less than whole without him and it had taken a return to the faith to make me see that.

When oh when would my Achille return?

Would he return at all? Who knew! I tried to be resolute in the face of my doubts, but could not stop them from spilling out from time to time when wayward tears would appear at the corner of my eyes. Though I tried to hold these thoughts at bay, as a practical reality it now felt like I was the wife of no one and the princess of nowhere.

The calendar relentlessly turned and the new year of 1841 began with a celebration at the bay front home of the Barkleys, my favorite friends of fathers. I especially enjoyed the company of their daughter Clara who was only a few years younger than I. Clara had recently married a Mr. Vienne of New Orleans and their tender expressions of love on that New Years Eve forced me to think about my long-absent husband more than ever. I moped all evening immersed in self-indulgent sorrow for my long-absent husband. All I could think as the party swirled about me was how Achille would have loved the evening, for Mrs. Barkley was French and the conversation drifted, much as our social events in Europe had, in and out of several languages. At midnight the mistletoe was especially lonely. I had tried to fend off the desperation of self-pity but tonight I felt as flat and listless as a deflated balloon, allowing myself to wallow in the "poor me" syndrome. On the clip-clopping carriage ride back home, the fresh midnight air and glittering moon over the bay cleansed my muggy mood for a time, but as I readied myself for bed, the empty bed itself taunted me until sleep came.

The following week it seemed as if Achille had read my mind. After months of silence I received a letter in that familiar chicken-scratch handwriting of his . . . the first in five months. He wrote page after page of accounts of his frustrated efforts to secure the Murat fortune from King Louis Philippe of France. He praised the abortive *coup d etat* attempt by his cousin Louis Napoleon to overthrow the Louis Philippe monarchy. This was the same Louis Naploeon with whom we had spent such joyous time in London, Hortense's son. Like Achille, Louis Napoleon had not given up the notion that it was the God-given destiny of the Bonapartes to rule Europe, starting with France. Alas like Achille he lacked a sufficient political base for so lofty a goal.

After seven pages of news and some idle chatter toward the bottom of the letter, almost as an afterthought, Achille wrote the most wonderful news of all.

He was coming home! In the springtime! I shrieked and waved the letter around the kitchen with Bessie looking on as though I had lost my mind. In fact I had lost my mind with joy.

My excitement was such that father and I opened a bottle of champagne that night as a celebration of the survival of my marriage to a whirlwind named Charles Louis Napoleon Achille Murat, the Crown Prince of Naples. Our love had won out over *la dolce vita* of Italy and had defeated the powerfully nostalgic influence of his father King Murat's unfinished business.

After the surface conversation about Murat fortunes, Louis Napoleon's escapades, Queen Caroline's estate, and the luxuries of courtly life in Italy, my long-suppressed jealousies exploded. I took off my mask of bravado and finally admitted to myself and to father that it was really the threats of Europe's female suitors seeking to lure my prince away which had worried me most. But our love had won. I had won. The seductions of royalty and the supposed sophistications and courtiers of Europe had lost. Though just a simple southern girl, our love had won out over the many seductions which Europe had paraded before him. With the deepest of deep breaths, I sighed and turned toward the future.

At dinner that evening I felt like thumbing my nose at the marble bust of Uncle Napoleon which sat on the sideboard. I didn't need royalty, I needed my husband back and it was that conversation which animated our dinner table well into the night.

As a full moon rose over Pensacola Bay I took it as an omen of good fortune and for the first time in weeks relaxed enough to drift off to sleep with thoughts of love and the renewal of our interrupted life.

Before sleep came I focused intently on the moon, wondering if my beloved husband was looking at the same moon, having the same thoughts, feeling the same loneliness. Somehow it was comforting as I extended my arm with the palm of my hand toward the distant moon. I was reaching out to my distant Achille. It was a communion almost like touching him.

After so many lonely nights, with a feeling of contentment and security, I snuggled deeper under the covers with the thought that this was surely our private moon.

Reunited, 1841

WHEN BESSIE BROUGHT pancakes for breakfast one morning in March of 1841, I slathered them with molasses. It slowly clung to the rim of the pitcher as in slow motion, exactly like the calendar since learning of Achille's planned return. Though I had developed more spring in my step, lost a few pounds, which had come my way due to the bounty of Father's table and started attending church more regularly since his "I'm coming home letter," the weeks dragged mercilessly. Checking off the days on our calendar, while a comforting ritual, was also a daily reminder of just how slowly the days pass when one is eagerly awaiting an event. "Slow as molasses."

I could not dismiss the thought that it was the Episcopal God of my upbringing, who inhabited Christ Church down on Seville Square, who had personally answered my prayers. He would have my eternal thanks in return. Each Sunday in church, I felt privately but firmly chastised for drifting with my husband into the murky forests of atheism. Some days, it felt like God was personally scolding me. At times like that I solemnly swore that my faith had brought me through the ordeal of Achille's absence and that He would once more be honored as a pillar of my life as he had been in my youth.

Achille would be away almost exactly two years if his planned return took place as scheduled. I anxiously anticipated. The spring days dragged. And dragged. And dragged. I spent as much time as possible with my little brother Mu, for when Achille and I returned to Econchattie, Mu would remain in Pensacola with Father while the pseudomotherly role I had played for two years would slide away into the mists of memory. Inevitably, I would revert back to the less-important role of big sister.

Forever two things would stand out for me concerning my two years in Pensacola: being Mu's stand-in mother and keeping Father company during his protracted adjustment to the cruel world of life without his beloved wife. I felt renewed at having been useful as both devoted daughter and surrogate mother even though my primary roles as wife and princess had rusted away into insignificance.

My little brother Mu was now a precociously bright thirteen-year-old, and I adored him. He was a very expressive child and reciprocated my love in the touching manner of an emotionally needy young adolescent. Though Father loved him dearly, Mu clearly was in need of a female mother figure in his life, and I tried my best to fill that role.

The opportunity for me to play surrogate mother to him had filled some very deep psychological needs for us both as well as filling our daily lives with the simple joys of spending time together. In Pensacola, my loneliness had often gotten the better of me, but I had nevertheless tried my best to fill the large shoes that Mother left as a result of her untimely death. I prayed that she would approve of my ministrations in her name.

As I checked off days on the calendar until Achille's return, I was filled with both the twittery anticipation of a long-separated wife as well as, I must say, some trepidation. He had been away so long! During that time, he had been captive to all of the sophistication and royal attentions of a European prince and drinking deeply from the well of his Bonaparte and Murat past. I on the other hand had lived such a simple life with Father and my little brother in a small town on the Florida frontier, where the *Pensacola Gazette* still carried reports of nearby attacks by the Creek and Seminole Indians, and the biggest news was the arrival of a boat from nearby New Orleans.

My prince was now in his forties. How would he look? How would I look to him? When we returned to our small plantation of Econchattie near Tallahassee, how would it measure up to Queen Caroline's Florentine villa at which he had been living? How indeed would Tallahassee, Florida, and the United States look?

Daily, a wild carousel of thoughts and emotions spun in my brain until I was dizzied. Would there be the deep love we had known? Had his foray to the Continent remade him in ways I could never understand? We had no common base of memories for this two-year hiatus in our lives. Would there be enough commonality from which to rebuild our marriage? Would there be love? No love? Happiness? No happiness? Success. No success?

Satisfaction or . . . ?

Who, indeed, would he be, and how would we be?

Having dealt him failure after failure, how could the down-and-out Florida Territory hold a candle to his last few years in one of the world's most celebrated cities? The hub of Achille's world, despite the sadness of his mother's death, had been the refined city of Florence, home of the renaissance, center of art, culture, science, and a storied history filled with names such as Da Vinci, Medici, Michelangelo, and more. Though ostensibly a princess, I was actually just a Virginia girl impatiently passing the days with my father and brother, dressing in clothing I had made from old sheets. That I worried about a disconnect upon his return I believe is quite understandable.

In many respects, I had felt like a widow during the last two years, an emotional state into which I slumped when night after night his space in the bed remained empty and his pillow unruffled. *Widow*, I thought. *Geographic widow.*

It was an apt analogy. My husband would soon be returning, not from the dead but from the seductive abyss of pleasures that had surrounded him in Florence. His letters had been vague to say the least, but for an attractive forty-one-year-old prince alone in the exciting city, imagination easily ran rampant. Was I afraid of what I knew? Or was I afraid of what I didn't know?

As spring turned to summer of 1841, the long-awaited day finally arrived. I had lain awake most of the night, unable to calm my nerves, and I buzzed with a curious blend of excitement and trepidation. Not knowing the exact arrival time of his coach, we remained at home where I nervously paced the floor under the stony gaze of Uncle Napoléon's marble bust. As I waited, my fluttery combination of excited anticipation was tinged at the edges with a hint of apprehension. Where exactly did I fit into his life now?

I dreaded my own answer.

At half past three in the afternoon, Little Mu came enthusiastically bursting through the door with an early warning that Achille's carriage was at the head of the driveway. I had pulled my hair back severely as he liked it, and my ebony hair was pulled to a perfect widow's peak. *Appropriate,* I thought, *for this southern-belle-cum-widow for the last two years.* I walked out onto the shaded porch under the big oak tree and tried my best to look princesslike.

Faithful old William, Achille's manservant who had been with him for years, was turned out in Murat livery in honor of Achille's return, and took the reins of the carriage as it stopped on the oyster-shell drive. As the door opened, it was as though every lonely minute of the years had evaporated. Charles Louis Napoléon Achille Murat, my prince, alighted from the carriage and spoke only the word "Kate!" before pulling me tightly to him. Though he had come only from Italy, for me he looked as though he had come straight from heaven. Though he was slightly paunchier and moved more slowly, still his expressive eyes danced as they had in youth. Beneath the older exterior, those eyes and their puckish sparkle suggested that both his lively intelligence and his Mediterranean zest for life still smoldered within.

Or was I reading too much into the moment?

I scarcely knew how to respond and, as much as I had been eagerly awaiting this moment, stiffened in his arms. He looked much the same but had gained weight, no doubt from years of the indulgences of Italian food, and he now affected gray-flecked wings at the temples. Was I really married to this man? How did I feel to him? Had his arms held others while he was away for so long?

Sensing my unease, holding both of my hands, Achille stepped back and looked penetratingly into my eyes in a gesture both comforting and disquieting. The old Mediterranean machismo at that moment prompted him to fall upon both knees. It was vaguely reminiscent of that chivalrous moment so long ago when he had drunk from my slipper at a picnic in Tallahassee when his courtship commenced in earnest.

With a deep sigh, he half-said half-gasped, "Kate, I have missed you so terribly. The days have been long, but the nights longer. You must know the depths of my love, for I wished for you every lonely moment."

As for me, I had planned so much to say but was speechless in the tension of the moment.

Fine, I thought privately, with a slightly catty edge, *If you had asked, I could have come to you.* I let my sarcasm pass without voicing it, however, as William lumbered up the stairs with Achille's traveling valise.

I had rehearsed in my mind so many times our first few moments together, but nothing had prepared me for the awkwardness of it. Mu broke the electric moment with a child's question. "What did you bring me, sir?" How to address Achille had always been unclear to Mu. Calling him by his first name seemed too presumptuous and informal for a child to address the son of a king. At the other extreme, for a family member, prince was too stilted, so he had settled on the safe middle ground, sir.

"Mu, you will have some of my father the king's trinkets for now, and when you are old enough, you shall have a pistol which he carried at the Battle of Aboukir."

"A real pistol?"

"Yes, and one which saved his life in battle. May it protect you against all harm as it did for him," said Achille, reaching up to tousle Mu's hair.

At this, he realized that he was still kneeling and arose, stiffly and awkwardly, with a hand up from Mu.

"Hello then, my love," seemed to me a nice neutral phrase with which to restart our interrupted reunion and marriage. "Shall we go inside?" I took the crook of his elbow, and as William proudly held the door, we stepped across the threshold of the rest of our lives both literally and figuratively.

After a few minutes of idle chitchat, the tension began to melt away. Physical contact still seemed inappropriate, so we sat across from each other in Father's living room in a pair of new wing chairs upholstered in maroon velvet. The summer humidity of Pensacola soon urged Achille's jacket off, and as he placed it on a nearby table, I noticed a faint twitch of the sort I had come to recognize as a symptom of his nervous affliction.

"Are you all right, my dear?" I inquired.

"Quite, Kate, but I have been under enormous stress with the many family disputes over Mother's estate. Then I have had a series of unpleasant correspondence with Louis Philippe over the monies and lands. He sees me as still threatening his throne, though just how I would attain it is a mystery. In any case, I came home empty-handed. We have none of the Murat or Bonaparte money though Joseph is sitting on a horde of it, and I believe part of that should be ours. He will fight us for it though."

Just then, white-haired Bessie arrived with a tray of lukewarm lemonade. "Can't get no ice, mastah, and I sho' am sorry." For the special day of his homecoming, Bessie had proudly worn the Willis livery brought from Willis Hill and loving patched over the years. Her uniform seemed somehow symbolic. It stood for the formal elegance of a bygone era at the peak of Virginia society, yet it was a bit tatty and held together with various repair jobs over the ages. Like the Willis family.

So here we awkwardly sat, Achille and I, surrounded by the elegant contradictions of two different servants, wearing different liveries, representing two different families, from two different cultures, even two different nationalities, and in a still-primitive town on the Florida frontier. It struck me as emblematic of our strange and wonderful marriage. Completing the incongruity of the moment, the servants, who had served us for decades, all turned out in family formality of the past seemed a mocking anachronism. Perhaps Achille and I were both stuck in the past. We faced an uncertain financial future in which such finery seemed to rise to the ridiculous, but for today, it was a gesture of honor for my long-awaited husband.

At dusk, Father arrived from the navy yard driving the shay he now preferred over the larger coach and for which he had driven when we lived in Fredericksburg. The shay's one-horse rig was better suited to life in Pensacola where he lacked the huge acreage for grazing a large herd of dray animals. As was his habit, Father's shay was drawn not by a Percheron or other heavy work animal but by a sleek silky-black thoroughbred whose coat glistened like polished ebony.

Hugs and pleasantries of the sort that men affect between them consumed a good hour between Father and Achille, with more backslapping and laughter than had occurred in the Willis home for years. Father genuinely liked Achille, but no one quite knew if Achille's seemingly enthusiastic response was genuine or simply feigned, a well-acted part played to satisfy the demands of family politics.

Before the week was out, I set the help to packing my things for our return to Econchattie and the life that had been on hold for two years. Because of Indian attacks in the region, we planned to travel by boat between Pensacola and Saint Marks, the nearest port to Tallahassee on the Gulf of Mexico. Achille never unpacked his gear from the sojourn to Europe, and with my trunks now packed, we began a few social calls to begin the process of my exodus from the city, which had been my home for two years. Saying good-bye to the people who had supported me while I was a geographic widow was more difficult than I thought. There was a quality of genuineness here I had never felt in the social stratosphere of Europe.

Achille sent his manservant William ahead to Econchattie to have it readied for our arrival. Meanwhile, I tried as best I could to fill Achille in about events in the Tallahassee area as reported by friends and relatives. He, of course, inquired about our friends and neighbors: the Calls, Gadsdens, Nuttalls, Bellingers, Moores, and the Gambles. It was a mixed report. Scattered Indian attacks were on everyone's mind, the territorial legislature was in turmoil as usual, a long-sought move toward statehood seemed stymied, population was declining, the territory was flirting with insolvency, and the condition of Tallahassee's first bank, the Union Bank, was the most significant business development.

Having brought from Florence a bank order for $15,000, his share of Queen Caroline's estate, Achille planned to deposit the amount with the new bank except for a yet-specified portion with which to increase the number of slaves for the plantation. We had many overdue bills, which needed paying first, and I gulped but held my counsel as he laid out grand plans for our modest plantation's expansion. The Murat genes, as I had long pushed to the depths of my mind, tended to the grandiose in all things. It had gotten us in trouble in Louisiana, and I hoped that the same fate would not overtake us again once more.

My love for my husband was deep and abiding, and having weathered the two-year uncertainty of his flight to Italy, I now felt more strongly than ever. My worries now were not about Achille succumbing to the seductions of Florence or its temptations of the flesh but of our ability to reconstruct a future of substance using the inheritance as wisely as possible. It was clear now that King Louis Philippe of France had no intention of relinquishing control over the Murat assets seized after Joachim and Caroline's betrayal of the emperor. Further exacerbating the problem, Uncle Joseph had made it equally obvious that the $400,000 entrusted to him by Napoléon would remain under his personal control and not divided among the scattered remains of the Bonaparte family.

We would have to make it on our own or not at all.

I knew we would survive, but since marrying my prince I had harbored hopes that a more comfortable lifestyle would be our lot. Except for a brief period when we lived above our means, so far it had not. Princely wealth had not accompanied his princely title. Our marriage was rich in love, adventure, and memory but not in the financial sense.

My dear husband had eagerly immigrated to the United States, full of confidence in both America and himself. He had arrived with a blank slate upon which the fates, his impetuous nature, the financial crash of the mid-1830s, and perhaps a misunderstanding of the American business world had written the sobering word *failure*. We were both demoralized, but our marriage survived even if his investments had not. Our drastically altered financial position hit Achille, the child of limitless wealth, especially hard. With his return from Italy, the fires of the old Murat passion were now only charred ashes of unfulfilled destiny.

I felt especially deeply for Achille during these first months back in America. I knew in the very depths of my being that his heart was mortally wounded by the litany of failures, which reached back over many years and now robbed him of any sense of purpose or accomplishment. My dreamer was now bereft of dreams. In my darker moments, I even wondered if his many disappointments had driven him to the brink of madness as I watched in dismay as his self-esteem imploded on him. Poor Achille was now struggling both physically and emotionally.

These were the most bittersweet of times. Though it was wonderful to be together again, Achille was a changed man, and I knew that somehow things would never be the same again. The sun had set on Achille's dreams of power and wealth. All that was left now was the shriveled and dried detritus of once-lofty ambition, blown away by the winds of fate. The brilliant visions and ambitions, which once inhabited his imagination, were now only twisted parodies of what might have been.

Tragically for both of us, his track record as a planter and investor left something to be desired. I thus tried to quietly influence him to spend our newfound funds more judiciously while adjusting my own expectations to the new reality. As I had aged, I harbored fewer of the illusions with which I had started married life with him. Most of those illusions had been thrown overboard during our financially disastrous time in Louisiana, swept down the muddy Mississippi along with most of our assets.

My new attitude had nothing to do with love and everything to do with the practicalities of life and preparing for the eventual rigors of old age. We might be still officially prince and princess, but the endless wealth with which Achille had been raised was now a thing of the past. Achille was having a hard time dealing with that inconvenient fact and seemed somehow a harder and more withdrawn man, quite different from the ebullient optimist of fifteen years ago. I suspected that his proud dignity had evaporated with the rest of his dreams.

I wondered if it was that optimism that had brought him to this point by causing him to charge into venture after venture without fully considering the consequences. On top of his string of business failures, the once-supportive family now shunned Achille with devastating consequence. His uncle Joseph firmly slammed the door on that portion of a $400,000 inheritance from Emperor Napoléon, which he believed was his due. It had been originally intended for Napoléon's son, the so-called King of Rome, but upon his death, Joseph diverted it to his own purposes and the detriment of other Bonapartes. Finally, the death of Achille's mother put the final nail in the coffin of empire and any residual wealth for which he had hoped. For the royal son, the crown prince, the child of luxury and privilege, these were hard times indeed. Adjustment to primitive plantation life in the North Florida wilderness promised to be a rocky road. Starting over at Econchattie meant that we would be threadbare.

But we couldn't delay any longer. Econchattie and our American life would have to fill the bill for us both. It had been a privilege to aid my devoted father during my two years in Pensacola and to experience firsthand the joys of motherhood even if the child was my younger brother, not my biological son. Now, however, it was time to get on with life.

For Better or For Worse. Our Florida Home, Mid-1840s

*T*HE SHORT TRIP by steam packet from Pensacola to Saint Marks south of Tallahassee was marked by fair weather and the accompaniment of hundreds of dolphins, which led us into the bay all the way up to the dock. Forever the optimist, I took both as omens of good luck as we turned to the next phase of our lives.

After a night at a portside boarding house, a hired wagon took us northward toward our beloved Econchattie outside Tallahassee. The cloying humidity of a summer afternoon was almost tangible. The rasp of cicadas was muted by the heavy air while billowing thunderheads rose like cotton palaces toward the blue-black sky. As we turned into our gate under a drenching thunderstorm, once again the stark contrast of our life together was made real; just when you think it will turn for the better, a new storm will arise. This was the story of the elder Murats, it was surely our story, and perhaps I should reconsider omens.

Unlike the return to Lipona a few years ago, even in the rain Econchattie looked in splendid condition, having been lovingly tended during our absence by my sister Attie and her husband Samuel Duval. We had brought fresh seafood from the coast and enjoyed an oyster feast with them before they set out for their own home. Thoughtful Achille had brought for them several gifts of the gilded woodwork for which Florence is famous and some of the softest leather goods I have ever felt.

As their wagon pulled away at sunset, Achille and I were now alone, replanted in the world of the Florida frontier with all of its promise, hardships, and overhanging legacy of failures. It was then that the blunt reality of our situation dawned like a gunshot upon Achille.

His father, King Joachim, was long dead. His mother, Queen Caroline, was recently dead and buried. His illustrious deceased Uncle Napoléon was now widely derided in newspapers and periodicals as having been nothing more than a bloodthirsty egotist who sucked the life and treasure from Europe for personal gain. The supposed Bonaparte mystique was now ridiculed and largely depicted as a cruel myth. As a result of the flood of anti-Bonaparte books and periodicals, a stench now attached to the name of Napoléon Bonaparte and his dynasty of hangers-on. For the nephew of the emperor raised amidst Napoleonic glories, this was a crushing load to bear. The Bonapartes, as it turned out, were not immortal after all.

Even Uncle Joseph, Achille's other Bonaparte uncle, had slammed the door on any Napoleonic inheritance. It was this cold dose of reality that created the somber mood for our first month at Econchattie. Rather than the excitement we had craved, it was one of depression, and it twice set off Achille's nervous fits, now exacerbated with a new favorite drink, whiskey and milk. In hindsight, I now understand that it was his way of numbing the pain, but it befogged the stern reality of life for him and on occasion left me without a coherent partner in navigating our way back to financial stability.

With icy clarity, Achille now understood that the family was no longer a resource to him and that no one gave a damn about his former pretentious title as the crown prince of Naples. Uncle Napoléon, to whom he was once a potential heir apparent, was now portrayed as a villain rather than a world-changing leader, and the criticism stung Achille like a lash whenever it surfaced in conversation or in the press. Against the long-standing Bonaparte tradition that family came first and would always take care of its own, the collapse of family relations was the cruelest cut of all. I pretended that none of this was of consequence, tried to forget that I was a princess somewhere in the now-defunct Bonaparte constellation, and confined my activity to working quietly at improvements in both Econchattie and our finances.

Despite it all, I nudged us toward incremental improvements at Econchattie. With funds from his inheritance, Achille added to our holding of slaves, which made possible an efficient farming operation, and we soon planted, harvested, and made tidy profits from seasonal cotton and sugar crops. Immodestly, I believe that my influence helped to stabilize our precarious economic posture, and without Achille's knowledge, I commenced to slowly pay down some of our overwhelming obligations.

Though we were still in debt, I tried valiantly to reconstitute our once vibrant social life. Our lifestyle at first seemed to take a turn for the better when we once more attempted to get into the swing of Tallahassee society. Though at a much reduced level from the galas we once hosted, we sought to wedge our way back into the social circles which had once celebrated our royal status.

For a time, I was quite put off and had difficulty understanding why some of our old acquaintances seemed to hold us at arm's length. Through a combination of private confidences and widespread rumor, I learned that Achille's eccentricities had become so bizarre as to cause them concern, if not outright discomfort, a revelation which had to remain locked within for fear of further shattering his frail ego.

Clearly, we were no longer the darlings of society. Rather, Achille's business failures had become legendary, and his personality quirks the butt of scurrilous tales and coarse territorial humor. His dress became increasingly unkempt, and soon even his manner devolved into a vulgar pantomime of the prince of bygone years.

In addition, the once-proud and optimistic Achille Murat, who had perceived himself as leader of a worldwide political nation and a global voice for freedom and democracy, was relegated to insignificance all the way from Tallahassee to the throne rooms of Europe. I can scarcely find words adequate to describe the change in his demeanor and personality as he withdrew into the deep recesses of depression and drink to hide from the world.

The psychological effect of his depression soon took a physical toll. His seizures became more frequent and severe. His moodiness often led to overindulgence of his new favorite of whiskey and milk, leading to many nights of incoherent babble over lost fortunes, titles, and power until he passed out. In these moments, angry words, dammed up for years behind a polite social facade, flooded forth in confused torrents of English, French, and Italian as though the verbal catharsis would change anything. Of course, it could not and did not. In the quiet that followed these emotional maelstroms, I worried deeply that my beloved husband was losing touch with reality.

Though our marriage continued to be a source of joy and strength for me most of the time, there were some trying times in this era. Even in the best of times when Achille was totally sober and unaffected by the physical symptoms of his seizures, our happy banter of yesteryear seemed suffocated under a gray melancholy as though the sun had gone behind a cloud. Though he professed his undying love for me daily, it seemed more an echo of the happiness of youth rather than a reassuring validation of the moment. He seemed suspended somewhere between our glittering past and the moribund present, never quite fully here in the moment. Introspectively, I was forced to admit that though we were both in our forties, autumn had come to our lives, and the winds of winter howled just outside.

I was saddened that Achille had given up his dreams and had little to live for except riding herd on our cattle as they foraged the North Florida woods. Some days when he scoured the forests on horseback searching for wayward cattle, I would accompany him in jodhpurs and ratcatcher pretending to be out for a canter across the Virginia hills of my youth. As I look back now, I see these poignant days for what they really were, a mental voyage back to a happier time. It was escapism pure and simple.

In thoughtful moments after Achille had passed out from drink at night, I gave in frequently to the magic carpet of the mind, indulging in sweet reveries of our courtship and our lives of fantasy. Alas, these reveries of mine were but wistful echoes of a bygone era and a far cry from our diminished lives on America's southern frontier.

In addition to moping about in silent humiliation, my prince was wasting away before my eyes. During this adjustment to our new reality, it struck me that his acute and well-developed mind was shriveling up for want of anything more intellectual than hunting down a recalcitrant old bull in the south forty. He rarely spoke of abstract theories of government or his perceptive insights of America. He never again wrote intellectual treatises or sharply descriptive letters to his friend Count Thibedeau and his publishing days were over. Sad. Knowing that his energetic mind needed stimulation and that he needed something to restore lost self-confidence, I urged him to reread some of his own extraordinary works. I pulled out beautiful leather-bound copies of *"Exposition des principes du gouvernement republicain tel qu'il a ete perfectionne en Amerique"* (He had written this in both in French and German.); *"Esquisses morales et politques sur les Etats-Unis d'Amerique, Lettres d'un citoyen des Etats-Unis a ses amis d'Europe,"* written in French; *"A Moral and Political Sketch of the United States of North America; With a Note on Negro Slavery"*; and *"The United States of North America"* (written in English); *"Daretellung der Grundsatze der Republikanischen Regierung,"* written in German; and *"Brieven,"* written in Dutch. These important treatises my Achille had written a decade before now appeared in over thirty editions, were translated into many other languages, and had become the bible of the democratic movement in Europe.

His able mind grasped the significance of his contributions to the political thought of the day and began to wean him away from his evenings of stiff drink. Often, I would find him, book in hand, beside a whale-oil lamp in our sitting room deep in reminiscence, a half smile upon his handsome face. The sorrow for us both was that such intelligence was now, both literally and figuratively, lost in the wilderness.

When daybreak's soft colors flushed the North Florida woods, he could often be found still reading but would then yawn and turn to the practical realities of plantation life. A priority for Achille was to reconstitute our scattered herd of cattle, a task he frequently undertook alone despite the discomfort of his gout and assorted physical ailments of aging. Often he would be gone for days at a time, and I suspected that the solitude of the pine barrens gave him private time to ponder his life and its many accomplishments and disappointments. As well as time for reflection, his forays into the wilderness provided an escape from the discomfort of depression and social rejection he now felt so acutely. Week after week, I would supervise the work of the plantations while Achille rode off in brooding isolation, mentally mired in a toxic mix of disappointment, sorrow, and the Greek tragedy of his collapsed life. He would return in hard-worn clothing and battered boots, wearing a silly little hat of woven palm fronds and a corncob pipe stuck in his mouth where a fine-carved meerschaum once resided. Was this the man who was once touted as heir apparent to the great Napoléon? The almost king of Belgium? The heir to the kingdom of Naples?

That his already-tenuous emotional state frayed at the edges is completely understandable. The wonder is that he was not stark-raving mad.

Through it all, I made every effort to retain the Southern-belle composure and manners of my Virginia upbringing. Despite having lost my beloved mother to a virulent attack of yellow fever in Pensacola in 1834, her memory remained a calming and persistent presence in my life. The genteel qualities I had learned at her knee had stood me in good stead from royal coronations all the way to rough-and-tumble Tallahassee.

Indian problems in the Florida Territory resumed the ferocity we had known earlier. Ever since Andrew Jackson's edict for their removal throughout the 1830s and now into 1843, Seminoles, some Creeks, a southern tribe known as the Mikasukis, and the Muscogees in our area raided isolated farms, ambushed travelers, and occasionally fought pitched battles with army forces. For reasons I never fully understood, the local chief, Tiger Tail, promised us security and pledged to Achille that he would not hurt Murat's squaw. I, of course, was the "Murat's squaw" of which he spoke but felt only haltingly secure under this promise of safety. The sorry litany of broken promises between white man and Indian, both ways, left me wondering when the next violation would occur. Stories of cruelty and midnight bloodletting by both sides fueled a paranoia among settlers. A siege mentality began to evolve, and plantation owners grouped together at night for mutual security.

Our slaves, though largely loyal and hardworking, were subject to increasing bombardment of news and propaganda from abolitionist rabble-rousers who had drifted south from their poisonous nests in the north. Naturally, we chafed at this disturbance of our neighborhood and throughout the plantation-based economy of the South. Malaise now poisoned our plantation help, and in the year 1841-42, eight of our slaves ran away to join insurgent Indian bands and were never heard from again. As before, Achille's disciplinary tendency with our slaves was far harsher than my own and soon became a source of friction between us. I chose to hold my own counsel on the matter to prevent a family argument, which could never be won.

Privileged child of generations of plantation owners that I was,
I was no abolitionist but saw the handwriting on the wall that the
institution of slavery was doomed. Good. It had never been justifiable
from the beginning of the republic but, for want of a solution that
would satisfy all parties, had been swept under the rug by generation
after generation. In this belief, I was the realist while Achille clung
stubbornly to his proslavery views, which had their origins in his
privileged and royal upbringing where unlimited servants were de
rigueur.

Much of our disagreement over slavery was a matter of perception. I
understood completely the need for a large agrarian workforce for the
South's plantation economy and that this role was filled by Africans
forcibly relocated to America. The difference was that I saw them as a
workforce of essential helpers with human emotions while Achille saw
them as mindless chattels to be owned, bought, and sold. I continue
to believe that fair and honest treatment and the satisfaction of their
needs for shelter, food, and clothing produce both loyalty and willing
labor for our fields while Achille and most slave owners resorted to
severe discipline enforced by the lash.

Achille was akin to other plantation owners who sought to alleviate
their consciences with tortured logic and opinions masquerading as
fact. For example, he once wrote to Count Thibedeau that "if slavery,
in political economy facilitates the population of our Southern states,
its effect on society is not less disadvantageous. The planter, released
from all manual labor, has much more time to cultivate his mind. The
habit of considering himself as morally responsible for the condition
of a great number of individuals gives to his character a sort of austere
dignity favorable to virtue, and which tempered by arts, sciences, and
literature contribute to make the Southern planter one of the most
perfect models of the human race. His house is open to every comer
with a generous hospitality; his purse is too often equally so, even to
profusion. The habit of being obeyed gives him a noble pride in his
intercourse with his equals, that is to say, with any white man, and an
independence of views in politics and religion, which form a perfect
contrast with the reserve and hypocrisy to be met with but too often
in the north. To his slaves, he is a father rather than a master, for he
is too strong to be cruel."

Under the lash after fourteen-hour days in the field for month after
endless month, I could only wonder how our hands felt, and if they

shared Achille's enthusiasm that their enslavement provided dignity to the master, while their labors freed the master to cultivate his mind. As I aged, I simply saw such expositions by slave owners as so much poppycock.

There is no way that slavery can be rationalized with the elegant rhetoric of my forebears who established this nation on the principal that "all men are created equal." Having said that, more than a hundred slaves continued to serve us, and I reluctantly, as a matter of practical economics, had to side with the slave-owning South in the great debates that raged about as the 1840s wore on.

Who was the greater hypocrite I wondered, Achille or me?

We muddled along through the mid-1840s, slowly urging our plantations along the painful path from liabilities to assets. Visits to Father in Pensacola revealed that though he had achieved the restoration of a measure of wealth due to his Pensacola brickyard ventures and contracts for building Pensacola's forts, life in his mid-sixties provided little true satisfaction. He never regained his joie de vivre after Mother's death, and while financial success smiled upon him, I sensed that he was just going through the motions of life, not really living but putting on a grand front for Pensacola society. It did not surprise me when he announced that he would leave Pensacola and the life he had created there in order to return to his beloved Virginia. Brother George had provided the final motivation for this move when he purchased a grand plantation at Wood Park, Virginia, and once more donned the mantle of the Virginia squire. My father, the aging lion of the Old Dominion, would similarly return to the comforts of old and familiar haunts of his youth to live out his days. It was sad for me but a comfort for Father that my young brother Achille Murat Willis, now nineteen, chose to remain with Father, and he too abandoned life in the Florida Territory to apprentice for the first time the role of Virginia gentleman played so convincingly by so many of his forebears. In 1846, my father, who epitomized the Virginia squire, passed away to spend his eternity atop his beloved Willis Hill overlooking the City of Fredericksburg.

For Father, young Achille Murat Willis, and for brother George, Florida had been but a way stop. To be sure, it was an important one of decades' duration, but Virginia was so ingrained in the Willis family that it won out over the lure of the southern frontier. Sister Mary Byrd

Willis had found her soul mate in Florida and became an important fixture on the arm of her successful husband at the Pensacola Navy Yard, Commodore A. J. Dallas. Sister Attie, remained in Tallahassee near Econchattie, but we rarely saw her. Brothers Lewis and John had died in Florida and now lay under her rich soils in final peace. Florida was struggling into the sunlight of American democracy after the dreadful financial crises of the late 1830s, and we were playing our small roles in it.

A huge and long-standing goal of Achille's was attained in 1845 when Florida became the twenty-seventh state of the Union. I was flattered when we were asked to attend the celebration. As the proclamation was read at the statehouse, this daughter of democracy, reared in Virginia in the traditions of the nation's founders, stirred with pride that the American experiment begun so many years before by my own forebears was indeed flourishing. We welcomed Florida to the Union, and it was a moving experience.

And as for me, in Florida I had found my prince, and from Florida had launched, lived, and lost a life of glamour and adventure. As we struggled through the mid-1840s together, Achille and I were content that we had planted our flag on America's southern frontier, and it was forever and ever my home.

Farewell, My Prince, 1846-47

RHEUMATISM AND GOUT plagued Achille increasingly through-out late 1846. There seemed to be no relief from pain for him, and by Christmas, his life had morphed into one of quiet desperation. Not even visits from occasional well-wishers seemed to lift his spirits. In his discomfort, there now seemed a deliberate look over his shoulder and a posturing of the courtly speech, manner, and protocols of old. I believed this innocent facade to be a conscious nod to the royalty of his youth and his way of saying "I am a still a prince."

By February 1847, he was bedridden twenty-four hours a day, the color was gone from his ashen face, and the sparkle of his Mediterranean eyes gave way to a vague focus on what seemed a thousand miles away. I think his focus was indeed on a past now many thousand miles away, in Paris, in Naples, and in a bygone world long disappeared from the world scene. I instinctively knew that the grimaces, which crossed his countenance, were as much psychological pain as physical pain. We both knew that the life that had seemed one of inexhaustible promise had failed to materialize. It was a hard pill to swallow.

Bonaparte fame, Murat wealth, and fancy titles counted for nothing here on the Florida frontier, but as I consoled him with hours of quiet nostalgic conversation, I kept up a facade of long-lost grandeur and stoked his illusion of hope. I swore a dozen times that I would undertake his lifelong effort to unfreeze the confiscated Murat millions from the French crown of Louis Philippe, redeem the family's sullied reputation, and burnish the name of Murat for posterity. I had no idea that my petitions to Louis Philippe would come to anything, but I could not let Achille down, and the promises that I made seemed to buoy his mood but cost me nothing.

Achille's manservant of years ago, old William (who had no idea when he was born, but I guessed to be about seventy now), sat with Achille every moment I could not. He emptied bedpans, brought soup, massaged his back, changed soiled bed linens, and to the end was as devoted to my husband as I was. I was glad that he could not read so that Achille's pejorative view of blacks remained forever out of sight.

In April 1847, I think it was about the fifth, William tapped gently on my boudoir door around midnight. "You bettah come, Miss Kate, he askin' fo' yah." With a lump in my throat and silent tears cascading down my cheeks, I took my candle to Achille's bedside where, wordlessly and without a sound, reached he for my hand. In the silence of the wilderness night, punctuated by the plaintive call of a whip-poor-will, he pressed the flat of my palm against his cheek and drifted off into a sleep so deep that he didn't awaken at all the next day.

By the tenth, he alternated between shivering cold and a pervasive dry, hot fever. Much of his speech, though in a whispered voice, fell out in jumbles of French and Italian, though when he would open his eyes and with great effort focus on me, he snapped back into his accented English.

"Tell my younger brother Lucien that he will become the dauphin, the crown prince, when I am gone. He must uphold the family's honor and serve our father's memory with dignity and pride. Make him promise to continue to work for the overthrow Louis Philippe. Urge him to revise the history books, which now treat our father, Joachim, so harshly. Murat is an honorable name, not the butt of some author's evil idea of dishonoring our glory and fame."

I began to see that he had accepted the inevitability of what now appeared imminent and that he was trying to achieve in death the things he left unaccomplished in life. In a voice grown increasingly raspy, more like breaths than words, he told me tales of his palatial boyhood in Paris and Naples and happy times at the family's seaside palazzo at Positano.

Achille's calm demeanor was marvelously reassuring to me. If there was even a trace dread of the hereafter, he hid it carefully, no doubt to alleviate my natural spousal worry. I knew he was possessed of a powerful persona, but his strength enabled a positive atmosphere at Econchattie though we all knew that the end was nigh. The bravery of his father Joachim was obviously manifest in the son. Both were able to stoically scoff at the face of impending death.

I cried alone in my room with dread that if Achille remained an atheist until the end, even a merciful God might lock him out of the gates of heaven. I could not visit in my worst nightmares the vision of my soul mate burning forever in the fires of hell. Fingering the little gold crucifix around my neck, I privately pleaded with God that he would forgive my husband for his vanity and reminded the Almighty of Achille's beliefs in the nobility of each human being and the right of every man to determine his destiny. In prayerful desperation, I hoped that by reminding God of Achille's views on the dignity of man, this might trump his atheism and earn him at the eleventh hour a dispensation and a place among the saints.

At such deeply religious moments, Achille's denigration of blacks and his vehement defense of slavery came awkwardly crashing into my mind. I hurriedly skipped over those inconvenient thoughts just as the founders of America and generations thereafter had done. Were all men indeed created equal? Were our slaves entitled to life, liberty, and the pursuit of happiness?

Could God forgive the discord of slavery or Achille's defense of it? Even as he teetered on the brink of eternity, the question remained too difficult to confront. In my cowardly haste to dismiss those inconvenient thoughts, I hurriedly skipped over them as had my ancestors, prominent early settlers of America. It was a topic more easily procrastinated than solved.

William once again summoned me in the depths of night to respond to a whimper from Achille. In the dim light, he looked better this time, and I was momentarily encouraged that his condition might be improving. He boldly spoke of the Bonapartes' belief in their privileged position in God's hierarchy, an inherited arrogance more wish than reality. He spoke like a lonely little boy of his love for his mother and father. He spoke nostalgically about all that he had accomplished and all that remained to be done.

With eyes closed and hands folded across his chest, he spoke of destiny and his quest for the meaning of his life. Achille, I knew, had spent his entire life searching for and fretting about his destiny.

I remained silent and let him ramble, for it was clear that he had things to say before God's chariot called for him. I hoped that he was at peace that his destiny had not been in Naples. It had not been in Paris. In Brussels. His destiny had not been fame. Or riches. Or glory.

Achille's destiny had been the love he shared with this Virginia-born girl here amid the simple blessings of America. It was my prayer in this moment that this was destiny enough for him.

From all corners of his mind, he spoke with perfect recall and crystal clarity of the amazing life adventures we had shared, the Prince and Princess Murat. And then in a moment of finality, he spoke of love, uttering words forever emblazoned on my heart.

"Farewell, Kate, my dear good wife, you have been the sunshine of my life."

And with a sigh, closed his eyes and went forth into that unknown place from which we all emanate and to which we all return.

Son of a king and queen, nephew of the most powerful man on earth, and a crown prince in his own right, Charles Louis Napoléon Achille Murat did not die of any identifiable disease or malady. My prince died from having lived, and he lived as fully as is humanly possible.

Deaths Aftermath, 1847

*F*OR THE REST of the night and into the next day, I was completely disconsolate and unable to comprehend the incomprehensible. I consulted a worn calendar, and it was only then that I learned that my husband, the first Bonaparte to die in America, had quietly and without evident pain eased from this earth to God's dominion on April 15, 1847. As though time mattered.

When I could bear it, I returned to the bed where he lay frozen in the moment of his passing and laid upon his chest a yellow rose from my garden. Like me, its roots were in Virginia, but it too had weathered the Bellamy Road, storm and squall, drought and good times, but just in my hour of need, it had found the courage to bloom here on America's southern frontier. I somehow found it consoling; perhaps a sign from God that life and beauty would prevail even in tragedy.

I next sent four servants on horseback to the neighboring plantations of friends who needed to know of Achille's passing. The first to respond was Colonel Robert Gamble, who thankfully took over the mournful affairs of Achille's final arrangements. As Achille had desired, the body was straightaway removed to the Gamble residence where the Andrew Jackson Lodge of Masons lifted from me the sad burden of handling funeral details. The thought fleetingly crossed my mind that in death the religious overtones of the Masons were a silent concession from my proud atheistic husband that there just might be a God after all, and that perhaps the two of them should mend fences.

Having in his last years retreated into the quirky side of his personality, the death notice in the Tallahassee *Floridian* snidely commented that Achille was a "man of great eccentricity of character." He remained misunderstood in death as he had been in life. It went on to partially redeem itself by acknowledging that he was "gifted with a high order of mind which was enriched by solid literary accomplishments."

Though Achille had by naturalization become a proud American, no other American news reports so much as acknowledged the life or death of my Napoleonic prince. Thus slighted, I vowed then that I would insure that his extraordinary life would not be forgotten. I could do no less for him as a small recompense for the incredible life he had given me. The catty introduction of his obituary notice prompted me to dedicate my life to restoring the reputation my royal husband had once held but which, like the clothing he wore during his final years, had become a bit tatty.

For the most part, Achille had been better and more accurately known in Europe than he was in America. Though he was indeed a man of eccentricity, he was, first and foremost, a man of intellect and character. From that, he never wavered. He was withal a cyclone of brilliance with whom the common man could not keep pace. Those who knew him best knew that his so-called eccentricities were merely his way of approaching life from an unconventional direction.

Of those who knew him best, I knew him best of all. I would set the record straight!

From the Masonic Lodge, on a lovely spring day filled with the promise of earth's rebirth, a small coterie of friends followed the casket to the graveyard of St. John's Episcopal Church, Tallahassee. Burial there, in the company of believers, was yet another bow of my stubborn atheist to the deity whom he had refused in life.

William and about forty of our slaves followed respectfully at a distance, but their weeping could be heard above the intonations of the service. There seemed a unique authenticity to their grief while some of the townspeople who came for pro forma reasons seemed to treat Achille's funeral as a social occasion.

Curiously and without comment, I noted that several Seminoles also came to pay final respects to the man they regarded as a white man's chief of some sort. I briefly wondered if they understood any of the Episcopal ritual but dropped the thought when I realized that even I had trouble fathoming the concept of resurrection of the body and ascension into heaven.

I nonetheless took deep personal comfort from the service that laid my Achille to rest among God's faithful. The arcane ritual of the Mason's passed over my head, but my abiding faith in God and the familiar words of the Book of Common Prayer gave me a calm reassurance. Though Achille had disavowed the church in life, I prayed that my Episcopal beliefs were not misplaced and that my beloved husband now looked down upon us in renewed life.

Because Achille's love for his gallant father Joachim was so deeply ingrained, I hoped in my Christian soul that the two of them were at last reunited. Among the well-wishers at the service, I suspect that I was the only one who understood the depth of Achille's lifelong insecurity that he had not measured up to his famous father.

Whether other Bonapartes were plucking harps in heaven with Achille was an open question for me. It was difficult to rationalize since Uncle Napoléon had sent millions to bloody deaths in his quest for glory.

And so it was that when the mourners had left, when the tears had dried, I allowed myself to wander down the lonely halls of memory. What fates, I pondered, had collaborated to bring together in the unlikeliest of places a girl of old Virginia aristocracy with a quixotic prince of Bonaparte ancestry? Was it a match made in heaven or was our unlikely pairing an expression of the muses quirky sense of humor.

In the still of the night I realized that the more I knew the less I understood.

What I did understand to the depths of my being was that the curious interplay of my life with Achille had woven a tapestry of such richness that I would never be the same without him. The warp without the woof was incomplete.

I some respects I decided that our life together had been as one of his scientific experiments. Take two different ingredients, add a dash of this, a dab of that, stirred together to produce an unpredictable result. Forged in the crucible of life, our love had evolved through many stages; attraction, romance, novelty, excitement, pain, pleasure, struggle, sadness, indescribable joy, and finally a foretaste of the contentment of aging together. But just when we had reached that stage, my soul mate was gone too soon.

Achille had blazed across my life and the night sky like the meteor shower we had once observed, leaving me alone in the quiet to make sense of it all. Mankind's age-old questions whispered incessantly to me as I tossed and turned. As I lay alone in the bed we had shared, relentlessly voices as old as mankind itself turned over and over in my mind.

Where was Achille now? Exactly what is heaven? How did resurrection feel? Did he feel at all? Were there indeed angels and archangels? Cherubim and seraphim? Was Achille with God? What did God look like? Was he now with Joachim? Caroline? Could he talk with God?

The envelope of a body, which we had just committed to the ground, was not him; it was only the vehicle for him to make his presence here on earth known. This was a question as old as man himself and one which ultimately every one of us must answer for themselves.

In the silent satisfaction and security of my renewed Christian faith, I surely felt that my Achille could talk with *me*, as if to affirm the love we had shared. Perhaps it was just a wish, but in my overloaded whirl of thoughts and feelings, I think I heard him tell me that "it's all right, Kate. I am with God now."

By 3:00 AM, the only way that sleep would come was simply to turn my questions and my grief over to God. Once I did so, my burdens were lifted, and I slept until noon the next day.

In the weeks that followed, my younger sister Attie, married to Samuel Duval and living nearby, moved to my guest quarters at Econchattie, and I can scarcely describe the comfort she provided in the dark aftermath of Achille's death. Her support took many forms, but the most important was simply being a loving family presence in my life, which would have otherwise been unbearably desolate. I had never experienced being all alone, but now my prospects for the future appeared a long and solitary road to where?

It was premature to forecast how my life would evolve, so I just took it day by day with Attie's help and the visits of friends, who for weeks called solicitously, often bringing food from their kitchens and scuppernong wine from their vineyards. Especially touching for me, even my slaves, who had so little, brought fish caught from nearby creeks and simple dishes from their meager kitchens. The generosity that was baked into them made them so tasty that they would have done the royal kitchens of Europe proud.

The realities of settling in to life without Achille arrived abruptly when Attie's own family drew her back, leaving me now isolated and facing the administrative details of closing out his life efficiently and honorably. His will provided that I was to receive our Econchattie Plantation, sixty slaves, and assorted cattle, goats, a dozen horses, our carriage, three farm wagons, and assorted farm equipment. It seemed a reasonable distribution of assets with which to scratch out a living, for it was all we had left after the Louisiana debacle. Fortified with enough assets with which to live out my days, my sunny disposition, which had been in hiding since his death, made its first appearance.

Then the bills and debts began to arrive.

Achille's inattention to business details had haunted us for nearly two decades and nearly bankrupted him. A profligate spender, despite his prodigious intellect, he had no common sense whatsoever of how to alleviate the pall of debt that had hung over us since Louisiana. My life's work was cut out for me.

Thus motivated by anxiety, I set about to shepherd the assets with which I would have to support myself for the rest of my life and turned my full attentions to managing Econchattie. Determined not to make the same mistakes of my late husband, I sought advice from successful planters, placed every square inch into sugarcane, and before my first winter as a planter was out, was receiving accolades (and money!) for Econchattie's sugar production. Not only was this pleasing to me, but also it enabled me to nibble away at the mountain of Achille's debt, which I had received along with his assets.

Though it wasn't initially a priority for me, as a member by marriage of the extended Bonaparte family, within a few months of his death a unique issue of protocol arose. As an American whose royal connections were attained long ago in name only at the time I married Achille, I wondered if there were rules, restrictions, or expectations for the widow of a deceased prince of the blood. Though few in Tallahassee still addressed me as princess, I sometimes felt an undercurrent in the community, which never quite knew how to regard me and which questioned if was any reality to rumors of my supposed royalty. Though during my marriage I had indeed been the princess consort of the crown prince of Naples, that kingdom no longer existed when Achille and I married. Moreover, I had never even been to Naples. How could I be the princess of it? For a daughter of Virginia not schooled in the finer points of royalty, it was vexing to say the least. Since the Bonapartes placed great stock in maintaining the correct image and pecking order within the family legend, I suppose it was important to deal with.

In February 1848, it became evident that this was an issue of more consequence than I might have imagined.

The event, which Achille had for so many years longed for, exploded onto the international scene. Far removed from my simple life in Tallahassee, King Louis Philippe of France, the Bourbon king who steadfastly refused to release the Murat fortune from his coffers, was forced to abdicate! Spurred on by the very sort of liberal democratic movement which Achille had long advocated, the era of absolute French monarchy collapsed onto itself suddenly and without warning.

Responding to the wave of democracy sweeping over Europe, the French Chamber of Deputies cashiered Louis Philippe and called for a republic.

Who should show up as a contender to lead the French into the promised land of democracy? None other than an heir to greatest autocrat in all of history and successor to a self-crowned emperor, a Bonaparte! One with little ambition, no credentials, and little claim to leadership in France save his familial connection to his illustrious uncle Napoléon, none other than Lucien Murat, Achille's brother and also a nephew of Napoléon! In a classic example of Bonaparte clinging to past glories, at Achille's death, Lucien formally succeeded him in the ceremonial title of crown prince of Naples though the kingdom had not existed for some thirty years!

I was flabbergasted at the news of Lucien! This was the same slothful Lucien who loafed about at Joseph's New Jersey estate, squandered his inheritance on gambling and drink, and who was a laughingstock in many a tavern along the Atlantic seaboard. This was the Lucien Murat who had never spoken out for the principles of democracy, let alone authored eloquent treatises in many languages.

Lucien's singular accomplishment to date was his marriage in 1831 to Caroline Georgina Fraser. Caroline was the daughter of Thomas Fraser and his wife Anne Lauton of Bordentown, New Jersey, the locus of Bonaparte power in America thanks to Joseph's massive estate and the wealth he ostentatiously spread around there.

I admit to a certain amount of jealousy on behalf of my late husband, who would have leapt at such a chance to insert himself into the power vacuum that was France in 1851. It seemed so unfair! It was nevertheless my right, and I also believed it to be my duty, to speak up for my dead husband in the matter of the Bonaparte pecking order. It was Achille, the older of the two Murat brothers and the one with credentials who should have been, and doubtless would have been, at the head of the list for a leadership role in France.

It was the height of irony that the one Bonaparte who had spent his life promoting democracy and who could have truly led France into the era of representative government, my beloved Achille, had died only ten months before. Cruel fate; this opportunity should have fallen to him. Lucien was a relative unknown while the defining works written by my late husband were frequently consulted by liberal democrats of Europe who sought to empower the common man. It was a favorite theme of Achille's many published works on government. It was also best articulated by my own ancestors who had midwifed the birth of the United States.

What Achille had longed for and spent his life in pursuit of was to see that the moribund governments of Europe at last move toward representative government of "We the people," that powerful principle that headlined the U.S. Constitution.

What Lucien longed for was not as clear, though he too, following the lead of my late husband, had harangued Louis Philippe for years about the family inheritance. Oh well. Achille was dead. I wished the best for cousin Lucien and tried my best not to stew about the unfairness of it all.

Whether my wishes had anything to do with it or not, later that year Lucien was elected to the national assembly and given the task of reorganizing the French government. That position should have gone to Achille. The year after, 1849, when the Second French Republic was formed, he became a member of the Chamber of Deputies, under the presidency of his cousin Louis-Napoléon Bonaparte. This was the same Louis who had schemed with Achille for just such an outcome. Once again, the bitter irony that my prince had died too soon stuck in my craw.

Louis-Napoléon, you will remember, was the son of Hortense de Beauharnais, and Achille and I had taken him under our roof during his less felicitous times in London. This was also the same Louis who admired America and had taken a particular liking to me as his American cousin. Louis had, in fact, promised that his "dear Cousin Kate" would never want for anything. Now he was president of the French Republic, and I wondered if he would remember those halcyon days in London.

Grand were the pronouncements of the democratic foundations of Louis's Second Republic, but having been a part of the Bonaparte inner circle for many years, I well knew that with the Bonapartes, nothing was as it seemed. With curiosity, I watched the events in Paris from faraway Tallahassee. In a flash of insight, it occurred to me that Bonaparte hunger for power never lay far from the surface. This was a fact I had learned by having been married to one for more than twenty years. Could—would—Louis accede to a vote of the people to legitimize his government as a real republic?

The coup of December 2, 1851, provided the answer. President of France Louis-Napoléon Bonaparte, our dear cousin Louis, summarily dissolved the national assembly. It was a raw power grab in which he became sole ruler of France. In a classic Bonaparte sleight of hand, Louis masked this move by the introduction of universal suffrage and a referendum that legitimated the whole notion of return to empire and extended his mandate for ten years as its emperor.

Validated by the referendum, on December 2, 1852, clever cousin Louis had made himself Emperor Napoléon III.

Louis Napoleon, elevated to the title of Napoleon III, was a close colleague of Achille and Catherine Willis Murat. He invested her as a princess of France and offered her a position at his glittering court. Though she declined the offer to remain in France as a member of his imperial court, the emperor supported her financially for the rest of her life.

Just as I suspected. Those Bonapartes loved power! Cousin Louis, now styled the emperor, immediately concentrated absolute power in his throne and with the functionaries of his administration. I knew that he was, at heart, a liberal democrat, but from faraway Econchattie on the distant southern frontier of America, it appeared to me that the seductions of absolute power were blinding him and that France may have exchanged one despot for another. I wished so many times that he and Achille could sit down and work together as they had in theory at our flat in London. Once again, I was saddened by Achille's premature death. He was born to do the things that others were now doing, and I knew he could do them as well or better. To punctuate that thought that others were governing where Achille should, I next learned that his brother Lucien was made a senator and given honorary titles of *monseigneur* and highness for his role in assisting the coup that had elevated Louis to emperor.

The Bonapartes enjoyed the pretentious trappings of power and fancy titles almost as much as they enjoyed the reality. Monseigneur Lucien Bonaparte, the ne'er-do-well of Point Breeze, was almost too much for me to bear though.

Despite my misgivings about the coup with which Louis had attained the throne and some of his autocratic moves, I liked him as both a friend and family member and was supremely happy that he had at last pushed out the last Bourbon. I regretted only that it was not Achille who had done so. Maybe I had lived with a Bonaparte so long that I now thought like one.

With a smile in my heart, I sometimes perceived Louis, now ruling as Napoléon III, as a sort of surrogate for Achille who was now hovering about God's throne rather than that of France. Much of Louis-Napoléon's political acumen had, after all, come from their months of intense discussion in our Mayfair flat in London, so I thought it likely that Achille's words and ideas would play a paramount role in the new government of France. Perhaps he might prevail in death where he had failed in life.

Just when I had accommodated these thoughts magnanimously and wished the whole lot of power-seeking Bonapartes well, I would once again be struck with the selfish thought that Achille should have sat upon that throne in the flesh, not just the chance to influence it from the heavenly realm above. Having been so immersed in Bonaparte politics for so long, it was difficult to get these royal thoughts out of my mind, but frontier Tallahassee helped me by treating it all with a giant yawn of indifference.

I must say that it was both frightening as well as intriguing how close I had been to becoming the empress of France's Second Empire had Achille lived a few more years.

It was not to be, but with Louis thus ensconced as Emperor Napoléon III, I knew that in heaven Achille wished nothing but good fortune for his cousin. With a premonition that Louis would not forget his "dear Cousin Kate," so did I.

The Momentary Empress, 1850's

*W*HEN I RECEIVED a gracious invitation in 1850 from cousin Louis-Napoléon, now reigning as Napoléon III, for a visit to France, I first consulted aging black servant William and requested that he prepare appropriate belongings for me for a transatlantic voyage and a stay at the Tuileries for several months. Oddly enough, faithful old William was the best-traveled person in all of Tallahassee. He had traveled abroad extensively as Achille's valet and bodyguard for decades and was expert at the ropes of international travel and the arcane world of royal fashions.

What an exciting opportunity! Getting Econchattie back on a sound footing had been something of a drudge, and my Tallahassee social life, while pleasant, was definitely lacking since Achille's death. I had only recently given up my black clothes of mourning and was ready for a little joy in life. Thank you, Cousin Louis!

In order to cope with rigorous foreign travel, I would need William's help, for I was now nearing the age of fifty and no longer the spry belle who thrilled to European travel with my prince more than twenty years ago. When I looked with jaundiced eye at my clothing William laid out, I realized that it was suitable for a plantation mistress but otherwise far too dowdy for a royal visit to a dashing emperor in the world's most exciting capital. I would have to shop upon arrival in Paris—every woman's dream!

Louis was a man of his word. He had not forgotten his "dear cousin Kate," and with the wealth of all of France at his disposal, forwarded with his kind invitation a bank order for 40,000 francs. I was excited and knew that my late husband would have been also. It was somehow very satisfying that Louis's elevation to emperor had not gone to his head and that his memories of our support in London those many years ago was to now be reciprocated.

Still a bon vivant bachelor, Louis's reputation preceded him. Having seen him with at least a dozen ladies in London, I was more than well aware of his proclivities regarding women but was not intimidated. I knew Cousin Louis well and hoped I could trust him. I privately wondered, nevertheless, if there were strings attached to the 40,000 francs and the invitation to his opulent court in Paris. Louis reputation as Europe's raconteur was well-known even as far away as rural Tallahassee, and some who traded in that sort of gossip suggested that he had some unusual, even bizarre, tastes. I could handle it. Thanks to my Willis genes and Mother's sternly insistent upbringing, I had the inner fortitude and ready manner of dealing with unwanted advances should that be on the mind of *l'empereur.*

Upon arrival in Paris in 1852, I was both pleased and relieved when Louis introduced me straightaway to his new love, and how charming she was! Overnight, Eugenie and I became fast friends, and her hospitality and disarming manner were a highlight of my visit. Eugenie was of Spanish extraction but had been raised in Scotland, Doña Maria Eugenia Ignatia Augustina de Palafox-Kirkpatrick, styled the Countess of Teba. Aside from her beauty, I found her keenly intelligent and ambitious; in short, a likely match for a Bonaparte. She had made a seamless transition to the glittering life of Paris on the arm of the emperor, and it was evident that she would make an extraordinary empress and first lady of France. Louis's wandering eye had alighted on exactly the right partner!

Paris was bustling with energy and enthusiasm after decades stuck in the mire of France's ever-present political turmoil. Under Cousin Louis, it was exciting that Paris was to recapture the former glories of the City of Light. Louis had grand plans and had engaged Baron Hausmann to completely remake the capital into elegant public spaces, grand avenues and boulevards, and a series of bridges over the Seine. Ostensibly, this was for aesthetics, but the reality was it that it was to allow for use of cannon and cavalry in the city in the event of insurrection against his government. Cousin Louis was, after all, a Bonaparte with more than a touch of their well-known paranoia.

Given his Bonaparte ancestry, part of Louis's rule included an eternal search for power, and he now seized on an avenue more from my world across the Atlantic than his. By the 1850s, it seemed in America likely that the slavery issue was going to boil over, possibly into open warfare. Informally and delicately, Louis inquired of me how this might be exploited for his advantage. I was stunned that he might have designs on some sort of intrusion into affairs in the Americas and let him know most forcefully that any French gambit across the Atlantic would not be welcome. The French had aided the United States during our revolution, but our sovereignty and pride would not allow French meddling into internal affairs in the Americas, and the Monroe Doctrine was still operative in the foreign affairs of the United States. The United States would not tolerate meddling by foreign powers! As it later turned out, Louis was beginning to formulate an idea for French intervention south of the U.S. border, in Mexico, and these were just his feelers. He was fishing in troubled waters, and I told him so.

While Louis attended to matters of state, Eugenie and I enjoyed the theater, the opera, the historic sights of Paris and engaged in enjoyable conversation. Because of my sad frontier wardrobe, we shopped from the dressmakers and milliners of Paris, who brought their wares to the Tuileries for our approval. Can you imagine a more stark contrast to that of a frontier plantation mistress?

One evening of particular note, Louis was hosting a state dinner with all of the finery that the elegant French capital could muster. I dressed in some of my new haute couture and presented myself at the door. Immediately, there was among the attendees a murmuring of "*la princesse*," "Princesse Murat," and all eyes turned toward me. Public accolades as a princess had been almost forgotten, for I had been only a princess consort and my prince was now dead. With much pomp, I was escorted to the vacant seat of the empress and, puzzled, seated in her place. Almost immediately, the murmur struck up again, "*l'empereur, l'empereur!*" and Louis made his grand entrance, sans Eugenie. He greeted me most affectionately and assured me that I was seated properly. Eugenie, he explained, was not feeling

Catherine Daingerfield Willis Murat; early 1860's at the time of being created a princess of France. Photographed en route to a state dinner at the court of Emperor Napoleon III where she was seated in the place of Empress Eugenie and accorded the honors of empress. Image courtesy of the Archives of the State of Florida.

well and would not be joining us that evening. A magical evening for this daughter of Virginia ensued, flowing with champagne, good wishes, and witty conversation as I sat at the elbow of the emperor in the place of honor reserved for the empress of France. It was breathtaking.

After the dinner and entertainments, Louis escorted me to the royal apartments where, to my surprise, a perfectly hale and hearty Eugenie awaited. She effusively treated me like a sister and insisted that I should consider myself part of the royal family. You cannot imagine how good it made me feel to be accepted in this manner now that my Bonaparte husband had passed away. Firmly ensconced in the royal family as Louis-Napoléon's cousin I was publicly, and for all the world to see, still celebrated as Princess Kate. Both humbled and flattered, I loved it. Achille had always told me that I could hold my own in any company, and now I actually believed it.

The entire imperial event had been orchestrated for me so that I might be the guest of honor of the emperor, as exquisite gesture of courtesy as I could possibly imagine. More than mere protocol, there appeared a genuine sense of affection for this Virginia girl within the historic Tuileries and throughout the hierarchy of the Second Empire of France.

Such was my elegant and royal treatment under the care of Louis and Eugenie from the moment of my arrival until it was time to go. It was extraordinary. I doubted that any American had been so honored in all of the history of the world. For me to now relate to you that it was flattering would grossly understate my reaction at being tendered a position of nobility in the world's most fashionable court. I was overwhelmed with the honors tendered a simple Southern girl by no less than Emperor Napoléon III and his elegant empress.

The week before my departure, Louis surprised me exceedingly when he formally created a princess of the Second Empire and insisted that I should not depart but rather take up a permanent position at his court. Aghast, I hardly knew what to say; in America, there are no protocols for such an offer to join the royal court of a foreign land, and not just a single state but an empire! To sweeten his offer, he assured me of my own chateau, a cadre of servants, an annual stipend from his treasury, and use of the royal livery of France. All of this for the little girl who danced in her mirror in Fredericksburg, Virginia,

Princess Kate enjoyed a particularly close relationship with the Empress of France's Second Empire, the Empress Eugenie.

atop Willis Hill! I had lived many magical moments but forever would regard the generosity of Louis's offer as a high-water mark.

Louis-Napoléon, how could I thank Cousin Louis? He was a dear, and Eugenie his perfect royal counterpart. During my several months as his guest, not a hint of the lechery for which he was famous surfaced, for he was completely besotted with Eugenie. I chastised myself for having had such thoughts!

My few months in Paris were filled with more gaiety than all of my years in Tallahassee, but I yearned for America and the simple pleasures of Econchattie. When it was time to leave, I boarded the ship with gratitude to Louis and joy that I was going home to my beloved America.

Fifty and Beyond, 1853

On AUGUST 17, 1853, I celebrated half a century of life! I could, like most who achieve that benchmark of life, scarcely believe it. The whirlwind I had lived, before, during, and after my marriage to Achille, was cause enough to celebrate, and I did so with friends who came to honor me with flowing champagne and the bounty of our fields and farms. Hams, turkeys, casserole dishes of many varieties, venison, oysters from the bays bordering the Gulf of Mexico, scuppernong wine, and more. What a celebration my friends hosted for me!

Of course, it was marred by the conspicuous absence of my beloved husband, now dead for more than six years. With an inner glow of satisfaction, I remembered and thanked my maker for the extraordinary life I had been afforded, due in no small measure to the prince who had drunk from my slipper at San Luis so long ago. So while the assembled crowd toasted me, their princess in residence, in return, I toasted the late Prince Achille Murat.

It was very much a celebration of the quality and excitement of my life, not just the fifty-year quantity of it.

Even in the sad aftermath of Achille's death, I had much to celebrate. I would soon be able burn the mortgages, which had hung over me like the sword of Damocles since our Louisiana debacle. The generosity of Cousin Louis on the throne of France had enabled me to pay down much of the debt, but the part that gave me the greatest pride was that I had proved an able and independent plantation mistress.

Econchattie and the larger estate of Lipona were now profitable. The blacks who worked the property on my behalf were now owned free and clear, and I refashioned their lives now to provide each and every one positive incentives for their work rather than simply punishment for infractions. I had proved to the community, and to the surprise of many townspeople, that I could manage a plantation with the best of them.

For a widow, as much as I rejoiced in having brought our acreage back from the brink, I felt isolated and lonely in the wilderness of the Wacissa district outside town. From my brother-in-law Samuel Duval, in 1854, I purchased a smaller home nearer town and sited on a parcel of 470 acres. With my annuity from Louis, I was now blessed with the wherewithal to farm two plantations and to achieve a status in life not attained since we fell from grace in Louisiana. Achille would have been proud of me, and in his honor, I named the new property Belle Vue in honor of the elegant hotel in Brussels where we had spent our happiest days. It was my very personal tribute to him and was dedicated to his memory.

Princess Kate's beloved "Belle Vue" plantation is today a part of the Tallahassee Museum and open to the public.

Thenceforth, I divided my time between the two plantations and slipped into the tranquil grace of aging.

Belle Vue and its more convenient location allowed me a more active social schedule in Tallahassee. The more I was with friends, the less my life felt empty without Achille. As incongruous as it may sound, the royal livery of France could now be unveiled in Florida, thanks to my having been granted its use by Louis. As far as I know, no one else in America had that royal privilege. As I unveiled the Napoleonic finery, I must say that my recherché breakfasts, dinners, and parties were soon the idol of Tallahassee's elites. I set a pretty table with sterling serving pieces, china, and crystal, which dated to the empire of Uncle Napoléon and to my father-in-law's kingdom of Naples. These artifacts were elegantly complemented with my own family's heirloom silver, which had graced the now-burned-out Willis mansion in Fredericksburg since the 1700s.

When guests were served by my household help dressed in the royal livery of France, it created quite the scene! Faithful old William in Napoleonic livery took as much pride as I and told me in a sweet and poignant moment that he felt a kinship with his deceased master Achille whenever he wore the finery bearing the laurel-crowned *N*.

In his mind, I think he was more family member than slave. I found his affection for the late prince touching and very much in keeping with my beliefs as to the relationship of master and slave.

As to slaves, and that subject was on everyone's mind, there much lore about my great-uncle George Washington and his beliefs in that regard. Many criticize that our nation's father did not free his slaves in his lifetime, not realizing that he harbored wishes to do so but was frustrated by the laws of the era, particularly state law in Virginia where he made his home. The great Washington, my forebear, was especially troubled at the slave trade's effect of breaking up families. To his credit, he is quoted as saying that "I am principled against this kind of traffic in the human species." I had vocally defended Washington in Europe and was determined to set the record straight here as well.

Though I believe history would have been kinder to him had he not employed slaves at his plantation, the famous Mount Vernon, Washington was economically trapped in the South's plantation economy. My own family was also a part of the dichotomy and conflict of slavery. I accept history's verdict that the heinous practice had to end if America was to fulfill its promise that "all men are created equal."

Slavery was tearing at the heart of America by the late 1850s, and Florida was not immune. My home in middle Florida was especially vulnerable to the incessant drumbeat of conflict between slaveholders and abolitionists. It broke my heart that this pot might soon boil over into war, but there was no middle ground. You were for or you were against.

The likelihood that my beloved United States would tear itself apart increased daily. When at last I was forced to make that difficult choice, I stood firm with the only life I had ever known, the slave-based economy of my beloved South. In my heart, there remained an unresolved angst, yet I could do no other. Once decided, I knew this could not be a halfway measure and set my bonnet to support the hard road that lay ahead.

Florida, my adopted home, seceded from the Union on January 10, 1861, and I was honored to fire the cannon at the statehouse to announce to the world that we would seek our own way, create our own laws to accommodate our way of life, and if need be, fight for those rights. The political turmoil, which Achille and I had hoped would spare America, had come home to roost. The states of America were no longer united states.

By February 1861, Florida joined with Alabama, Georgia, Louisiana, Mississippi, South Carolina, and Texas to form a new republic, the Confederate States of America. Having irrevocably cast my lot, I became a vocal supporter of the Confederate cause.

Despite the hurricane of controversy that raged, my two plantations seemed to go on, season after season, much as they always had, and my daily life was blissfully unaffected by the political bluster on both sides. From my quiet and self-contained little plantation world, I got the impression that neither side believed that the other would actually go to war. It was the calm before the storm.

Political rhetoric, I had learned in Europe, tends to develop a life of its own however, and soon there were bellicose actions to back up the overheated rhetoric. The new president in Washington swore he would resolve the conflict without resort to war, but few believed him. Mr. Lincoln was untested and, as a son of a state not reliant on the slave economy, seemed not to appreciate the depths of hostility that poisoned the land.

In March 1861, the federal's Fort Sumter in South Carolina was captured by Southern sympathizers, and by April, the war we all feared had begun in earnest. By summer, Southern forces forced a federal retreat at Bull Run, and precious American blood was shed on both sides. It was the first of many a bloody field where America's sons in both blue and gray would die in agony.

Through it all, my little daily world at Econchattie and Belle Vue remained one of overseeing the planting and harvesting. The ancient rhythms of the South were seemingly unchangeable, yet I knew I was avoiding the obvious. My field hands and house servants went about daily chores as though there were no guns sounding over the horizon. They sang as they tended fields, their children grew up before my eyes, and they, like all of America, wished that the nightmare might end peacefully or avoid us entirely.

I could see the fear in their eyes that the only lives they knew might soon be overturned by forces they could not understand. I sympathized deeply. All they wanted was a humble home, food on the table, an honest day's work, and family. They neither knew of nor cared about politicians who manipulated us all, black and white, in a great clash of ideas. Together we all hoped and prayed that we would be immune to the bloodshed which had started and that we might continue to go about our lives as usual. Though I could not speak for everyone, at Econchattie and Belle Vue, this sentiment was shared by slave and slaveholder alike.

Though no shots were fired on my plantation properties, there was tragic evidence, even in Tallahassee, that a great civil war inflamed America. The horribly wounded from distant battlefields soon filled our meager medical buildings. Newspapers, pamphlets, and posters depicted ghoulish scenes of death and dying thanks to a new contrivance, the photograph. Never before had the brutality of war been seen at home. I could scarcely believe the scenes of gore which Americans inflicted on each other.

The carnage of the battlefields was an extension of the political carnage loosed upon the land as America made war upon herself. Tearfully, while I grieved for the soldiers of both sides, I prayed that the illustrious South would soon prevail and the peace of God once more pervade the land.

My friends and I raised funds for the Confederacy, knit socks for our brave men, and spent endless days feeding and comforting the bloodied soldiers who filled our hospitals. We of Tallahassee's Soldiers Aid Society despaired that we could not do more.

Confederate Causes, French Money, and Mexican Madness, 1861-1867

*T*HE ANNUITY SO generously settled upon me by Cousin Louis-Napoléon became a bankroll for Confederate causes, and I spent it willingly as my small contribution to the glorious cause of the Confederacy. I was a daughter of the South, and my soul bled with the men whose bandages I changed. Each bandaged soldier who took my hand from his deathbed reminded me that my meager money was small beer compared to those who did the dying. Some days as I labored as a volunteer at the hospitals, amid the stench of gangrene and the moans of the dying, I wondered if I could go on.

Had Achille still lived, I was sure that he would have taken command of a Confederate unit of cavalry. It was in his blood, it was in his heart, and it was an unfulfilled mandate of his past that he step into his gallant father's shoes. I wondered how Confederate forces would have responded to his leading them into battle astride a great warhorse with white ostrich plumes flying. For Achille, the names of Antietam, Gettysburg, and Bull Run would have been echoes of Jena, Aboukir, and Borodino.

My every penny soon went to the cause, and ere long, I felt the familiar breath of austerity breathing down my neck. Damn the Yankees! If my fortune must be spent to stop them, so be it! If tens of thousands of brave Southerners could march into battle for the cause, I could march into poverty behind the proud flag of the Stars and Bars!

With my powerful connections in France, I wrote desperately to Louis soliciting support for the Confederacy. Surely the French, whose support had facilitated our freedom as a nation, would rise to support the rights of the Southern states to determine their destiny. Surely Louis would send money, if not troops. Surely the photographs of bloody battlefields would move him to help bring the war to an early close.

My reply was silence. The slavery question and the war it had spawned was a risk Louis could not afford. If he acknowledged the right of some American states to secede from their central government, what would that mean to the integrity of France and to the security of his throne? France's course remained one of neutrality.

For Cousin Louis, the American Civil War was an abstract idea. For me, it was personal. Two of my brothers, George and Mu—my "little" brother Achille Murat Willis—and two cousins, Byrd Charles Willis II, and Thomas Hayward Willis, wore the Confederate gray. Mu in particular, perhaps motivated by his namesake's connection to the cavalry, placed himself in the thick of the fighting. He first served as aide to General Jubal Early at First Manassas, where he was singled out for bravery, and again as the commander of a company of cavalry under the gallant Turner Ashby, the so-called Black Knight of the Confederacy.

Rallies were held throughout the South, and I spoke passionately at several of the need for the South to stay the course. Crowds cheered. Tinny-sounding bands played off-key. Troops marched. Flags waved. Young men with no idea of the horrors of battle signed up. In retrospect, it is hard for me to now admit that my words of bravado may have sent impressionable Southern youth to their deaths. But these were desperate days, and as 1865 dawned, we could foresee a grim end to the glorious cause of the Confederacy. It was evident to me that we were seeing the death of a way of life as well as the deaths of so many brave men of both sides. It was a carnage that I prayed we would never experience again.

Some six months into his second term of office, Abraham Lincoln was felled by an assassin. He died a month before the Confederacy and all that it stood for also died.

The war was over.

In the aftermath of the horrid war, which split the very fabric of America, a different sort of struggle ensued. For proud Southerners, it was an insidious, even demeaning psychological battle. The South's economy was in tatters, and hundreds of thousands of our finest young men lay maimed or dead. Sixty percent of the rural South lived in poverty, now bereft of its young men. These were the young generation of farmers, carpenters, merchants, and more. Who would replace them in the prostrate economy of my beloved Dixieland?

These were the South's husbands and fathers, sons and cousins, brothers and uncles. In a male-dominated society, the vacuum left by such a loss could scarcely be overstated. Those lucky enough to have survived the war had no place to turn.

I know all too well. My brothers fought. My cousins fought. My friends fought. And when it was over, and the plantation-based world they had grown up in no longer existed, they were physically exhausted and psychologically adrift. The South and its proud warriors were not just defeated, they were humiliated.

My own dear brother, Little Mu, no longer little but every inch a man, was captured in an engagement near our Father's ancestral home at Orange, Virginia, and described in a northern newspaper as "a distinguished prisoner."

Our money issued by Confederate authorities was devalued to nothing. I lost thousands. Some counseled saving it until a glorious day when the South would rise again. Sweetly sentimental but naive. Clearly, the South was not destined for resurrection.

Some picked up their hoes and went back to the farm. Some moved to the cities, far away from the humiliation of returning home in defeat. Few had skills. Many were amputees. Some lost their minds. Some swallowed hard and joined the opportunists who moved south in droves seeking a livelihood on the back of the defeated South. These carpetbaggers were the worst of all. To survive in the shadow of the Confederacy's remains, the proud men of the South had to learn to cope. Many couldn't, and some resorted to suicide during the era of so-called reconstruction, a euphemism for the federal government's boot on the neck of the prostrate South.

I had been in regular communication with Cousin Louis-Napoléon in Paris, reigning now as the Emperor Napoléon III. Several themes emerged from these correspondences and from news dispatches. First, it was evident that Louis had both a grand sense of his own destiny and the same adventuresome tendency in foreign policy as his predecessor namesake Napoléon Bonaparte. The Bonapartes were obsessed with extending their power. Louis intervened in the so-called papal states conflict in Italy, invaded an area of Southeast Asia he called Cochin-China, sponsored incursions into Korea and Japan, and sent troops to China during their Second Opium War. Closer to home, he promoted a three-part "Grand Scheme for the Americas," which involved not only teasing the Confederacy with notions of support, but also an active deployment of French forces to intervene against the Mexican government of Benito Juarez. The legitimate government of Mexico was overthrown to be replaced with Napoléon III's chosen puppet, the (so-called) Emperor Maximilian and his Empress Carlota.

Emperor Maximilian of Mexico. Louis Napoleon, ruling in France as Emperor Napoleon III of France's Second Empire supported the installation of Archduke Ferdinand Maximilian Joseph of Austria as puppet emperor of Mexico. After the defeat of the Confederate States of America in the American Civil War, Maximilian encouraged former members of the Confederacy to relocate to Mexico. Among these were members of Princess Kate's own family, who were abetted by her close ties to Napoleon III. Emperor Maximilian was opposed from the outset by Mexican rebels led by Benito Juarez and eventually executed in 1867.

When Emperor Napoleon III of France's Second Empire supported the installation
of Archduke Ferdinand Maximilian Joseph of Austria as puppet emperor of Mexico,
his wife Marie Charlotte Amelie Augustine Victoire Clementine Leopoldine better
known as simply Carlota, became the figurehead Empress of Mexico. Carlota was
the daughter of Princess Kate's friend, Queen Louise-Marie of Belgium and this
relationship abetted members of Princess Kate's family in their relocation to Mexico
after the defeat of the Confederacy in the American Civil War.

Louis-Napoléon's Mexican adventure had all been brewing under my
very nose at the height of the American Civil War. It had not properly
registered on me due to my preoccupation with our own war at home
but now played out a strange role in the evolution of the defeated
Confederacy. When our so-called Civil War ended and the Confederacy
disbanded, Mexican Emperor Maximilian encouraged displaced
Southerners to join his cause in Mexico. If the defeated soldiers and
sympathizers of the Confederacy were no longer welcomed in the
United States, open arms awaited south of the border.

In this environment, major U.S. colonies were cobbled together in
Mexico. Veracruz was a hotbed as were the Carlota Colony and the
Virginia Colony. Effectively, U.S. communities south of the border,

they offered solace, opportunity for work, and an escape from the severe judgments handed down against former soldiers and sympathizers in the former Confederacy, now harshly ruled by the U.S. federal government.

Some disgruntled Confederate veterans and sympathizers straggled south on their own, some assembled in a sad approximation of military order and fled under the leadership of Confederate General Jo Shelby. Many did not make it at all. It was a disheartening exodus to Mexico for proud Southerners with nowhere to turn.

Maximilian's colonies thus became a mecca for disaffected and defeated Confederate soldiers including both my nephew Byrd Charles Willis II and my cousin Thomas Hayward Willis.

I, of course, had a link with Louis-Napoléon (Napoléon III) and his empress Eugenie. These two were, of course, Maximilian's patrons in Paris. Though I had not formally met Maximilian, through Louis I stoked a relationship with his young bride, the Empress Carlota, daughter of my dear friend from years gone by, King Leopold I of Belgium. Through these channels, I brokered a clandestine introduction to the circles of empire for my family members who had fled to Mexico. Their political activities in Mexico remained sub rosa and were doomed to failure. Rumors abounded however that they were in league with the forces of Maximilian and had some quasi-government authority at the edges of his ill-fated empire.

In Mexico, my relatives disappeared into oblivion, and I have no more facts. I cannot speculate further, but both of these family members lived successfully in Mexico for the rest of their lives under the aegis, if not the protections, of Louis, Eugenie, Maximilian, and Carlota.

Maximilian's days would not play out so pleasantly. He was put to death by firing squad under order of Benito Juarez.

In the Wake of War, 1866

*T*HE TRAGIC CIVIL War and its wake created malaise and confusion for all Southerners, and I was not immune. For those like me who had grown up in the agrarian plantation lifestyle, both a cherished belief system and an economic way of life were turned on their heads. Of course, the old bugaboo of slavery was at its core, and what to do now was the most vexing issue of all.

Under the sweeping Emancipation Proclamation of 1863 and later the Thirteenth Amendment to the U.S. Constitution, the hardworking men and women who worked my fields and home were told by faraway strangers that they were free to go.

But go where? To do what?

A few went, but for the most part, they had nowhere to go, no skills with which to earn a living, no transport to go anywhere, and no alternatives.

They were as quizzical as I about what the political leaders in Washington expected them to do, so most did the obvious. Nothing.

For those who choose emancipation and left my plantation, I could only wish the best for them, for they were about to learn the difficult lesson that with freedom comes responsibility. *Freedom* means the freedom to fail as well as to succeed. With a scant few exceptions, for all of their lives my field hands had lived in the cradle-to-grave security of the plantation. They knew little of the competitive world, and I feared for their futures should they choose to leave. In fact, those who left were rudely awakened. Chastened by an outside world far harsher than life at Econchattie or Belle Vue, within a year, many moved back into their former cabins and happily took up my new offer of compensation as sharecroppers. I had never called them slaves anyway, so little was changed.

For those who remained on my plantations, it was, of course, a reciprocal arrangement. These farmhands sustained me much as they always had while I sustained them. Amid the confusion of newfound emancipation, at Econchattie and Belle Vue, the daily world of both master and servant trundled along pretty much the same.

Having spent virtually all of my money to no avail on Confederate causes, I socialized less. It was just as well, for the war had driven many of my friends away, and in the environment of the postwar period, there was little to celebrate anyway.

Austerity was now my byword; poverty my handmaiden.

But God, as my mother had taught me, works in mysterious ways. Just when it looked most bleak, in 1865, my world was brightened by yet another invitation from Cousin Louis-Napoléon and Eugenie, the emperor and empress, for Cousin Kate to visit them in Paris. Well into my sixties then, I fretted to my sister Mary that the voyage might be too strenuous. (Sister Mary was married to Commodore A. J. Dallas, commandant of the nearby Pensacola Navy Yard, the same one that Father's brick had helped construct.) Mary had the immediate solution. Their son Trevanion, more than forty years my junior, could accompany me to France as my escort, traveling companion, and helper. In the process, I felt sure he would receive an imperial orientation in Paris at the knee of Emperor Napoléon III, my very dear Cousin Louis-Napoléon.

It was an opportunity made in heaven. Trevanion was a dear, the trip went smoothly, and the City of Light was more enchanting than ever after Louis-Napoléon's huge public works projects, which paved the city's broad boulevards and built stunning bridges and public edifices, including an opera house the likes of which bespoke wealth and sophistication beyond anything I had seen in America. He called it the Palais Garnier after the architect who had designed it, and I was to learn that he was of the Garnier family with whom Achille and I had lived so long ago in New Orleans. It is, indeed, a small world.

I expressed my dismay to Louis that he might have materially altered the course of the American Civil War had he been forthcoming with tangible support. In many a private conversation, he confirmed his philosophical agreement with the South but made it clear that French domestic politics rendered it impossible for him to aid the Confederate States with troops as France had so long ago for my great-uncle General Washington in the struggle with Britain.

Had Louis openly sanctioned the dissolution of the American union, his ministers feared a similar fate for France. The Second Empire might have come unraveled if Louis acknowledged the right of groups or regions to sever from their central government, and his own throne would have likely fallen; perhaps even his head.

Despite undercurrents of political differences, my stay in Paris was a welcome rejoicing after the sad chapter of the American Civil War. Especially, the lovely Empress Eugenie was more charming than ever. It was the sort of natural friendship that never needs coaxing. We spent glorious days together both in the Tuileries and reveling in the cosmopolitan joys of Paris, especially the art collections of Le Salon Carré within the Louvre Museum, which I had first visited with Achille.

I took quiet pleasure that my well-tutored upbringing as a Virginia aristocrat, buttressed by Mother's example of ladyhood, stood the test of time. Now it served me to the nines in this personal foray into the world of empire. Aside from the Bonaparte credentials of my late husband, my connection to George Washington also opened many a door and carried many a conversation.

Cousin Louis tempted me repeatedly with a standing offer that I might become a permanent member of his court with a chateau of my own and all of the accoutrements of elegance accorded to French nobility. Though that might have been a diversionary path of life for me, my heritage and, indeed, my entire life was American. After such royal pampering in Paris, I wondered though how I would adjust to my simple home in Florida.

As I pondered the offer of the emperor in the still of night, the voices of my patriotic ancestry steered my thinking, persistently reminding me of a solemn obligation to my most wonderful country. Though I accepted Louis-Napoléon's astounding offer of investiture as a princess of his court, I could not go the extra mile to leave America for immersion in the Second Empire or the chateau and luxuries that would have provided. I would forever proudly carry the honorific title Princess of France just as I had proudly borne the title of Princess Consort of Naples. Though both were honors beyond imagining, in reality they were mere contrivances. I was neither a courtier nor bred to royalty. I was neither French nor Neapolitan. I was by birth a Virginian and by choice a Floridian.

And always an American! But how did I get here, in Paris, as a princess?

My royal connection to the house of Bonaparte had started with a marriage license issued in Tallahassee, to Achille Murat, son of Napoléon's sister. To that was now added the head-turning honor of being named a princess of France by yet another Bonaparte of imperial status and international renown. I could scarcely believe that this little Virginia born girl was honored in this manner. So far as I know, I was the only person in the history of the world to be accorded such amazing recognition, not once, but twice a princess. Yet my American roots called their siren song, and I resolved again to make my home not in a French chateau at the knee of the emperor, but across the Atlantic in the land of the free and home of the brave.

And so after a flirtation with the Second French Empire, Trevanion and I packed our bags for home. Gracious, ever generous Louis and Eugenie, without fanfare, insisted that each year for the rest of my life I would receive an annuity of 40,000 francs. In the desperate straits in which I had lived during and after the war, it was manna from heaven. Along with the huge cash payment of 125,000 francs he had made to me previously, Emperor Napoléon III, my friend, my companion, and my dear Cousin Louis, made possible a life of security for me and for the varied people and causes of my home in the American South. From his lofty pedestal overlooking the entire world, I often wondered if he had any appreciation for the unpretentious simplicity that characterized my life.

In the vein of Lafayette and Rochambeau, France thus came to the aid of America once again, not with armies marching, cannon blazing, or banners waving, but quietly, personally, and privately. Funds from the emperor would provide security for my old age, which was closing in fast, would help wounded veterans of our savage Civil War, and would support my aging servants who had nowhere to turn.

Louis's generosity also would help me in my campaign to help preserve an icon of American history, the proud ancestral home of my great grand-uncle, George Washington. Mount Vernon became my new cause. Upon return from France, I proudly took up the invitation of a group of selfless American ladies to serve as the state of Florida regent for the for the Mount Vernon Ladies Association. Single-handedly, I raised the goodly sum of $3,791. Mount Vernon survives today, a monument of America and a sweet reminder of the Washington legacy that flows in my veins.

Princess Catherine Willis Murat, "Princess Kate", took special pride in her relationship to the Washingtons. (Her great grandmother was Betty Washington, only sister of George.) She served as State Regent for the newly formed Mount Vernon Ladies Association and proudly raised funds for preservation of Mount Vernon. Photo by the author.

War Weary and Surviving, 1866-67

*A*T HOME AT Belle Vue near Tallahassee, I continued to marvel in disgust at the opportunists, rabble-rousers, carpetbaggers, and abolitionist troublemakers. With their cause now brutally resolved in their favor, they flooded into the South with signs, pamphlets, newspapers, and street demonstrations whose only visible benefit was to give them something to do when they were otherwise unemployed and unemployable. The way the scalawags leapt upon the corpse of the Confederacy reminded me of disgusting vultures feasting on the dead. Solidly grounded in the proud values of the old South, I thought the whole lot of them devoid of any sense of the decency and honor best personified by the great Robert E. Lee.

I detested especially the vitriolic rhetoric they brought to the public discourse and which poisoned so many, regardless of color. My poor blacks, who had expected the world to become their oyster when the North won the war, were the greatest victims of all. All the fine talk in the world would not feed their babies.

I would.

Between Econchattie and Belle Vue, I now employed sixty-two, of whom twelve were downtrodden black mothers whose men folk, incited by Yankee propaganda, abandoned them in search of the glory and bounty that they were told awaited them just around the corner.

My twelve black mothers had thirty-two children among them, children who should have had a father at home to look after their welfare and eke out a living, which is all that any of us were doing. White-haired old William, Achille's valet for so many years, clung to his homespun version of an aristocratic manner and served as a liaison between myself and the destitute little community that called Belle Vue home.

Clearly, all were free blacks who could come and go at will. Everyone knew of this theoretical freedom, but no one had any place to go. As meager as it was, at least here I made sure they had a roof over their heads. I paid them a tiny wage on which to survive, and together, we shared a fate of austerity, simple foods grown on the property, fish from the streams, scrawny chickens, oysters from the Gulf to our south, and the occasional cow from the herd, which I selectively thinned.

Our homegrown efforts at Belle Vue were supplemented by the generous charity of Cousin Louis-Napoléon in Paris, without whose largesse many of my people would have starved. Though I tried to explain to the beat-down black workers who hung on with me exactly who was footing the bill, the notion that it came from an emperor across the sea was lost on most of them.

By 1866, hunger knocked at our door regularly, and at last, I was forced to sell off some of my exquisite jewels, which had their origins in the lavish courts of the Bonapartes and Murats. There being no market in Florida for such finery, I sent them via steamer bound for New York and hoped for a quick turnaround and enough money to tide us all over for another few years. En route north, the ship sank off the stormy coast of Hatteras. My heart sank with the ship for with those jewels the last wealth of empire went to a briny grave and left all of the residents of Belle Vue to scratch out life as best as possible from the earth, forests, fields, and streams that surrounded us. We would survive together or not survive at all.

As the winter of 1866-67 turned, my health began to turn also. Now sixty-three, I seldom left Belle Vue and was attended by the black sharecroppers, many older than I, who clung to life alongside me. We told each other stories, their children, grandchildren, and great-grandchildren amused me with their antics, and we commiserated about each other's aches and pains. They brought my meals from their simple kitchens, they sat beside my bed fanning me through the heat of summer, they sponge bathed my body when I was feverish, they sang beautiful hymns and old African chants, and the simple truths of the great American patriots of years gone by took on a deeper meaning.

"All men, indeed, ARE created equal." Profound words written so long ago.

The great American paradox had come full circle. It was never possible for slavery to be reconciled with the ideals on which America was founded. Freedom and slavery are opposite and cannot coexist. I and other generations of slave owners had wrongly subjected thousands to the degrading and inhumane practice. By looking the other way, we naively thought that we could wish the problem away until at last it festered and finally exploded into war. That horrid tragedy of my native land, that bloody cataclysm of body and soul, wrote for all time in American blood that the ideals of equality of man must mean equality for *all* men.

As I lay for weeks on end in my bed at Belle Vue, with more than ample time to think, I grew melancholy that it had taken such a devastating war to transform the promise of America into the reality of America. The Civil War had been an epic struggle for the soul of my homeland. Brave men in both blue and gray died on famous battlefields, in anonymous forests and fields, in ditches, in hospitals, in sanitariums, on the byways of the land, in the arms of fellow soldiers, in the arms of loved ones, but mostly alone.

All alone.

In the twilight of my years, I was forced to swallow a bitter pill. It was this.

In avoiding honest resolution of the slavery question, the Founding Fathers of America, including those of my own ancestry, had sown the seeds of that bloody debacle, which pitted brother versus brother.

Someone far away had labeled it the Civil War. There was nothing civil about it.

In declining health, I stared for the first time of my sixty-three years down the long darkening corridor that led to heaven and my eternity. My lifetime of support of slavery appeared to me now as an abyss on the pathway of my salvation. I needed to make peace with God on that score so that I might enter His kingdom. I prayed that God would forgive me and looked to His guidance as to how I might atone for that.

He answered me as He is wont to do. Not in flashes or shouts or roars from a thundering Old Testament God. He answered me in a whisper.

"You already know, Kate, you already know."

And I did. I did God's bidding in my own small way, shepherding my little flock at Belle Vue. In the final epoch of life, I provided my people a simple home, I provided them food for their table, I urged the younger ones to learn to read and write and pursue the learning needed to succeed in the new postwar world after I was gone.

None of this was grand or heralded across the land. It was not an act anyone will ever remember or write about. But I meant it from the bottom of my heart. It was mine and mine alone.

My penance to God by caring for the servants and sharecroppers of Belle Vue was so sincere that some of the neighboring plantation owners who came to call actually chastised me. They thought it an excessive, even inappropriate display of black sympathy. I had, after all, so recently been an avid supporter of the Confederacy that many now labeled me a turncoat.

Nonetheless, in the bitter brew of reconstruction, I never felt more confident in all of my life that I was doing the right thing.

In soulful moments by candlelight, I shared my Episcopal view of the Almighty with the elderly blacks who called Belle Vue home and who tended me at all hours of the day and night. They, in turn, shared their God with me. Their God, I thought must indeed be a powerful one. He had seen them through the vicissitudes of slavery and had sustained them for generations.

The little white-haired band of residents at Belle Vue found solace together as I drifted toward the end of that corridor toward heaven.

In the cool green days of spring 1867, I experienced something amazing. Others had told me of this experience with their loved ones as they approached heaven's door. The fog of failing memory lifted like the ground fog through which I used to canter in the days of my youth. Once the fog of mind burned off, like a clear mountain stream the recall of my life gushed and tumbled without letup, sharp, incisive, but now enriched by a more complete understanding of the meaning of those events in my life. No longer just isolated events, I pieced together the puzzle of this American girl's life of richness and adventure. I had even become twice a princess, and it was a story worth passing on to succeeding generations.

I summoned Sophronia to bring me some paper, and I began to write. I was determined to remember it all and to write the details of my voyage upon the waters of life. Most days, I would write from sunup to sunset. I had encyclopedic recall of it all. My life story would survive me even when I had left my earthly home to join my God.

Catherine Daingerfield Willis Murat; a very early photograph done by C.D. Fredericks and Company, Tallahassee when she was in her mid sixties. Image courtesy of the Archives of the State of Florida.

Finis, 1867

*A*S JULY 1867 lapsed into August, I was never quite sure whether I was experiencing fever or simply the oppressive heat of the North Florida woods in summertime. All I know is that the heat was unrelenting. In this disturbed state, from my bed at Belle Vue, my very being seemed to flicker as a magic lantern show. Where was reality? Where was fantasy? Where was the line between then two? What was fact? What was imagination? Where was the princess? I seemed to remember that I was one, but it was so unlikely, could that be? Lightning bolts of thought blazed across my brain.

Long ago, there was my dapple gray mare Lizzie cantering across the sweet fields of my youth.

Long ago, when I was a child there was a terrifying fire on Willis Hill, and my home was left in ashes.

Long ago, I struggled across the wilds of Florida. Somehow the name Bellamy kept intruding, but I could not fix its place in the tangled fabric of my thoughts.

Long ago, there was a man, a beautiful man, who drank from my slipper. He was a prince. My prince. I became his princess. I was Princess Murat, an American part of the Bonaparte saga. Did I visit a king in New Jersey, or did I imagine it?

Lipona. What was Lipona? Pink dresses. Roast buzzard. Long ago.

*The final home of "Princess Kate" was her simple plantation home "Belle Vue"
outside Tallahassee, Florida, named for the elegant hotel "Belle Vue" in Brussels,
Belgium where she and her prince spent halcyon days as he supported King Leopold
I with command of a foreign legion. The dazzling life of an American princess ended
on August 6, 1867 at her homespun plantation in Florida.*

Long ago, I lived in a foolish carnival world beyond reality in New
Orleans. And a sugar plantation. And masques. And sadness and a
retreat. Lipona? Again the name, but what did it mean? Who were
the Seminoles, and why did I fear them?

Long ago, my prince and I sailed the stormy ocean. Wet. Tossing.
Seasick. But then to glory in Europe. Somewhere in my confused
mind.

London seems my home. And Brussels. Did I really live there? Did I
befriend kings and queens? Was it real? My prince might have become
a king. I would have been his queen. Long ago.

Lonely, lonely, lonely me. Long ago, my prince died, and with him, a
part of me. Long ago.

My homeland was torn by a civil war. There were bandages and socks
and moans and smells of the dying. But I seem, in my muddled mind,

to be transported to Paris. How could that be? Was I in Paris now? With Cousin Louis? Eugenie? Belle Vue? Was that Brussels or Florida?

A fantasy Bonaparte court of unimaginable wealth and glitter where courtiers whispered "Princesse" as I passed. Was I was a French princess or a proud American?

Reality? Delusion? Imagination?

In my fevered mind, thoughts came and went in torrents. Sometimes I tottered to the very brink of sanity while the gentle blacks of my little farm hovered over me. In the fog, I recall a voice saying, "Missus caint be dyin', she ain't gwine to go am she?"

Heat. Incessant, stifling heat. And whirling confused thoughts.

Bessie? William? Sophronia? Bucky? Are you there?

I summoned every last ounce of strength in my body and, like the croak of a frog, asked to be wiped down with a cool wet towel. In the dark behind my closed eyelids, I heard familiar voices but could not respond. I heard a voice softly singing the familiar strains of "Amazing Grace." It comforted me as a sound from long ago. So quiet it was barely audible, it sounded as though it was wafting to me from afar, perhaps from heaven. My constricted throat wanted to join in, but I could only hum, and even then doubted that any sound emerged. Long ago, I knew that hymn.

Wails from what could only be African voices vaguely pierced the muddle of my consciousness. Or was I conscious at all. Oh, beautiful life. Oh, my prince. Oh, Father, Mother, my family, my friends.

In my mind's eye, hands reached down from above. There was Mother. Oh, long ago. And Father's bear hug embrace. Long ago. Gasping. I saw them. Here. In my room.

Though the room was dark, it brightened until a glaring white light of great intensity suffused my mind's eye. The quiet voice across the room softly took up "Swing Low Sweet Chariot." I sang it long ago, but now I could see God's chariot. The moment was gentle, peaceful, reassuring as a deep breath filled my lungs.

I was a princess.

Long ago.

I . . .

Princess Catherine Willis Murat acquired "Belle Vue", her final home in Tallahassee, Florida from her sister who was married to a nephew of an early Florida governor. Her modest historic home provides a nostalgic link to the internationally prominent Murat legacy. It is preserved by the Tallahassee Museum and may be visited today. Image courtesy of the Florida State Archives.

In St. John's Episcopal Cemetery, Tallahassee, Florida twin obelisks mark the graves of Prince and Princess Murat. In their marriage the houses of Napoleon Bonaparte and George Washington were joined, representing a unique historic convergence of some of history's most powerful political dynasties. Image courtesy of the State of Florida Archives.

Epilogue

In Tallahassee's St. John's Cemetery the graves of Prince and Princess Murat are adorned with the coat of arms of the legendary Murat family.

CATHERINE WILLIS MURAT— Princess Kate—niece of George Washington, niece of Napoléon Bonaparte, princess consort of the Napoleonic kingdom of Naples, and princess of France, surrounded by her now-freed former slaves who loved and respected her died at her Florida plantation, Belle Vue, on August 6, 1867. She is buried in St. John's cemetery, Tallahassee, Florida, alongside her beloved husband of over twenty years, Crown Prince Charles Louis Napoléon Achille Murat, son of Joachim Murat, king of Naples, grandduke of Berg and Cleves, marshal of the Empire, admiral of France, and governor of Paris, the first horseman of Europe, and his wife, Queen Caroline Bonaparte, Napoléon's sister.

Achille Murat's father was born a commoner but raised to become Napoléon's greatest cavalry commander, close confidant, and king. In marrying Prince Achille Murat, Catherine Willis became an integral part of one of the greatest sagas of world history, the era of Napoléon.

The intermarriage of the houses of Bonaparte and Washington created a unique convergence of dynastic power not replicated before or since. Together they joined families, continents, and political powerhouses. Unique in the history of the world, she was twice princess yet never relinquished her American citizenship or her love for "the land of the free and home of the brave."

Princess Kate's beloved simple plantation house Belle Vue is on the National Register of Historic Places and may be visited today as part of the Tallahassee Museum, 3945 Museum Drive, Tallahassee, Florida, 32310. The graves of the prince and princess may be visited at St. John's Episcopal Cemetery, Tallahassee.

A State of Florida historic marker provides a tangible memorial to the lives of Prince and Princess Murat. Among the most interesting couples in Florida history, they represented a marriage of cultures as well as linking the politically powerful families of Napoleon Bonaparte and George Washington. Image courtesy of the State of Florida Archives.

Appendix A

Abbreviated Genealogy Chart

Illustrating the Linkage of the Houses of Napoleon Bonaparte
and George Washington
Through the Marriage of Catherine Daingerfield Willis ("Princess Kate")
and Prince Achille Murat.

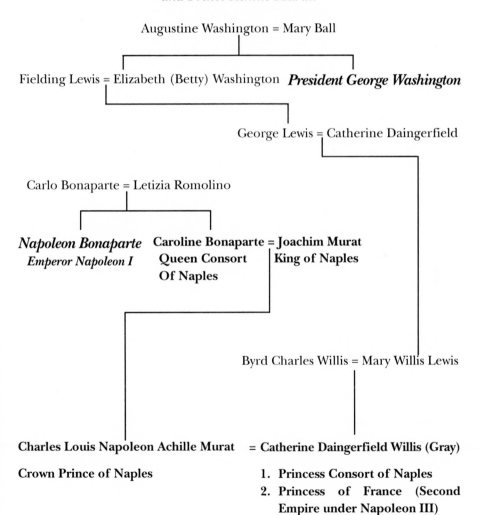

Augustine Washington = Mary Ball

Fielding Lewis = Elizabeth (Betty) Washington   ***President George Washington***

George Lewis = Catherine Daingerfield

Carlo Bonaparte = Letizia Romolino

Napoleon Bonaparte   **Caroline Bonaparte** = **Joachim Murat**
Emperor Napoleon I   **Queen Consort**   **King of Naples**
                              Of Naples

Byrd Charles Willis = Mary Willis Lewis

Charles Louis Napoleon Achille Murat   = **Catherine Daingerfield Willis (Gray)**

Crown Prince of Naples   1. **Princess Consort of Naples**
                                             2. **Princess of France (Second Empire under Napoleon III)**

TWICE A PRINCESS!

Bibliography
(MLA Format)

Anderson, Robert Gordon. *Those Quarrelsome Bonapartes.* D. Appleton-Century Company Inc.; New York; 1939. Print.

Arnault, M.A. and C.L.F. Panckocke. *Life and Campaigns of Napoleon Bonaparte.* Porter & Coates; Philadelphia; 1876. Print.

Arnould, Maurice A., *Achille Murat en Belgium, Un Citoyen Americain at Service de Notre Revolucion.* (in French). Brussels, Carnets de Fouraggere, 1938. Print.

Arthur, Anthony. *General Jo Shelby's March.* New York. Random House. 2009. Print.

Atteridge, A. Hilliard.. *Joachim Murat: Marshal of France and King of Naples.* New York. Brentanos. 1911. Print.

Bannon, Lois E., Carr, Martha Y., and Edwards, Gwen A., *Magnolia Mound.* Gretna, LA., 1984, Pelican Publishing Company Inc. Print.

Barnes, Nancy, *Carlota, American Empress,* Julian Messner Inc., New York, 1943. Print.

Black, Shirley Jean, *Napolean III and the French Intervention in Mexico* University of Oklahoma, 1974. Print.

Blackford, L.M. *Comment and Query: Achille Murat, Again.* Saturday Review of Books and Art. The New York *Times.* April 23, 1898. Print.

Blackthorne, Mister. *Following the Yellow Brick Road.* http:// curiositychronicle.blogspot.com/2009/10/following-yellow-brick-road.html. Web. October 31, 2009. Accessed July 1, 2010.

Bresler, Fenton. *Napoleon III: A Life.* New York, Carroll and Graf Publishers, Inc., 1999. Print.

Brown, William Garrott. *Andrew Jackson.* New York: Houghton, Mifflin & Co., 1900. Print.

Caulaincourt, Armand. *With Napoleon in Russia, The Memoirs of General de Caulaincourt.* New York, William Morrow and Company, Inc., 1935.

Cole, Hubert. *The Betrayers: Joachim and Caroline Murat.* London. Eyre Metheune Publishers, 1972. Print.

Collier, Margaret Wootten. *Catherine Daingerfield Willis Gray Murat: Biographical Sketch.* Biographies of Representative Women of the South.. N. p. Volume 2 (1920-1923). Page 33. Print

Connelly, Owen. *Napoleon's Satellite Kingdoms.* New York: Free Press, 1965

Covington, James W. *The Seminoles of Florida.* Gainesville: University Press of Florida, 1993. Print.

Croce, Benedetto. *History of the Kingdom of Naples.* Chicago: University of Chicago Press, 1970

Davis, Burke. *Old Hickory: A Life of Andrew Jackson.* New York: Dial Press, 1977. Print.

Davies, Catherine. *Eleven Years' Residence in the Family of Murat, King of Naples,* London. How and Parsons. 1841. Print.

Deaton, Linda. Tallahassee Museum. *Achille & Catherine Murat: Tallahassee's Napoléon Connection,* http://www.napoleonexhibit. com/for-kids.php#Anchor-Achille-3800. Date of publication unknown. Web. Accessed 12/20/2009.

Dodd, Dorothy, PhD. *Florida Becomes a State: Social Life in Florida in 1845.* (Copyrighted 1846) Florida Centennial Commission. 1945.

Donald, Eugene Emerson. *Metternich and the Political Police: Security and Subversion in the Hapsburg Monarchy (1815-1830).* Martinus Nijhoff. 1968. Print.

Doty, Franklin A., *Florida, Iowa, and the National "Balance of Power,"* 1845 Florida Historical Quarterly , Vol. 35 No. 1 (Jul. 1956), pp 30-59.

Du Bellet, Louise Pequet., *Some Prominent Virginia Families.* Baltimore, Genealogical Publishing Company, Inc., 1976. Print.

Du Coudray, Helene. *Metternich.* Yale University Press. 1936. 415pp. Print.

Duff, David. *Eugenie and Napoleon III.* New York: William Morrow and Co. Inc., 1978. Print.

Espitalier, Albert. *Napoleon and King Murat.* London. John Lane Publishing Company, Inc., 1911. Print.

Field, Catherine. *Joseph Bonaparte at Point Breeze.* http://www.flatrock. org.nz/topics/new_jersey/new_jerseys_ex_king.htm. Website undated. Accessed April 9, 2010.

Foster, John Watson, *'Maximilian and his Mexican Empire',* The George Washington University Bulletin, IV(4), 1905, 5-21. Print.

Geer, Walter. *Napoleon and His Family; The Story of A Corsican Clan.* Vol. I, II, III. George Allen & Unwin Ltd.; London; 1928. Print.

Gilder, Joseph B., *Bordentown and the Bonapartes.* Scribnere's Monthly, Volume 0021, Issue 1, 1880. As reproduced at http://dlxs2.library.cornell.edu/cgi/t/text/pageviewer-idx?c=scmo;g=moagrp;xc=1;q1=Achille%20Murat;rgn=full%20 text;view=image;cc=scmo;seq=0040;idno=scmo0021-1;node=scmo0021-1%3A3. 9 May, 2010.

Golden, Jennifer. Tallahassee Museum. *Frenchtown*. http://www. napoleonexhibit.com/for-kids.php#Anchor-Achille-3800. Date published unknown. Web. Accessed 02/02/2010.

Gooch, Bryson D. *Belgium and the February Revolution*. Amsterdam. M. Nijhoff. 1931. Print

Grab, Alexander. *Napoleon and the Transformation of Europe*. New York: Palgrave MacMillan, 2003

Green, Harry Clinton and Green, Mary Wolcott. *The Pioneer Mothers of America*. New York. G. P. Putnam and Sons, 1912. Print.

Gulland, Sandra. *Tales of Passion, Tales of Woe*. New York: Simon and Schuster, 1998. Print.

Hall, Frederic, *Life of Maximilian . . . Late Emperor of Mexico, with a sketch of the Empress Carlota / Invasion of Mexico by the French; and the reign of Maximilian I., with a sketch of the Empress Carlota*, James Miller, New York, 1868. Print.

Hanna, A. J. *A Prince in Their Midst: The Adventurous Life of Achille Murat on the American Frontier.*, Norman, OK, 1946. Print.

Hanna, A.J., and Hanna, Kathryn Abbey, *Napoleon III and Mexico: American Triumph over Monarchy*, Chapel Hill, The University of North Carolina Press, 1971. Print

Harden, Clara Ryder. *When America Harbored a Nephew of Napoleon*. Daughters of the American Revolution Magazine, Volume LIII No. 1, January 1919. Pp 602-606. Print.

Hibbert, Christopher. *Napoleon: His Wives and Women*. London. Harper Collins Publishers, 2002. Print.

Johnson, David. *Napoleon's Cavalry and its Leaders*. B.T. Batsford Ltd.; London; 1978. Print.

Johnston, R.M. *Napoleonic Empire in Southern Italy*. New York: MacMillan, 1904

Kenyon, Frank W. *My Brother Napoleon: the Confessions of Caroline Bonaparte.* Hutchinson Chambers Biographical Dictionary. Chambers Harrap Publishers Ltd. 1996. Print.

Klamkin, Marian. *The Return of Lafayette.*, Charles Scribner's Sons, 1975. Print.

Lee, James W. and Luccock, Napthali. *Prince Murat as an American Citizen.* The American Illustrated Methodist Magazine, Volume 4, pp 23-26, September 1900.

Lewis, Carl L., *Achille Murat, His American Wife, and the Career in the South.* The New York *Times*, March 29, 1898. Print

Lindsay, J.T., *French Exiles of Louisiana.* New York. W. B. Smith and Company. 1881. Print.

Lockhart, John Gibson. *The History of Napoleon Buonaparte.* J.M. Dent & Sons (London & Toronto) and E.P.Dutton & Co. (New York); 1919. First printed 1906. Print.

Lomax, Elizabeth P., *An American Princess.* City and title of publication and date not specified. Print.

Long, Ellen Call., *Princesse Achille Murat, A Biographical Sketch.* The William Byrd Press, Inc., Richmond, VA., 1931. Print.

Long, Ellen Call. *Florida Breezes.* Jacksonville. Ashmead Brothers. 1883. Print.

Macartney, C.E. and Dorrance, J. G., *The Bonapartes in America,* 1939. Print.

McConnell, Matilda L. *The Prince and Princess Murat in Florida,* The Century Illustrated, Volume XLVI-68. Pp 515-520. Print.

MacDonell, **A.G.** *Napoleon and His Marshals.* London: MacMillan And Co., 1934, Reprint 1950. Print.

McLynn, Frank. *Napoleon; A Biography.* Pimlico; London, England; 1998. Print.

Meacham, Jon. *American Lion: Andrew Jackson in the White House.* New York: Random House, 2008. Print

Millar, Stephen. *Napoleonic Titles in Italy: 1806-1813*
Research Subjects: Government and Politics, The Napoleon Series. http://www.napoleon-series.org/research/government/italy/c_ italytitles.html. Website undated. Accessed August 7, 2010.

Mitchell, S., *A Family Lawsuit: The Story of Elisabeth Patterson and Jérôme Bonaparte,* 1958; Print.

Murat, Achille, *Esquisse morale et politique des Etas-Unis de l'Amerique du Nord.* Par Achille Murat. Paris. Crochard, 1832. Print.

Murat, Achille. Translated from the French by Henry J. Bradfield. *America and the Americans.* Buffalo, N.Y. George H. Derby and Company. 1851. Print.

Murat, Achille. *A moral and political sketch of the United States of North America. With a note on Negro slavery.* London. Efingham, Wilson. 1833. Print.

Murat, Achille and Redivivus, Junis. *The United States of North America.* London, J. and C. Adlard. 1833. Print

Murat, Charles, Prince . *Prince Achille Murat, a Citizen of Florida.* A lecture at Rollins College. 1931.

Murat, Ines. (with translation by Frances Frenaye). *Napoleon and the American Dream.* Baton Rouge. Louisiana State University Press. 1976. Print.

Mustaine, A. *The Prince and Princess of Tallahassee,* Tallahassee. Rose Printing Company, Inc. 1946. Print.

Palmer, *Metternich.* New York. Harper. 1972. Print.

Palmer, Alan. *An Encyclopaedia of Napoleon's Europe.* St. Martin's Press; New York; 1984. Print.

Pappas, Dale. *Joachim Murat and the Kingdom of Naples: 1808 - 1815.* Reseach Subjects: Biographies, The Napoleon Series. Website undated. Accessed Mar 12, 2010.

Potter, Maud. *The Willises of Virginia.* Chapel Hill, N.C., Von Press, 1964. (Revised 1968)., Print.

Rath, R. John. *The Fall of the Napoleonic Kingdom of Italy 1814.* New York. Columbia University Press. !941. Print.

Renfroe, Joan. *SPOTSYLVANIA: CEMETERY RECORDS - WILLIS CEMETERY* (Based on research by Gordon, Sue K.) http://files.usgwarchives.net/va/spotsylvania/cemeteries/willis01. txt. 1937. Web. Accessed 02/12/2010.

Rickard, J (9 August 2008), *Portrait of Marshal Joachim Murat,* http:// www.historyofwar.org/Pictures/pictures_murat.html. Web. 2010.

Riehn, Richard K. *1812: Napoleon's Russian Campaign.* McGraw Hill Publishing Company, Inc., 1990. Print.

Riley, J.P. *Napoleon and the World War of 1813.* Portland, Oregon: Cass, 2000. Print.

Rolle, Andrew. *The Lost Cause: The Confederate Exodus to Mexico.* University of Oklahoma Press, Norman, OK and London. 1965. Print.

Rush, Peggy Frances. *The Willis Family of the Northern Neck in Virginia, 1669-1737.* Bowie, Maryland. Heritage Books, Inc. 1998. Print.

Sandler, Roberta. *"Florida Woman Vital in Saving Mount Vernon".* http:// www.tcpalm.com/fiftyplus/v09t108.shmtml. Date of publication unknown. Date accessed 04/02/2010

Schneid, Frederick. C., *Napoleon's Italian Campaigns 1805-1815.* Westport, CT., Praeger Press. 2002. Print.

Schom, Alan. *Napoleon Bonaparte.* New York: Harper Perennial, A Division of Harper Collins Publishers Inc. 1997. Print.

Seward, Desmond. *Napoleon's Family.* New York. Viking Press. 1986. Print.

Smith, K.C., Museum of Florida History. *Marquis de Lafayette: The Absent Landlord Frenchtown.* http://www.napoleonexhibit.com/ for-kids.php#Anchor-Achille-3800. Date of publication unknown. Web. Accessed 02/02/2010.

Somit, Albert. "Andrew Jackson: Legend and Reality." *Tennessee Historical Quarterly* 7 (December 1948): 291-313. Print

Sorley, Merrow Edgerton. *Lewis of Warner Hall.* Baltimore. Genealogical Publishing Company. 2000. (Originally published 1935). Print.

Stacton, David. *The Bonapartes.* Simon and Schuster; New York; 1966. Print.

Tebeau, Charlton. *A History of Florida.* Coral Gables: University of Miami Press, 1987 rev. ed. Print.

Tippett, Irene Cowan. *An American princess, and other sketches.* Cedar Rapids, IA., The Torch Press. 1921. Print.

Turquan, Joseph. *The Sisters of Napoleon, Elisa, Pauline, and Caroline Bonaparte.* New York. Charles Scribner's Sons. 1908. Print.

Tyree, Benjamin. *Champagne toast: Vive Napoleon! Society is dedicated to life of emperor.* Washington, DC. The Washington *Times.* September 18, 1997. Print.

Webb, Mrs. Samuel. *"Prince and Princess Achille Murat".* *Southern Magazine.,* Volume 1, Number 4, July 1934. Pages 6-7. Print

Wilentz, Sean. *Andrew Jackson.* New York: Times Books, 2005. Print.

Williams, Edwin L., *Negro Slavery in Florida,* in Florida Historical Quarterly, October, 1949. Print.

Willis, Adelaide R., *The Willis Family of Virginia.,* Mobile, AL., Paper Work, 1967. Print.

Willis, Byrd C., *A Sketch of the Willis Family: Fredericksburg Branch., Richmond,* Whittet and Shepperson, 1909. Print.

Womack, Marlene. *Napoleon Bonaparte's Nephew Enjoyed Frontier Florida.* Tallahassee *News Herald.* January 26, 1997. Print.

Woodward, E. M. *Bonaparte's Park and the Murat's.* Trenton, N.J., McCrellish and Quigley. 1879. Print.

Young, Peter. *Napoleon's Marshals.* Osprey; Berkshire, England; 1973. Print.

References by Unnamed Authors

*M*ANY REFERENCES USED by the author are websites, various magazine articles, or manuscripts in which the author's name is not specified. Though they may not be perceived with the same level of academic rigor as sources in which the name of the author is cited, they are nonetheless essential references in understanding the life, times, and associates of Princess Catherine Willis Murat.

Author unknown. *European Royal Houses, History of the Princes Murat (King of Naples), Genealogy of the Princes Murat.* http://chivalricorders.org/royalty/gotha/murat.htm. Date published unknown. Date accessed 11/03/2000.

Author not specified. *Carolyn (sic) Bonaparte; Queen of Naples.* Napoleonic Historical Society. http://www.napoleonichistoricalsociety.com/articles/Caroline.htm. Website undated. Accessed 6 June 2010.

Author unknown. *BelleVue: The Home of Princess Murat: Tallahassee.* "Explore Southern History". http://www.exploresouthernhistory.com/belleview.html. Date published unknown. Web. Accessed 15/10/2010.

Author unknown. *Personal Remembrances of Madame Murat.* Potter's American Monthly, Vol XVIII, No. 122. (Feb, 1882). Pp 152-156. Print.

Author unknown. *Catherine Willis Gray. Academic Dictionaries and Encyclopedias.* http://en.academic.ru/dic.nsf/enwiki/2564012. Date published unknown. Web. Accessed 03/03/2010.

Author unknown. *Catherine Murat.* The Great Floridians Program: 2000.   http://flheritage.com/services/sites/floridians/?section=t#Tallahassee. Date Published unknown. Web. Accessed 04/04/2010.

Author unknown. *Prince Murat House, 1790.* http://www.old-staug-village.com/prince_murat_house.shtml.   Old   Saint Augustine Village. Date published unknown. Date accessed 04/02/2000.

Author unknown. *Biography of Achille Murat.* The Murat (Achille, Prince) Papers. Stanford University. http://www.oac.cdlib.org/dynaweb/ead/stanford/m0079/@generic_booktextview/134. Date published unknown. Date accessed 04/02/2000.

Author unknown. Florida Memory. State Library and Archives of Florida. *Painted portrait of Catherine Willis Gray Murat, Tallahassee, Florida.*   http://www.floridamemory.com/Photographic Collection/display photo.cfm?IMGURL=http:/ . . . Date of publication unknown.
Date Accessed 3/5/2010

Author unknown. *Caroline Bonaparte Murat, Queen of Naples.* Napoleonic Historical Society. http://www.napoleonichistoricalsociety.com/articles/Caroline.htm. Date published unknown. Web. Accesssed 07/15/2010.

Author unknown. *Obituary of Catherine Willis Murat.* Tallahassee "Sentinel." August 8, 1867. Print.

Author unknown. *Achille Murat, the Prince of Tallahassee.* http://ufdcweb1.uflib.ufl.edu/ufdc/?s=amura. University of Florida. Date published unknown. Date accessed 4/5/2010.

Author unknown. *Women of Courage (Catherine Willis Murat).* http://www.geocities.com/darla1776/lagal.html#WomenofCourage. Date of Publication unknown. Date accessed 31 August 2001.

Author unknown. *Louisiana Timeline: Year 1820.* http://enlou.com/time/1820.htm. Page 2 of 3. Date published unknown. Date accessed 11/10/2000/

Author unknown. *Magnolia Mound (Murat House).* http://www.ebrpss.k12.la.us.community/building.html. Date published unknown. Date accessed 11/10/2000.

Author unknown. *Texas Land Company.* The Handbook of Texas Online., Feb 15, 1999. http://www.tsha.utexas.edu/handbook/online/articles/view/TTdsl2.html. Date accessed 02/06/01

Author unknown. *Portraits/Biographies of Regent and Vice Regents to 1874.* Mount Vernon Ladies Association. http://www.mountvernon.org/visit/plan/index.cfm/pid/333/. Date published unknown. Web. Accessed 07/08/2010.

Author not specified. *Achille Murat Willis, Biographical Sketch.* Confederate Veteran. Nashville. v.17 (1909), p. 518. Print.

Author not specified. *Achille Murat Willis: biographical sketch.* In: History of Virginia. Chicago and New York : v.4 (1924), p. 139-140. Print.

Author not specified. Achille and Catherine Murat: *Tallahassee's Napoleon Connection.* http://www.metrojacksonville.com/forum/index.php/topic,5707.0.html. Metro Jacksonville. August 8, 2009. Accessed May 4, 2010.

Author not specified. Marquis de Lafayette: *The Absentee Landlord Frenchtown.* http://www.metrojacksonville.com/forum/index.php/topic,5707.0.html. Metro Jacksonville. August 8, 2009. Accessed May 4, 2010.

Author not specified. *The Bonaparte Family: The Emperor's Three Sisters.* Volume 2 Chapter 40, The Napoleon Society. http://www.napoleonicsociety.com/english/chap40a.htm. Website undated. Accessed Feb 2, 2010.

Author not specified. *Joachim Murat.* The Columbia Encyclopedia, Sixth Edition, 2008. Print

Author unknown. *Prince Achille Murat.* http://en.wikipedia.org/wiki/Prince_Achille_Murat. Date published unknown. Date accessed 4/06/2010.

Author unknown. *Murat.* Fayard; Paris; 1999. Print.

Author unknown. *The Prince and Princess Achille Murat in Florida.* http://lcweb2.loc.gov/cgi-bin/query/r?ammem/ncps:@field(DOCID+@lit(ABP2287-0046. Date published unknown. Date accessed 11/10/2000.

Author not specified. *Belle Vue Plantation (Florida).* http://www.answers.com/topic/bellevue-plantation Website undated. Accessed Mar 01, 2010.

Author not specified. *The Princess Murat, nee Catherine Daingerfield Willis.*, in The Household., City of publication and date not specified. Print.

Author not specified. *The Murats of Florida,* in The Cornell University Making of America Series. Date and publisher of original text not specified.

Author not specified. *The Princess Achille Murat.* Tallahassee, The Southern Magazine. July 1934

Genealogical Information

*M*any of the above cited bibliographic works constitute important genealogical sources for the story of Catherine Willis Murat. The genealogies of the Murats, Bonapartes, Willises, and other families portrayed in *Twice a Princess* may also be found at ancestry.com, genealogy.com, familysearch.com, usgenweb.org, rootsweb.ancestry. com, genealogy.archives.com, or other similar genealogy websites. Websites come and go, but these were current as of the date of publication. As always, sources should be confirmed.

Index

CPSIA information can be obtained at www.ICGtesting.com
Printed in the USA
LVOW090959201211

260257LV00001B/10/P